KU-778-599

International Migration and the Globalization of Domestic Politics

Increasing international migration, the information revolution and democratiz-ation have propelled a globalization of the domestic politics of many states and, although diasporic politics is not new, emigrant political participation in homeland politics has grown as well as adapted to the new methods of the information revolution.

International Migration and the Globalization of Domestic Politics examines the partici-pation of emigrants in their home-country politics. It considers the consequences of such participation for domestic and foreign policies in both host and home country, and explores the theoretical implications for democracy, nationalism, the state and the shape of world politics in the future. The book includes detailed case studies of Turkish emigrants in Europe, the US and Saudi Arabia, Kurds in Europe, Israeli emigrants and the American Jewish community, Mexicans in the US, Chinese throughout the Pacific Rim, Indians in the US and Russians who found themselves outside of Russia when the Soviet Union collapsed.

By supplying extensive documentation of emigrant political activity with significant impact on homeland politics and foreign policies, this work provides ammunition to the argument that international migration, globalization and transnational phenomena pose serious challenges to the nation-state and the international system of states. It will be of interest to anthropologists, sociologists and area studies specialists as well as political science and international relations scholars.

Rey Koslowski is Associate Professor of Political Science at Rutgers University, Newark. He has held fellowships at the Woodrow Wilson International Center for Scholars, Princeton University and Georgetown University. He is author of *Migrants and Citizens: Demographic Change in the European States System* (Cornell University Press, 2000) and co-editor of *Global Human Smuggling: Comparative Perspectives* (Johns Hopkins University Press, 2001).

Transnationalism

Series Editor: Steven Vertovec
University of Oxford

"Transnationalism" broadly refers to multiple ties and interactions linking people or institutions across the borders of nation-states. Today myriad systems of relationship, exchange and mobility function intensively and in real time while being spread across the world. New technologies, especially involving telecommunications, serve to connect such networks. Despite great distances and notwithstanding the presence of international borders (and all the laws, regulations and national narratives they represent), many forms of association have been globally intensified and now take place paradoxically in a planet-spanning yet common arena of activity. In some instances transnational forms and processes serve to speed-up or exacerbate historical patterns of activity, in others they represent arguably new forms of human interaction. Transnational practices and their consequent configurations of power are shaping the world of the twenty-first century.

This book forms part of a series of volumes concerned with describing and analyzing a range of phenomena surrounding this field. Serving to ground theory and research on "globalization," the Routledge book series on "Transnationalism" offers the latest empirical studies and ground-breaking theoretical works on contemporary socio-economic, political and cultural processes which span international boundaries. Contributions to the series are drawn from Sociology, Economics, Anthropology, Politics, Geography, International Relations, Business Studies and Cultural Studies.

The "Transnationalism" series grew out of the Transnational Communities Research Programme of the Economic and Social Research Council (see http://www.transcomm. ox.ac.uk). It is currently associated with the Research Council's Centre on Migration, Policy and Society located at the University of Oxford (see http://www. compas.ox.ac.uk).

The series consists of two strands:

Transnationalism aims to address the needs of students and teachers, and these titles will be published in hardback and paperback. Titles include:

Culture and Politics in the Information Age
A new politics?
Edited by Frank Webster

Transnational Democracy
Political spaces and border crossings
Edited by James Anderson

Routledge Research in Transnationalism is a forum for innovative new research intended for a high-level specialist readership, and the titles will be available in hardback only. Titles include:

1 New Transnational Social Spaces
International migration and transnational companies in the early 21st century
Edited by Ludger Pries

2 Transnational Muslim Politics*
Reimagining the umma
Peter G. Mandaville

*Also available in paperback

International Migration and the Globalization of Domestic Politics

Edited by Rey Koslowski

Routledge
Taylor & Francis Group

LONDON AND NEW YORK

First published 2005
by Routledge
2 Park Square, Milton Park, Abingdon, Oxon OX14 4RN

Simultaneously published in the USA and Canada
by Routledge
270 Madison Ave, New York, NY 10016

Routledge is an imprint of the Taylor & Francis Group

© 2005 editorial matter and selection, Rey Koslowski; individual chapters, the contributors

Typeset in Baskerville by
Book Now Ltd
Printed and bound in Great Britain by
Antony Rowe, Chippenham, Wiltshire

All rights reserved. No part of this book may be reprinted or reproduced or utilised in any form or by any electronic, mechanical, or other means, now known or hereafter invented, including photocopying and recording, or in any information storage or retrieval system, without permission in writing from the publishers.

British Library Cataloguing in Publication Data
A catalogue record for this book is available from the British Library

Library of Congress Cataloging in Publication Data
International migration and the globalization of domestic politics/[edited by] Rey Koslowski.
    p. cm.
    Includes bibliographical references and index.
    1. Immigrants–Political activity–Case studies. 2. Emigration and immigration–Political aspects. 3. World politics–1989– 4. Globalization–Political aspects.
I. Koslowski, Rey.
    JV6124.I68 2005
    325'.1–dc22   2004013104

ISBN 0–415–25815–4

Contents

Illustrations

Tables

Figures

Contributors

Asher Arian is Distinguished Professor of Political Science at the Graduate Center of the City University of New York, a Senior Research Fellow at the Israel Democracy Institute, and Professor of Political Science at the University of Haifa.

Amy L. Freedman earned her PhD at New York University and is an Assistant Professor of Government at Franklin and Marshall College. She is the author of a number of articles and a book on ethnic politics in Asia and is working on a project that looks at the 1997 economic crisis and democratization.

Rey Koslowski is Associate Professor of Political Science at Rutgers University, Newark, and a recent fellow of the Woodrow Wilson International Center for Scholars. He is the author of *Migrants and Citizens: Demographic Change in the European States System* and co-editor (with David Kyle) of *Global Human Smuggling: Comparative Perspectives*.

Prema Kurien is Associate Professor of Sociology at Syracuse University. She is the author of *Kaleidoscopic Ethnicity: International Migration and the Reconstruction of Community Identities in India* (Rutgers University Press, 2002) and is completing a second book, *Multiculturalism and Immigrant Religion: The Development of an American Hinduism*.

Gallya Lahav is Assistant Professor in the Department of Political Science at the State University of New York at Stony Brook, and Visiting Scholar at the Center for European Studies at New York University. She is the author of several articles on migration and the book *Immigration and Politics in the New Europe: Reinventing Borders*.

Alynna J. Lyon is Assistant Professor of Political Science at the University of New Hampshire. Her research focuses on international organizations, ethnicity and political violence. Her recent publications include "International Influences on the Mobilization of Violence in Kosovo and Macedonia," in the *Journal of International Relations and Development* (2002), and "Policing after Ethnic Conflict," in *Policing: An International Journal of Police Strategies and Management* (2002).

Nedim Ögelman received his PhD in Political Science from the University of Texas at Austin.

Robert A. Saunders is an instructor at Wagner College (Staten Island, New York), where he teaches courses on Soviet and Eastern European history and global politics. He is also a PhD candidate in Global Affairs at Rutgers University, where he is completing his dissertation on the impact of the Internet on national identity.

Robert C. Smith is an Associate Professor of Sociology and Immigration Studies at Baruch College, City University of New York. He is the author of *Mexican New York: Transnational Worlds of New Immigrants* (University of California Press, 2005), and co-editor of *Migration, Transnationalization and Race in a Changing New York* (Temple University Press, 2001). He is a co-founder of the Mexican Educational Foundation of New York.

Emek M. Uçarer is Associate Professor of International Relations at Bucknell University. She holds a PhD in International Studies from the University of South Carolina. Her research interests include cooperation on immigration and asylum matters in the European Union, the role of EU institutions in cooperation, human trafficking and smuggling, and political mobilization of ethnic diasporas in host countries.

Acknowledgments

Many thanks to Rutgers University's Center for Global Change and Governance and the International Studies Association for the financial support they provided for the May 1999 workshop on *International Migration and the Globalization of Domestic Politics* at which drafts of the chapters by Rey Koslowski, Nedim Ögelman, Alynna Lyon and Emek Uçarer, Gallya Lahav and Asher Arian, and Robert Smith were presented. Yossi Shain served as a discussant for all of the papers presented at the workshop and provided helpful suggestions for the project as a whole – we greatly appreciate his comments and help. My contribution to this volume benefited greatly from discussions with the volume contributors as well as Peggy Levitt and Sarah Wayland. The "globalization of domestic politics" conceptual framework was first articulated in a chapter of my 1994 dissertation, "International Migration, European Political Institutions and International Relations Theory." For their comments on this earliest version of my writing on this topic, as well as subsequent paper presentations, I thank Daniel Deudney, Rod Hall, Martin Heisler, Peter Katzenstein, Ellen Kennedy, Friedrich Kratochwil, Yosef Lapid, Jack Nagel and Amir Pasic.

I also thank Steven Vertovec for his initial support for the book project and his ongoing patience. I am very grateful to the Woodrow Wilson International Center for Scholars for a fellowship that gave me time away from my normal teaching and administrative responsibilities and facilitated manuscript preparation. Most of all, I thank my wife, Susan McKenney, who has sustained me through the years of this project (as well as all the others).

Finally, I thank the following publishers for their permission to republish earlier versions of several chapters.

An earlier version of the chapter by Alynna J. Lyon and Emek M. Uçarer, "Mobilizing Ethnic Conflict: Kurdish Separatism in Germany and the PKK," appeared under the same name in *Ethnic and Racial Studies*, vol. 24, no. 6 (2001), pp. 925–48 (http://www.tandf.co.uk).

Robert Smith's chapter, "Migrant Membership as an Instituted Process: Transnationalization, the State and the Extra-Territorial Conduct of Mexican Politics," is a shortened version of an article that appeared under the same name in *International Migration Review*, vol. 37, no. 2 (2003), pp. 297–343, published by the Center for Migration Studies, 209 Flagg Place, Staten Island, NY 10304.

Earlier versions of Prema Kurien's chapter, "Opposing Constructions and Agendas: The Politics of Hindu and Muslim Indian-American Organizations," were published as "Religion Ethnicity and Politics: Hindu and Muslim Indian Immigrants in the United States," in *Ethnic and Racial Studies*, vol. 25, no. 2 (2001), pp. 263–93 (http://www.tandf.co.uk), and as "Constructing 'Indianness' in Southern California: The Role of Hindu and Muslim Indian Immigrants," in Marta Lopez-Garza and David R. Diaz (eds), *Asian and Latino Immigrants in a Restructuring Economy: The Metamorphosis of Southern California*, Stanford, CA: Stanford University Press, 2001.

Introduction

Rey Koslowski

Jet airliners, international telephone services, satellite television, fax machines and the Internet have made it easier for emigrants to maintain contact with their homelands and participate in homeland politics. Increasing international migration, the information revolution and democratization have propelled a globalization of the domestic politics of many states that is similar to the globalization of national economies. Just as firms may have an integrated production system with factories and research facilities in states other than the state in which corporate head-quarters is located, polities may have a political system with significant participants spread across several states other than that of the homeland. Just as even small firms use fax machines, Federal Express and the Internet to market their products globally, political movements and parties reach beyond state borders in organiza-tional and fundraising activities. As the Internet provides relatively inexpensive international communication with vast potential for political organization, emigrants have developed extensive networks of electronic bulletin boards and web pages through which members of diasporas communicate with one another as well as with political actors in the home country.[1]

This globalization of domestic politics is part and parcel of the larger pheno-menon of the politics of diasporas and transnational communities formed through recent or past migration (as well as the break-up of multinational states). Classical diasporas include the ancient Greeks, Jews and Armenians, and, as I will demonstrate below in chapter 1, emigrants in diasporas have influenced the domestic politics and the foreign policies of their home countries throughout history. Migrants have also become politically active in the host country to which they migrated, often in order to influence the foreign policies of their host countries toward their homelands. Governments of the homeland or "mother" country may engage their emigrants to further political agendas, view their emigrants as traitors for leaving, or simply ignore them. Diasporic politics in its many forms is not new. However, the scope and scale of emigrant political participation in homeland politics is increasing in today's world, as growing ranks of migrants from an increasing number of source countries living in a greater number of host countries produce ever more and increasingly varied diasporas.

Relatively new diasporas have become influential not only in their domestic politics but also in international politics on a global scale, as the role of Iraqi émigrés and refugees in the recent Iraq War amply demonstrates. Iraqis who had fled their country's Baathist regime in the 1960s, 1970s and 1980s were joined in Europe and the US by thousands of Iraqi refugees, primarily Shi'ites and Kurds, who left Iraq during and after the 1990 Gulf War. Some of these Iraqi refugees and émigrés formed the Iraqi National Congress, and then lobbied the US Congress and the Clinton and Bush administrations to depose Saddam Hussein. Ahmed Challabi, a leader of the Iraqi National Congress, argued that Iraqis were ready to be liberated and that the Hussein regime could be easily toppled. The Iraqi National Congress received moral support from the United States with the passage of the Iraqi Liberation Act of 1998 as well as covert and then overt military assistance. Challabi was particularly influential within the US Defense Department and particularly with deputy secretary Paul Wolfowitz, who initially argued that Iraqis supported by US air power and Special Forces could topple the Hussein regime, much as a US-supported Northern Alliance defeated the Taliban in Afghanistan. Eventually, US forces did invade Iraq. When they did so, armed Iraqi exiles participated in securing and occupying several areas. After the collapse of the Hussein regime, returning Iraqi émigrés and refugees made up half of Iraq's transitional governing council, which is considered the first step toward a new democratic Iraqi government.

As this brief example illustrates, emigrants can play a wide variety of roles in the domestic politics and foreign policy-making of host and home countries. This volume focuses on the emigrant involvement in home-country politics and its interaction with other dimensions of transnational diasporic politics. The first chapter provides a conceptual framework that elaborates on these various dimensions of diasporic politics and the relationships between them. The case studies that follow focus on one or more of the dimensions of diasporic politics as they relate to the globalization of the domestic politics of emigrants' home countries. The angle of analysis differs depending on the case at hand. In some cases, emigrants participate in the democratic processes of their home countries. In others, emigrants cannot participate in the electoral politics of their home country because it is not democratic, but then they oppose the existing authoritarian regime. In some cases, emigrants participate democratically in the host country and this, in turn, influences the foreign policy of that host country toward their homeland. In other cases, emigrants influence the foreign policies of their home countries, whether or not the outcome is in the national interest of the host country in which they reside. As the contributors to this volume examine diasporic political activity and evaluate the consequences of such participation for host- and home-country domestic and foreign policies, the chapters provide insights into the theoretical implications of the globalization of domestic politics for democracy, nationalism, the state and the shape of world politics in the future.

In the first chapter, Rey Koslowski argues that the extraordinary development of transportation and communication technologies over the past century and the information revolution of the past decade have transformed emigrant political activity in a qualitative way. After briefly describing the history of diasporic politics, he elaborates on how the combination of international migration, technological advances and democratization fosters a globalization of the domestic politics of many states that is similar to the contemporary globalization of national economies. The chapter then goes on to lay some of the conceptual parameters for analyzing multiple dimensions of diasporic politics and considers some of their broader theoretical ramifications for key issues of political theory, comparative politics and international relations. This introductory chapter not only sets out a conceptual framework for the examination of diasporic politics but it orients international relations scholars to the subject matter which has not been a central topic of the field – until recently, that is.

In chapter 2, Nedim Ögelman analyzes the political behavior of immigrant-origin actors linked to Turkey, using increasing migration, transportation and communications revolutions, and democratization as primary explanatory variables. Developments in four receiving countries, Germany, the Netherlands, the US, and Saudi Arabia, provide empirical evidence. Germany, with more than 2 million Turkish-origin inhabitants, receives disproportionate attention. The Netherlands and the US provide insight into Turkish-origin diaspora politics in different democratic settings. Experiences of roughly 130,000 Turkish-origin people in Saudi Arabia supply evidence on how diaspora politics fare in a more constrained institutional environment.

In chapter 3, Alynna Lyon and Emek Uçarer examine the internationalized politics of Kurdish separatism and argue that ethnic nationalism can and often does have consequences for countries other than traditional homelands. Segments of the Kurdish diaspora in Western European countries have been instrumental in bringing Turkey's treatment of its Kurdish minority to the attention of European states. Hunger strikes, protest marches and terrorist bombings in Germany are testimony to the increasingly transnationalized Kurdish separatist movement and to the political leverage of diasporic communities. Host to significantly large Kurdish communities, Western Europe, and Germany in particular, must now face the challenge of developing policies toward their Kurdish residents as well as toward Turkey. The chapter identifies the conditions under which the Kurdish diaspora and subsequently Kurdish separatism took root in Germany and explores the consequences of diasporic political mobilization for host and home countries.

In chapter 4, Gallya Lahav and Asher Arian examine the Israeli diaspora, the notion of which may seem contradictory since the basis of Zionism is an "ingathering of exiles." Yet, it is estimated that over 10 percent of Israelis live abroad, and their behavior is potentially important for Israeli domestic politics as well as Israeli foreign policy. This chapter explores ideological tensions between Israeli emigrants in the United States and their American-Jewish counterparts, who form "potential" citizens derived from the 1950 Israeli Law of Return. The ambivalent status of diaspora Israelis for Jews and Jewish organizations has evolved substantially since the formation of Israel fifty years ago, and needs to be interpreted as a function of the Israeli state. The chapter assesses the political and economic impact of these groups on the evolution of the Israeli state by examining their role outside and inside Israel, and it draws implications for the democratic nature of a maturing Israeli state which defines its *demos* through religion.

In chapter 5, Robert Smith examines the extra-territorial conduct of Mexican politics and the creation of a transnational public sphere between the United States and Mexico. He analyzes the Mexican state's efforts to create a thin form of diasporic membership for Mexican nationals abroad as well as efforts of migrants to "thicken" that membership by engaging with democratizing tendencies in Mexico. The chapter illustrates this interplay by comparing the political activity of migrants from the Mexican states of Zacatecas and Oaxaca and evaluating their differing practices and degrees of membership.

In chapter 6, Amy L. Freedman explains that there is a long history of links between Chinese politics at home and the diaspora community abroad. She then elaborates on how ethnic Chinese outside of the People's Republic have invested in the Chinese economy and supported movements for political change. The chapter examines how links between the Chinese diaspora and the Chinese government have changed over time and analyzes the possible impact that such a relationship can have on domestic politics in China.

In chapter 7, Prema Kurien focuses on the political mobilization of Hindu and Muslim Indian immigrant groups in the United States, based on their very different constructions of Indian identity. Hindu Indian-American organizations define India as a Hindu society and are strong supporters of the Hindu nationalist movement in India. In contrast, Muslim Indian-American organizations view India as a multi-religious and multicultural society and strive to safeguard India's secularism. This chapter examines how both types of organizations are working to influence Indian politics in line with their respective interests.

In chapter 8, Robert Saunders examines the politics of a new diaspora formed when the collapse of the Soviet Union left more than 25 million ethnic Russians marooned outside of Russia. Saunders argues that those Russians who chose to remain in the "near abroad" have effectively internationalized identity politics by playing on nationalist sentiment in the Russian Federation. This chapter considers the ways in which ethnic Russians outside of Russia have been able to garner support from within Russia to achieve indirect representation in their states of residence, while simultaneously generating unintended consequences for domestic politics and foreign policy in the motherland.

Note

1   Overseas Chinese and non-resident Indians have produced a myriad of websites, some of which are aimed at engaging emigrants in homeland politics. For example, "Silicon Valley for Democracy in China" (http://www.svdc.org) has raised money for disaster relief as well as publicized the plight of Chinese dissidents, and IndiaCause.com (http://indiacause.com/) seeks to defeat "Pakistan-sponsored terrorism" in Kashmir and "Pseudo-secularism in India" by using e-activism for email campaigns that have, among other things, pressured CNN not to use a map of India without Jammu and Kashmir.

1 International migration and the globalization of domestic politics

A conceptual framework

Rey Koslowski

Introduction

The combination of international migration, advances in transportation and communications technology, and spreading democratization fosters a globalization of the domestic politics of many states that is similar to the globalization of national economies. Just as the spread of new information technologies that connect headquarters, factories and distribution centers has enabled the globalization of production across borders, these technologies have enabled the globalization of domestic politics by connecting emigrants with their kin and political organizations back home. In addition to the transformation of the political environment brought on by the information and communications revolution, the globalization of domestic politics is driven by the confluence of two trends – increasing migration and increasing democratization of the world's states.

Over the past few decades, international migration has expanded to the point where there are now an estimated 175 million people living outside of their state of nationality. Moreover, these 175 million migrants are coming from a greater variety of source countries and moving to a greater variety of host countries. For example, until three decades ago, the US population was composed largely of the descendants of African slaves and European immigrants. Then, however, large-scale migration from a wide variety of migrant-sending countries in Latin America and East and South Asia transformed the United States into what the demographer Ben Wattenberg (1991) called "the first universal nation." Over the same period, migration flows out of historic migrant-sending countries in Europe, such as Germany and then Italy, Spain and Greece, reversed direction, and these countries have become hosts to a growing number of new diasporic communities.

Democratization in host countries provides more conducive environments for emigrant political activity while democratization of home countries increases the chance that emigrants are able to influence their homelands' politics. Moreover, democratization facilitates international migration (mostly by reducing the number of states willing to stop their citizens from leaving).

When the domestic politics of one state actually takes place in several states, it is a dimension of politics that is neither within individual states nor between several states. In that this political practice is not captured by state-centric international relations theories that conceptualize the world in terms of international anarchy in contrast to domestic hierarchy, the globalization of domestic politics challenges traditional conceptualizations of world politics. As the globalization of politics expands, the impact of migration on international politics grows, yet, as long as the anarchy–hierarchy dichotomy continues to govern mainstream approaches to the study of international politics, an adequate understanding of this phenomenon is not forthcoming.

My argument proceeds as follows: first, I review the implications of international migration for the conceptualization of world politics in general by examining migration with respect to two bodies of international relations theory that are divided on the conceptualization of world politics – state-centric theories, primarily realism and neorealism, and non-state-centric theories, which developed as alternatives to realism and focus on transnational interaction and non-state actors. Second, I build on the transnationalist approach by developing the concept of the globalization of domestic politics through the elaboration of several kinds of emigrant political activity and its expansion through increased migration. Third, I explain how democratization is expanding the globalization of domestic politics and consider the implications of emigrant participation for democracy and democratic theory in general. Fourth, I demonstrate how emigrant influence on host- and home-country foreign policy, as well as homeland political conflicts fought on foreign soil, transcends the globalization of domestic politics and becomes international politics as traditionally understood. Fifth, I examine the place of emigrant remittances and investment in the globalization of the international economy. Sixth, I examine the relationship between emigrants and nationalism and explore the potential for the development of alternative transnational identities within diasporas. Finally, I conclude by reviewing some implications of the above for the study of politics in general.

Migration, domestic politics and international relations theory

Refugee crises, human smuggling and the attacks on the World Trade Center and the Pentagon by terrorists who resided in the United States on student, business and tourist visas have recently thrown a spotlight on the role of international migration in contemporary world politics. The growing role of migration in the calculations of policy-makers has been reflected in an expanding literature on migration in comparative politics (Hollifield 1992; Freeman and Jupp 1992; Cornelius *et al.* 1994; Castles and Miller 1993)[1] and international relations (Mitchell 1989; Zolberg *et al.* 1989; Tucker *et al.* 1990; Heisler 1992; Hollifield 1992; Weiner 1993; Waever *et al.* 1993; Loescher 1993; Teitelbaum and Weiner 1995; Weiner 1995, 1996; Keely 1996; Posen 1996; Miller 1997; Muenz and Weiner 1997; Money 1997, 1999; Koslowski 2000, 2002). Still, migration is rarely considered in general works of international relations theory, and much of the recent work on the consequences of migration for international politics is written by scholars with backgrounds in demography, comparative politics and area studies. Although the role of diasporas in world politics has long been appreciated by foreign policy-makers (Mathias 1981) and analyzed by a few political scientists (Armstrong 1976; Sheffer 1986; Shain 1989, 1999; Shain and Barth 2003; Callahan 2003; Weiner 1995), mainstream neorealists and neoliberals downplay the significance of migration as a security issue (Walt 1991) and the factor of labor migration in the international economy (Keohane and Milner 1996). Some scholars developing alternative sociological perspectives, such as constructivism, have noted that migration is an issue that has "reemerged as deeply politicized from relatively taken-for-granted conventions of nationalism and citizenship . . . and could induce expansion in the conceptualization of security affairs" (Jepperson *et al.* 1996: 73). Still, they have shied away from analysis of such "new security issues" as migration so that their arguments will be taken seriously by neorealists and neoliberals (Katzenstein 1996: 7–11). Those international relations scholars who have systematically incorporated migration into their theoretical frameworks have placed the primary focus on the politics of immigration in host states and conceptualized the consequences of immigration for international politics in terms of "societal security" (Waever *et al.* 1993). In contrast, this volume focuses on the political activity of emigrants in their home countries, its international ramifications and theoretical implications.

With respect to the conceptualization of world politics, international relations theories can be divided into two groups on either side of a debate over the state as a unit of analysis. State-centric theories, primarily realism and neorealism (but also micro-economic-based, neoliberal institutionalism (Keohane 1984) and some forms of constructivism (Wendt 1994, 1999), are pitted against non-state-centric theories, which developed as alternatives to realism and focus on transnational interaction and non-state actors.

In state-centric theories, world politics is conceptualized in terms of an international system of territorially delineated states. Due to the existence of government within states, domestic politics is characterized by order and hierarchy; due to the absence of world government, politics among states is characterized by anarchy (Waltz 1979: 88–9). While both traditional realism and neorealism are state-centric, neorealist analysis is almost exclusively conducted in the "third image," or on the level of the international system, rather than in the "second image," or at the level of politics within the state (Waltz 1959). Unfortunately, third-image, state-centric, capability-driven analysis does not deal adequately with international migration because international migration can lead to changes in domestic politics that reverberate on the international level in the form of changes in foreign policies that are not necessarily the result of changes in military capabilities. Moreover, the concept of domestic hierarchy assumes a territorially contained polity, which obfuscates analysis of a diaspora that may be a part of a polity living outside of the territory of the home state.

As opposed to the state-centric approach of realism and neorealism, a host of theories taking a transnationalist approach have been advanced.[2] This group of theories includes functionalism (see Mitrany 1946), neofunctionalism (see Haas 1968), social communications theory (see Deutsch *et al.* 1957), interdependence theory (see Keohane and Nye 1977), world society theory (see Burton 1972) and epistemic community theory (Haas 1992). Theorists taking a transnationalist approach try to understand world politics in its totality. They point to non-state actors such as multinational corporations, international trade unions, international scientific, technical and functional organizations, etc., and argue that state-to-state relations represent only part of world politics and that many politically significant actions bypass states themselves. For instance, Keohane and Nye identified four global interactions: communication – the movement of information, including beliefs and ideas; transportation – the movement of physical objects, including merchandise and arms; finance – the movement of money and instruments of credit; and travel – the movement of persons (Keohane and Nye 1971).

While early work on transnational relations included analysis of international migration, most subsequent arguments challenging state-centric theories focused on economic interdependence arising from increasing international trade and monetary flows and neglected international migration. A more recent volume edited by Robert Keohane and Helen Milner emerged from a discussion of "What happened to interdependence theory?" and was entitled *Internationalization and Domestic Politics*. At first glance, one would think that the globalization of domestic politics resulting from international migration might be a prominent feature of the analysis. However, Keohane and Milner define internationalization as "the processes generated by underlying shifts in transaction costs that produce observable flows of goods, services, and capital" (Keohane and Milner 1996: 4). They did not consider migration as a part of internationalization "since labor moves much less readily across national borders than goods or capital" (ibid.: 256, n. 1).

Keohane and Milner are correct in arguing that labor does not move as readily as goods and capital. This should not, however, justify dropping migration from the factors of internationalization and minimizing its impact on domestic politics, because migration is often part and parcel of the cross-border movement of services and capital, and the actions of a state's nationals who reside abroad often have political consequences that are disproportionate to their numbers. While the international movement of services often conjures the image of software, financial data and legal information being communicated through transnational information networks, it also involves the migration of professionals who produce such information and services (about a third of Silicon Valley's engineers are foreign born; Sweeny 1996: 3) and lower skilled service workers (e.g., nurses and maids from the Philippines, Polish nannies, Chinese cooks and Mexican gardeners) who in turn provide services for highly skilled professionals. Only a small fraction of a country's citizens may work abroad, but capital movements in the form of migrant worker remittances may exceed merchandise export earnings, as is the case in many developing countries (see below). Similarly, emigrants and political refugees often participate in home-country politics with an influence that is disproportionate to their numbers due to the acquisition of education and skills, the accumulation of financial capital and the cultivation of influence on host-state foreign policies toward their home states. Even individual emigrants may change the course of their home country's political development. Moreover, the number of people who reside outside of their state of nationality understates the political consequences of international migration because it does not include the descendants of migrants, who may have the nationality of the state in which they reside but still identify politically with their parents' and grandparents' home-state and participate in home-state politics.

The neglect of international migration by scholars of transnational relations and international interdependence is unfortunate because in many cases the international movement of humans is potentially much more politically significant than the international movement of goods or money. As opposed to goods and money, migrants have a will of their own (Weiner 1989: 75, cited in Hollifield 1992: 21, n. 5) and can themselves become significant political actors. Migrants challenge assumptions of territoriality not just when they cross borders but also when they participate in home-country politics, influence the foreign policy-making of host and home states, and even develop alternative diaspora political identities which transcend existing borders. In this sense, the globalization of domestic politics refers not only to a growing political phenomenon. The concept of a diasporic polity existing in several states and influencing their domestic politics and foreign policies provides another way of understanding the relationship between domestic and international politics that builds on, but goes beyond, the "second image reversed" (Gourevitch 1978), "two level games" (Putnam 1988) or "agent-structure" debates (see Wendt 1987; Dessler 1989).

The international relations literature has a long tradition of theories of transnational relations but little analysis of diasporas. In contrast, anthropologists and sociologists have studied diasporas extensively; many virtually take it for granted that diasporas are majors factors of domestic politics and foreign policy in many parts of the world and some have made "transnationalism" a new analytical focus in their fields (see, e.g., Glick Schiller *et al.* 1992; Portes 1995; Kearney 1995; Appadurai 1996; Cohen 1997; Kyle 2000; Levitt 2001).[3] This chapter bridges this disciplinary divide by providing a conceptual framework that orients international relations scholars to the subject matter and helps anthropologists, sociologists and area studies specialists put their research into a format that will effectively register with international relations scholars and foreign policy-makers.

Emigration, diasporas and homeland political participation

Throughout history, victorious parties in domestic political conflicts often used banishment abroad as an alternative to killing or imprisoning political opponents, because exile was a more humane way of effectively eliminating political challengers (many of whom were related to the victor); it also avoided turning opponents into martyrs. The development of an international system of independent states facilitated both the expulsion of political opponents by states and the reception of political refugees by other states. In this way, the states system enabled opponents of any individual state's rulers to escape that state through refuge in another. The combination of an international system of states and better transportation and communication also opened up the possibility that exiles and political refugees could continue to influence the course of domestic politics in their home countries even after they left.[4] Emigration has long functioned as a release valve reducing revolutionary social pressure in the emigrants' home countries.[5] However, the greater the emigrant contacts with the home country, the greater the potential for emigrants abroad to foment revolution and national independence movements back home.

Diasporic politics is not a new phenomenon, as just one example from ancient Greece makes clear. Between 1050 and 950 BC Athenians and Ionian and other Greek refugees, as well as their Athenian-born descendants, moved from Athens to the central and northern coast of Asia Minor, which became known as Ionia and Aeolia (Forrest 1986: 20). Centuries later, the ties between the Athenian mother state and the Ionian diaspora were renewed during the Persian Wars. After Cyrus united the Persian kingdom in 546 BC and installed pro-Persian tyrants in Ionian cities, Ionians fled to Athens, and these Ionian refugees persuaded the Athenians to become involved in the conflict (Watson 1992: 57). Athenians responded to the Ionian revolt in 499 BC by sending twenty ships, while the Spartans refused to help.

In modern times, active involvement of refugees in the domestic politics of their home countries goes back at least to the Glorious Revolution of 1688, when James II received refuge in France and aspired to regain the English throne through mobilizing supporters in England, Scotland and Ireland (Mansbach *et al*. 1976: ch. 4). After the French Revolution, aristocrats who fled France attempted to moderate, if not reverse, the revolution (Roberts 1978: 45–6). These aristocrats eventually participated in the restoration of the monarchy in 1815 (Artz 1963). In response to the restoration, throughout the nineteenth century, liberal, nationalist and radical refugees and exiles organized groups, published manifestos and supported clandestine political activity in attempts to change the course of their home-country politics.[6] Although the influence of refugees, exiles and emigrants on their home country's domestic politics may be revolutionary, reactionary, liberal, conservative or nationalist in nature, contemporary emigrant political activity has been directed primarily toward movements of national self-determination and democratization.

During the struggle against communism and Soviet imperialism, the Polish diaspora supported the Solidarity labor movement of 1980–81 and underground Solidarity throughout the 1980s (Nash 1989; Blejwas 1995). For example, after General Jaruzelski declared a state of war on December 13, 1981, Jerzy Milewski (later National Security Advisor to the Polish president, Lech Walesa) and other members of the Solidarity leadership found themselves outside of Poland. They transmitted uncensored information from Poland to the West, and opened the Coordinating Office Abroad of NSZZ *Solidarność* in Brussels. The office itself was provided by European trade unions and staffed by recent émigrés, as well as volunteers from Polish immigrant communities in the United States and Western Europe. Underground Solidarity was supported by Solidarity International and other organizations of the Polish diaspora from the United States, Canada, Mexico, Sweden, West Germany, the United Kingdom, France, Norway and Denmark that came together in 1983 to form the Conference of Solidarity Support

Organizations. Perhaps the most important émigré, however, was Karol Wojtyla who, as Pope John Paul II, advised the Solidarity leadership and, it has been argued, collaborated with the Reagan administration, the CIA and the American Federation of Labor–Congress of Industrial Organizations to funnel supplies to underground Solidarity through its office in Brussels (Bernstein 1992). Although the combination of Solidarity's persistent opposition in Poland and Gorbachev's ending of the Brezhnev Doctrine were primarily responsible for a non-communist Polish government coming to power in the summer of 1989, inasmuch as Poles abroad were instrumental in sustaining the internal opposition to the Jaruzelski regime during the 1980s, they played an important role in its downfall.

Similarly, the Chinese diaspora proved critical to China's revolutions and attempted revolutions.[7] For example, Sun Yat-Sen raised money in Hong Kong, Malaysia, Yokohama, Hawaii, California and New York. He was in Denver when the revolution started in 1910 and later said that "The diaspora . . . is the mother of the revolution" (quoted in Kotkin 1993: 193). Likewise, in 1989 tens of thousands of Chinese university students studying abroad, primarily in the United States, supported their cohorts in Tiananmen Square with information, communications networks, publicity in the Western press and funds. By permitting Chinese students to remain in the United States after the Tiananmen Square protest was crushed, the Bush administration effectively granted them asylum (see chapter 6 below). Many of these students continued to support the democracy movement by publicizing human-rights abuses in China, which became a major point of contention in US–Chinese relations during the process of US renewal of China's Most Favored Nation trade status. The significance of overseas Chinese students' activities is underscored by the efforts of the Chinese government to discredit and split their ranks (Shain 1993).

Expanding migration enlarges the potential for emigrant political activity for the obvious reason that migration increases the number of possible political actors. The number of people living outside of their state of nationality has been growing – from approximately 75 million people in 1965, to about 105 million in 1985, to almost 120 million in 1990, to 175 million in 2000 (United Nations 1995, table 1, cited in Stanton Russell 1992; United Nations 2002). This figure does not include the 25 million Russians who found themselves outside of Russia after its collapse and the other displaced members of nationalities in the former Soviet Union and Yugoslavia, nor does it include illegal migrants, with an estimated 8 to 10 million in the United States alone. The prospects for migration escalating in the future is great given that projected world population growth is concentrated in the less developed parts of the world, thereby increasing prospects for migration from the less developed to the more developed parts of the world as well as migration among less developed countries (Hoffmann-Novotny 1997).

Emigrant politics, democratization and democracy

Whether or not this potential is realized depends largely on whether or not states permit more migration and emigrant political activity. The latest wave of democratization promotes an expansion of the globalization of domestic politics on both fronts. As democratization spreads, the number of authoritarian and totalitarian states with both the capacity and the willingness to interdict and expel migrants, as well as stop their citizens from leaving, decreases. Therefore, the potential for greater migration inherent in rising population growth is more likely to be realized if combined with increasing democratization.

Democratization also facilitates the political activity of émigrés in host states and opens up opportunities for participation in their home countries' politics. Migration to a democratic state often enables opposition that otherwise might not be possible. In a critique of Albert Hirschman's theory of exit, voice and loyalty, A. H. Birch argued that at times "exit was not an alternative for voice but a necessary condition for the exercise of voice" (Birch 1979: 79, cited in Shain 1989: 24). For example, while Polish and Chinese dissidents were routinely jailed by communist regimes in their home countries, émigré intellectuals supported by emigrant communities in Western Europe and North America were able to publish "unofficial" histories and banned literature as well as organize communication and support networks for opposition to communism in their home countries. Similarly, Algerian rebels may have been quickly suppressed in Algeria, but were much freer to organize, print literature, etc., in France (Castles and Miller 1993: 323–4).

The most poignant historical examples of emigrant political activity, noted above, took place in the United States and Western Europe not only because liberal ideologies fostered acceptance of political refugees, but also because liberal democratic governments exerted loose control over their own citizens, which, in turn, provided an atmosphere conducive to émigré political activity. This is the case because, practically speaking, many rights, such as guarantees against arbitrary search and seizure by the police, must be extended to all residents of a state if these civil rights are to be enjoyed by its citizens. It is necessary to note, however, that émigrés whose actions undermine the host countries' enemies are often not only permitted but encouraged and supported by non-democratic and democratic countries alike. For example, US interests during the Cold War coincided with the political activities of émigrés from Eastern Europe and the Soviet republics in support of national self-determination and resulted in official US support, such as the "Captive Nations" program (Loescher 1989: 12–15). Nevertheless, democratic checks on executive power and judicial protection of civil rights in the host country hamper the suppression of émigré political activity and organization if that activity runs counter to the host government's interests. For example, the United States did not stop the activities of Sheik Omar Abdel Rahman, an Egyptian cleric based in New Jersey who attempted to spark an Islamic revolution in Egypt, until some of Rahman's followers bombed the World Trade Center in 1993. This was the case even though Egypt was an ally in the Gulf War and is one of the top recipients of US foreign aid and Egyptian authorities wanted Rahman to stand trial. In the wake of the September 11, 2001, attacks on the World Trade Center and the Pentagon, the Bush administration took much more assertive actions, including the detention of nationals of Arab and Muslim states. However, these actions have come under increasing judicial scrutiny and public criticism.

Whereas democratization produces host countries that are conducive to émigré political activity, democratization of home countries increases opportunities for émigré influence. In the early stages of liberalization, emigrants are emboldened to attempt to influence the politics of their home countries because the costs of doing so are reduced and the chances for success increased. For instance, as authoritarian regimes in Spain and Portugal began to pursue more liberal policies during the 1970s, Spanish and Portuguese migrant workers who expected eventually to return home participated in demonstrations against their home-country governments (Miller 1981: 62–5). Home countries are often most open to emigrant participation as democratization enters the stage of the first free elections. It is at this juncture that emigrants have perhaps their greatest influence, in that this period of transition often sets the course for the subsequent development of the new democracy.

Emigrants who retain home-country citizenship are often permitted to vote in home country elections. For example, as free elections were held in Spain and Portugal, Spanish and Portuguese workers in France, Germany and Switzerland participated. Given that one out of ten Portuguese lived outside of Portugal at the time of the Portuguese revolution in 1974, emigrants could have had a major influence on the outcomes of the early elections. Portuguese emigrant participation remained low, however, in large measure due to the fact that citizens abroad were able to vote for only eight out of 263 parliamentary seats (Miller 1981: 48–52). Similarly, Poland permitted its citizens abroad to vote at Polish embassies and consulates in its first post-communist presidential election in November 1990. In the mid-1990s, the Mexican legislature considered a constitutional amendment to give voting rights to Mexican nationals living abroad (Dillon 1996) and the Mexican Congress is considering a proposal to allow some of the estimated 10 million Mexicans abroad (primarily in the US) to vote by absentee ballot (Brooks 2003). Perhaps most dramatically, in the 1990s, 12 out of 100 seats of the Croatian parliament were reserved for representatives elected by Croatian emigrants and their descendants with dual nationality. In the 1995 elections, fewer votes were cast to elect these 12 parliamentarians than were cast for the winning candidate for the seat from Istria (Pusic 1996).[8]

In addition to voting in the first elections of newly established democracies, émigrés participate in elections as candidates, sometimes even if they have naturalized to their host country. Such political participation has been quite prominent in the wake of communism's collapse in Central and Eastern Europe. For example, not only were Poles living abroad allowed to vote in Poland's first presidential elections, but a Polish-born Canadian citizen, Stanislaw Tyminski, ran for office. Although Lech Walesa won the election, Tyminski unexpectedly received more votes than Tadeusz Mazowiecki, the sitting prime minister, and this led Mazowiecki and his cabinet ministers to resign the following day. Somewhat similarly, in July of 1992, Milan Panic, a Serbian-born American citizen, was elected prime minister of Yugoslavia. At the time, Panic had the blessing of Slobodan Milosevic, the communist *apparatchik* turned nationalist leader, who viewed Panic as someone who could be used as window dressing for the West. In the following December, Panic challenged Milosevic in Serbian presidential elections and received over a third of the vote despite Milosevic's control of television coverage and alleged vote tampering.

Although voting and standing for election may be the most visible way in which emigrants influence newly emerging democracies, a less visible, but perhaps more influential, way may be through campaign contributions and other support for contending political parties. During the first free elections in East European countries, the relative influence of each individual emigrant's contributions in comparison to those of citizens in the home country was magnified by the high value of Western currencies in relation to local currencies which had been devalued by hyper-inflation. For example, a $50 contribution by a Polish American in the 1990 presidential campaign equaled the contribution by an average Pole of his or her entire month's wages. Much as corporations, unions and interest groups provide the major contributions to American political campaigns, diasporas of co-ethnics living in rich countries are a treasure trove for politicians from relatively poor countries undergoing democratization, as the following examples from the former Yugoslavia amply demonstrate.

Before non-communist political parties were even legalized in Yugoslavia, the Croatian Democratic Union (HDZ) of Franjo Tudjman and other newly created Croatian parties raised funds from the diaspora in the United States, Canada and Australia. Indeed, it has been estimated that as much as 80 percent of the money spent by political parties in the 1990 elections came from Croatian emigrants and their descendants (Pusic 1996). The lion's share, at least $4 million, went to Tudjman's HDZ (Glenny 1992: 63). It was raised primarily by Canadian Croats led by Gojko Susak, a refugee who arrived from Herzegovina in 1967 and became successful in the pizza business. After Tudjman won the election and Croatia declared independence on June 25, 1991, Susak became defense minister. Overseas Croats with dual nationality voting in the 1995 elections overwhelmingly supported the HDZ, which perhaps helps explain the diaspora's disproportionate allocation of representation in the parliament.

The role of campaign contributions described above highlights a growing discontinuity between the people who exert power through democratic decision-making processes and people who bear the consequences of the democratic decisions made. This discontinuity raises questions about the legitimacy of emigrant political participation in home-country politics from the standpoint of democratic theory as well as nationalist ideology.

David Held (1991) argued that the actions of a democracy often have international consequences for people beyond the democracy's borders, who in turn have no say in the actions of the democracy that effect them – for example, the American electorate's decisions about foreign aid, International Monetary Fund and World Bank financing, etc., have tremendous effects on the people of the developing world. Hence, the *demos* of a democratic nation-state may not necessarily coincide with the broader set of people affected by the decisions made by that *demos*. In contrast, if a democratic state's citizens who live abroad are permitted to participate in that state's democracy (e.g., through consular voting or through absentee balloting) then the *demos* is expanded beyond the borders of the state over which its decisions and laws have effect.

Democratic theory does not provide a good answer to the question of whether or not emigrants should be able to participate in the homeland's elections, campaign financing, and other activities of democratic rule, because democratic theory assumes a bounded *demos* (Whelen 1977: 15–16; Dahl 1989: 193–209). One could easily argue that emigrants and their descendants who have supported the homeland over the years, often with extensive economic contributions, deserve the right to participate. Or, one could argue that only residents of the homeland and those born there should be able to participate because it is they who must suffer the consequences of decisions made.

From the standpoint of nationalist ideology, legitimate exercise of power is based on criteria of belonging to the "nation," rather than the *demos* per se, and realizing the national interest, rather than following democratic procedure. Should emigrants who left the national homeland for a better life abroad be entitled to make decisions regarding the fate of those who stayed behind? While the descendants of emigrants may be considered members of the nation by virtue of ancestral lineage, regardless of the language they speak and the customs they practice, is their membership status legitimate when it comes to making decisions regarding the homeland? Again, nationalist ideology provides no clear answers to these questions, because "the nation" itself is often a politically contested concept, not simply among academics, but among nationalists themselves.

Emigrants and international politics

Much like the proliferation of international non-governmental organizations (INGOs), the political participation of emigrants is a transnational phenomenon whose importance was pointed out long ago (see Mansbach *et al.* 1976: ch. 4; Miller 1981), but subsequently failed to make much of an impact on the international relations literature because it failed to be seen as having a significant impact on international security. As is often the case with transnational phenomena, the globalization of domestic politics is, strictly speaking, distinct from international politics as traditionally understood in terms of state-to-state relations. When the actions of émigrés begin to influence the foreign policy-making of their host or home states, however, the boundary between the globalization of domestic politics and international politics as traditionally conceived evaporates.

In the post-war era, East European émigrés and Americans of East European descent lobbied the United States Congress and successive administrations to press human-rights issues in their home countries and maintain a hard line against the Soviet Union. American Jews who identified with Russian Jews did likewise with respect to the Soviet Union. The fight against Algerian independence spearheaded by the descendants of nineteenth-century French settlers in Algeria led to turmoil in French domestic politics and foreign policy throughout the 1950s and into the 1960s. Cuban refugees joined forces with the CIA and invaded at the Bay of Pigs in an attempt to topple the Castro regime. The Clinton administration's initiative in the Northern Ireland Peace process was prompted by years of lobbying by Irish-Americans (Guelke 1996).

The Croatian diaspora played an important role in Croatia's attainment of diplomatic recognition by the international community. Croats who went to Germany as guest workers lobbied German political parties, particularly the Bavarian Christian Social Union (CSU), and helped establish back-channel contacts between Tudjman and the Kohl government before Croatia declared independence. Then, in demonstrations during May 1991, thousands of Croatians called on Germany to recognize Croatian sovereignty. These activities helped place the question of self-determination long championed by West German politicians for Eastern Europe, particularly for East Germany, squarely before the German public and thereby contributed to forming a consensus among German political parties unilaterally to recognize Croatia despite the protests of their fellow EU members, particularly Britain and France (see Crawford 1996: 482–521, esp. 503). While the activities of Croatians were not in and of themselves decisive factors in the German recognition of Croatia, German recognition proved decisive for the break-up of Yugoslavia in that it forced the rest of the EU to recognize Croatia as well. Similarly, Croatian Americans helped establish Croatian diplomatic offices in Washington and lobbied for American diplomatic recognition after German and EU recognition.

African-Americans working through a coalition of TransAfrica and the Congressional Black Caucus induced a reversal of the Clinton administration's policy toward Haiti. Contrary to the position espoused by Bill Clinton as a candidate in the 1992 presidential campaign, as president, Clinton continued the Bush administration's practice of interdicting Haitian migrants on the high seas so that they would not reach US territory and thereby receive full asylum hearings and permission to stay in the United States until that hearing took place. Rather, Haitian migrants received only cursory on-board asylum hearings, and nearly all were then returned to Haiti. After the 1993 Governor's Island Agreement between Haiti's military leaders and its elected president Jean Bertrand Aristide collapsed, migration from Haiti to the United States increased and the Clinton administration stepped up interdictions at sea. Prompted by a hunger strike by Randall Robinson, the leader of TransAfrica, the Clinton administration removed the US State Department official in charge of Haitian policy, insured that Haitian refugees would get fair and extensive asylum hearings and began to house Haitians at the American base at Guantanamo, Cuba. Subsequently, the Clinton administration saw no other acceptable way to reduce refugee flows than to enforce the Governor's Island Agreement by inducing Haiti's military leaders to give up power in advance of an imminent deployment of US troops.

Emigrants may also influence home country foreign policy.[9] This influence is perhaps most clearly exemplified in those newly democratized countries where emigrants have assumed foreign policy-making portfolios in new governments. Much as Gojko Susak became Croatia's defense minister, an American, Alexander Eiseln, became the leader of the Estonian army. Americans, Raffi Hovannisian and Muhamed Sacriby, became foreign ministers of Armenia and Bosnia-Herzegovina, respectively. Of this group, Susak is perhaps most important, not only for his role in the rise of Croatian nationalism and the break-up of Yugoslavia, but also in the Bosnian War. Susak's so-called Herzegovina lobby pushed for Croatian military intervention supporting the ethnic Croats of Bosnia-Herzegovina and became what a Western diplomat called a "very substantial power, evidenced by the Croatian Government's commitment to recover what is basically a land of snakes and stones" (unnamed source, quoted in Kifner 1994). He subsequently became the primary Croatian power-broker in the Washington Agreement which formed the Bosnian Croat–Muslim federation.

Although the influence of emigrants and their descendants on host- and home-country foreign policy is the most significant way in which the boundary between the globalization of domestic politics and international politics is breached, the distinction also breaks down when the globalization of domestic politics entails violence between contending parties of a domestic political struggle taking place abroad. Such conflicts may be between factions opposed to the home-country government, as when Turkish groups fought one another in Germany and the rest of Europe (Abadan-Unat 1997). Emigrant political groups may also directly target diplomatic institutions or personnel of the home-state government. On June 24, 1993, Kurdish nationalists, believed to be coordinated by the Kurdish Workers' Party (PKK), kidnapped thirty people and attacked Turkish businesses and government offices in twenty-nine European cities (Fisher 1993). The German government responded by outlawing the PKK and other Kurdish nationalist groups as "terrorist organizations," raiding offices, arresting suspected members and deporting them (see chapter 3 below). Similarly, the attacks of al-Qaeda on US military and diplomatic personnel and facilities in Saudi Arabia, Yemen and East Africa can be understood as part of a globalized intra-Saudi conflict between Osama Bin Laden and a Saudi monarchy that Bin Laden condemned for allowing US military to be stationed in Saudia Arabia during and after the first Gulf War. When al-Qaeda joined forces with Egyptian Islamic Jihad, the conflict became less of a domestic Saudi conflict and more of an intra-Arab, intra-Muslim world conflict between radical Islamists and more secular Western-oriented governments supported by the US. In such cases, parties to the conflict often view these actions in terms of the continuation of domestic political struggles abroad, whereas the host countries in which this struggle takes place label it "international terrorism."

Although terrorist activity has generally come under the purview of cabinet ministers and executive departments dedicated to law enforcement and internal security, in the post-Cold War era, the phenomenon of international terrorism has increasingly become a matter dealt with by foreign and defense ministries. This shift has been motivated largely by the possibility of terrorists gaining access to weapons of mass destruction, particularly from the remnants of the Soviet Union. It was not, however, until the September 11, 2001 attacks that international terrorism became a primary mission of foreign and defense ministries and even, as in the case of the US, led to a reorganization of government to provide "homeland security." Hence, by the mid-1990s, international terrorism became recognized as a significant topic of security analysis. Now the September 11 attacks have led to a rethinking of national security itself. In this rethinking, it is worth pausing to remember that, just as Clausewitz defined war as "politics by other means," depending on one's perspective, certain forms of international terrorism may be considered transnational diasporic politics by other means.

Emigrants and the politics of the international economy

The question of international cooperation has become the focus of the few studies of migration and international political economy undertaken by migration specialists, and regime theory has become the primary theoretical framework (see, e.g., Mitchell 1989; Hollifield 1992; Zolberg 1992; Koslowski 1998). Although international cooperation with respect to migration is very important, it understates the significance of migration by relegating international migration to being considered as just one of many diverse issue areas. Since human migration across international borders differs from the movement of other factors of production or products because migrants possess the capacity to become significant economic and political actors themselves, the international economic and political consequences of migration go beyond questions of its regulation or lack of regulation by states.

It is perhaps more useful to examine the role of migration in the development of micro-economic linkages across state boundaries, the impact of migration on the macro-economics of host and home countries and the relationship of these micro-economic linkages and macro-economic consequences to the nature of political interactions among states. For instance, emigrant remittances and direct foreign investment by diasporas can have a very significant impact on the home states' economies, especially in developing countries. Given that emigrant capital is often politically fungible, especially in elections, this form of economic globalization often works in tandem with the globalization of domestic politics.

It has been estimated that all of the world's migrant workers[10] collectively sent home approximately $65.6 billion in 1989 and $71.1 billion in 1990 (Stanton Russell 1992: 286, table 3; Martin 1992: 162–72). With gross international capital movements at the end of the 1980s estimated at approximately $600 per year (Turner 1991: 9, cited in Keohane and Milner 1996: 1), remittances represented over 10 percent of the overall total. Although remittances were relatively small compared to total world merchandise trade of approximately $3.5 trillion in 1990 (UNSTAT 1994: 804–5, table 90), remittances of $71.1 billion become more significant if ranked with individual commodities, coming in second after oil (Martin 1992: 162). It is important to note that official remittance statistics do not capture all of the flows of remittances through informal funds transfer systems, such as "Hawala" operating in transnational Arab communities, "Fei-Ch'ien" among the Chinese, the Indian "Hundi," and Thai "Phei Kwan," among others (El-Qorchi 2002).

Moreover, remittances have had an increasing impact on many individual developing countries as well as developing countries as a group. In 2001, India received $10.0 billion in remittances and Mexico received $9.9 billion (World

Bank 2003: 198, table A-19). In terms of the proportional impact of remittances on developing economies, in 2001 migrant workers' remittances as a percentage of GDP were 37.3 percent in Tonga, 26.5 percent in Lesotho, 22.8 percent in Jordan, 17 percent in Albania and 16.2 percent in Nicaragua (ibid.: 159, figure 7.4). By the end of the 1980s, remittances exceeded the merchandise export earnings of many developing countries as well as the official development assistance they received (Stanton Russell and Teitelbaum 1992). During the 1990s, total remittances received by developing countries as a group exceeded total official development assistance received, and during the latter half of the decade there was a yawning gap between growing remittances and stagnant development assistance (see Table 1.1).

Given such trends, it should be no surprise that remittances are playing an increasing role in reducing poverty in developing countries. According to a recent World Bank study, on average a 10 percent increase in the share of a country's GDP that is made up of remittances will lead to a 1.6 percent reduction in the share of that country's people who live in poverty, defined in terms of $1.00 per person per day (Adams and Page 2003).

As temporary migrants become permanent residents and citizens of host states, their actions begin to affect capital flows in the form of foreign direct investment. That is, emigrants who have settled abroad permanently, and their descendants, also send money to the home country; however, they do so more often in the hope of making a profit than in order to support families. For example, by 1993, the flow of foreign investment to mainland China originating in Taiwan and Hong Kong was three times that of all other nations combined (Weidenbaum and Hughes 1996). Ethnic Chinese from South-East Asia, Japan, the Americas and Australia could well have provided a major portion of the investment coming from those countries other than Hong Kong and Taiwan, though solid statistical evidence is not available (Gungwu 1995: 278). Similarly, the investments of the approximately 10 million ethnic Poles who live outside of Poland provided much of the capital for the accelerated development of Poland's burgeoning private sector after the initiation of economic "shock therapy" in 1990 (Brzezinski 1993: 6).

These capital flows are not the only indicators of a significant economic phenomenon. International migration and the development of disporas help explain the internationalization of economies as defined by Keohane and Milner in terms of underlying shifts in transaction costs that produce observable flows of capital (Keohane and Milner 1996: 4). In the conditions of the information and

Table 1.1 Workers' remittances in comparison with net official development assistance (received by developing countries in billions of dollars)

	1995	1996	1997	1998	1999	2000	2001
Remittances received	48.1	52.6	62.7	59.5	64.6	64.5	72.3
Assistance received	61.0	51.9	46.6	50.3	52.4	50.5	52.0
Difference	−12.9	0.7	16.1	9.2	12.2	14.0	20.3

Source: World Bank 2003, Statistical Appendix, tables A-19 and A-21, pp. 198, 200.

communications revolution, individual emigrants are increasingly able to exploit the comparative advantage of the local information they possess through using diaspora networks formed by the migrant's predecessors as well as friends, relatives and business associates in the home country. As Hayek (1945) pointed out, the market works by coordinating the unique knowledge that every individual possesses. With the simple mechanism of a freely negotiated price, the information of individuals is elicited and then coordinated by exchange. If the possibilities of exchange are circumscribed by limits imposed by transportation or communications within political boundaries, the potential value of that unique individual knowledge is circumscribed in like fashion. If the limits of communication and transportation are lifted and the scope of exchange transcends political boundaries, the potential value of individual knowledge increases. Diaspora financial and information networks allow that potential value to be realized by reducing transaction costs of exchange as the scope of exchange expands to global dimensions.

Practically speaking, this happens when an individual is able to utilize knowledge gained by virtue of being a member of the diaspora in order to reduce costs and/or make profits in excess of what otherwise may be attained. This may involve learning about a new source for a product in high demand or about the opening of an underexploited market niche. Similarly, transaction costs of international trade and investment can be reduced by informal, but tightly binding, mutual understandings of agreement that are often possible among members of a transnational diaspora.[11] For example, informal funds transfer systems such as Hawala or Hundi depend on trust rooted in village, ethnic and even national solidarity (El-Qorchi 2002, 33). In contrast, agreements between private parties to an international deal from two or more different countries usually involve complicated contracts, sometimes requiring careful translations in order to avoid misunderstandings and sometimes saddled with the additional costs of private insurance or public guarantees against loss on investments. Communications networks, combined with language skills and informal contractual understandings, have enabled members of diasporas to share local knowledge in a way that has historically led to success in commercial undertakings.[12] Although it is unknown how much money passes through informal funds transfer systems, crude estimates put the figure in the billions (ibid.), and clearly these informal financiers are able to make a living in host and home countries.

In sum, migration can foster the process of economic globalization. Moreover, this form of economic globalization has very particular political implications in that remittances and foreign direct investment can be politically fungible. That is, such transnational financial flows can provide the resources for influencing homeland politics.

Emigrants, nationalism and alternative transnational identities

The end of the Cold War and the collapse of the Soviet Union and Yugoslavia have challenged the nation-state as a unit of political analysis and refocused the attention of international relations scholars on questions of culture, political identity and nationalism (see, e.g., Black and Avruch 1993; Lapid and Kratochwil 1996; Kupchan 1995). While the revival of political identities challenges existing states, such revivals are not necessarily home-grown affairs. The smuggled works of nineteenth-century émigré historians and poets provided the national histories and epic myths around which national identities coalesced in Central and Eastern Europe. Emigrants not only inspire but also finance and even lead movements, which project national visions that transcend existing state boundaries or revive dormant subnational identities that challenge multinational home states. In general, emigrants may transfer their political identities from their homeland to their new host state, become completely apolitical or continue to identify with and partici-pate in homeland politics. Emigrants may, however, resist homeland nationalism as well as complete assimilation in the host-state polity and instead develop a transnational identity, which is often marked by dual nationality. Such alternative transnational identities challenge uniform state authority and undivided loyalties, often assumed to exist with singular nationality in sharply delineated nation-states (see Jones-Correa 1998; Koslowski 2000, 2001; Levitt 2001).

The former Yugoslavia, the Soviet Union, and Czechoslovakia provide examples of nationalist revivals fostered by emigrants which led to the dismantling of these multiethnic states in the wake of communism's collapse. While Croatian emigrants supported Croatia's bid for independence from what they perceived as a Serb-dominated Yugoslavia, to the point of attempting to smuggle millions of dollars-worth of weapons to Croatia (Swardson 1993), Kosovo Albanian emigrants played an even more spectacular role in the Kosovar self-determination movement. By the end of 1998, an estimated 600,000 ethnic Albanians in Europe and 300,000 in Canada and the United States contributed to establishing independent education, social services and public administration in Kosovo (Hedges 1999). Led by Ibrahim Rugova, this non-violent movement to establish a civil society was similar to previous resistance movements to totalitarian regimes in the 1970s and 1980s in other parts of Eastern Europe. After the 1995 Dayton Accords led to EU recog-nition of Yugoslavia without having addressed the plight of Kosovo's Albanian majority, the more radical Kosovo Liberation Army (KLA) initiated attacks against Serbian police and eventually forged a political role that overtook the efforts of Rugova and other moderates. The KLA maintained a military command in Kosovo and a coordinating and fundraising operation in Western Europe (ibid.). To fund its activities, the KLA managed successfully to divert emigrant contributions for social services to military purposes and raise money directly – contributions to one KLA fund in Germany reached almost $1 million per month (Drozdiak 1998). The KLA also imposed "taxes" on Kosovo Albanian migrant workers who had hoped to remain less generous to the cause (Murphy 1998). Many Albanian emigrants and their children born abroad joined the KLA and returned to Kosovo to fight, as Serb police and paramilitary groups intensified attacks on Kosovo Albanian villages in the wake of NATO bombing. The Armenian diaspora – constituting half of the world's Armenian population of 6 to 7 million (Pattie 1994: 185) – supported the Armenian national independence movement and the Nagorno-Karabakh autonomy movement (Hovannisain 1993: 197–201).

Only a year after the collapse of Czechoslovakia's communist regime at the end of 1989, the Slovak League of America voiced its support for Slovak sovereignty. In 1991, Václav Havel declared that the 1918 Pittsburgh Agreement[13] was to be the basis for post-communist constitutional reform, and arrangements were made for Havel to bring the original document from the United States. On his trip, Havel was rebuffed by the Slovak League, which did not give him the document but instead supported parties in favor of Slovak self-determination during the 1992 elections. This, in turn, sealed Czechoslovakia's fate (Shain 1993: 295).

In contrast to such examples of emigrants supporting the revival of dormant subnational identities that challenge multinational home states, the Kurdish diaspora has supported a movement that projects national visions transcending existing state boundaries of several nation-states. Often depicted as a "nation without a state," the Kurds are spread across Turkey, Iraq and Iran.[14] Emigration has produced a Kurdish diaspora of approximately 400,000 souls, with the largest number in Germany (330,000) (O'Balance 1996: xxi). While Turkish politicians have gone as far as denying the existence of a Kurdish nation (referring instead to "mountain Turks"), the activities of diaspora Kurds reaffirm Kurdish national identity. In April of 1995, a Kurdish assembly-in-exile was formed in The Hague, including PKK representatives as well as members of the non-violent Democracy Party (DEP), which had just been banned in Turkey. The establishment of the assembly provoked Turkey to recall its ambassador to the Netherlands. Kurds in London produced a Kurdish-language television program that is broadcast via satellite throughout Europe and into Turkey. While the broadcasts feature children's programming and folk dances, the television shows are crucial to the maintenance of Kurdish identity in the diaspora and, given that Turkey does not permit Kurdish-language broadcasting within its borders, undermine Turkish efforts to suppress expressions of Kurdish identity in the homeland (Marcus 1995). West European states' tolerance of Kurdish diaspora political and cultural activities, in the face of Turkish protest, in turn, serves as a form of de facto recognition of the Kurds as a nation.

The communication networks and increased mobility that make homeland political participation possible can also facilitate the development of more ambivalent transnational identities among migrants. These act as alternatives both to complete assimilation to the host society and to the retention of homeland political identity that is often expressed in support of nationalist movements in the homeland.

In the classical model of assimilation based on the nineteenth-century experience of the United States, Canada and Australia, the political identity of migrants and their descendants shifts from the home to the host country. Eventually, the migrants' descendants, if not the migrants themselves, come to consider the host country to be their home country and lose interest in the politics of the ancestral homeland. The transfer of migrants' political identity from one country to another was usually marked by the act of renouncing home-country citizenship and taking an oath of allegiance during naturalization.

Sending countries often view such assimilation in terms of a demographic and national "loss." In response, countries experiencing great out-migration tended to base nationality primarily on ancestral lineage (*jus sanguinis*). This encourages emigrants to retain their nationality and pass it on to their children so as to facilitate their return and encourage closer ties with their homeland (Hammar 1990: 71–2).

The tug of war between receiving and sending states over the political identity of migrants increased the instances of dual nationality. This, in turn, led during the nineteenth century to legal and political conflicts between migrant-sending and -receiving states that prompted the negotiation of multilateral treaties codifying norms against dual nationality (League of Nations 1930a; 1930b; 1930c; 1930d); these also helped give citizenship in the host or home country a clear line of distinction of political identification (Koslowski 2000: ch. 7; Koslowski 2001). Recently, however, international norms against dual nationality have been eroding as host states, such as Switzerland and the Netherlands, are permitting dual nationality in order to facilitate naturalization of immigrants. Sending states, such as Mexico and Turkey, are making it easier for emigrants to keep their nationality after they naturalize in the hope that, as citizens, they might form stronger ethnic lobbies that can work to change host foreign policies in favor of the home states' interests. The migrant's act of taking on two nationalities, however, can be indicative of neither assimilation nor homeland political identification but rather of an ambivalent political identity, multiple political identities or even an apolitical identity.

Ambivalent, multiple and apolitical identities are just as much a part of diasporic existence as strong homeland identities or the transfer of political identity to host states. These alternative political and apolitical identities can also be considered part and parcel of the economic and political dynamics of globalization. As such, we can expect that, as the economic and technological processes of globalization intensify and states increasingly permit dual nationality and other forms of multiple membership, members of diasporas will sustain such alternative transnational identities to a greater extent.

Perhaps the interplay between assimilation, homeland identification and alternative identities existing between these two poles can best be seen emerging in the diasporic communication on the Iinternet. For example, soon after the Eritrean referendum on independence in May 1993, a group of Eritrean-American scholars formed list-servers and created home pages on the World Wide Web, which came to be known as "Dehai" (news from home). Operating on every continent,

> Dehai membership includes Ph.D.s, homemakers, college students, businesspeople, doctors, and government employees. Each member has a dual identity – Eritrean first, and American, British, Canadian, Swedish, or German second – and many have dual citizenship as well. English is the primary language of the network, but many Dehaiers (as they call themselves) use idiosyncratic English. . . . Dehaiers have enthusiastically joined in a worldwide debate on the content of the 1996 Eritrean constitution. The debate in cyberspace parallels one taking place in constitutional committees, attended by delegates who meet periodically in Eritrea, as well as in major cities in Europe and

North America. Since some members of the constitutional commission actively present their views on Dehai, while others silently "lurk," the virtual debate and the real one overlap.

(Rude 1996: 18–19)

Here we see the factors of globalization and the medium of communication come into play in identity formation. Even though the nation-state of Eritrea is very new, many members of Dehai have acquired dual citizenship in Eritrea and their state of residence. English, the language of global business, rather than Tigrina, the homeland language, becomes the common language of political debate. Calling themselves "Dehaiers," the participants in this political debate identify with the communication medium of the Internet, which, ironically, did not then operate in Eritrea itself due to the lack of an adequate telephone system.

In that the Eritrean case is one of the emergence of a new state in the middle of the information revolution, it may be considered somewhat atypical. Recent studies of other diasporas by anthropologists, however, have found similar technological impacts on changing patterns of identity formation and alternative transnational identity maintenance. For example, Armstrong (1976) identified the Greek diaspora as one of the classic diasporas, together with that of the Jews and the Armenians, yet many members of this very "traditional" diaspora have adopted new technologies with resulting changes in the reproduction of Greek identity in the diaspora (Panagakos 2003). The Internet is also playing an increasing role in the mechanics of identity formation of the much newer Iranian diaspora, which is now composed largely of those who fled the 1979 Iranian revolution and their descendants (Graham and Khosravi 2002).

Inasmuch as nationalism is a primary focus of domestic politics in modern times, the politics of nationalism have been projected onto the global level for those "nations" with diasporas beyond the territorial borders of their states. Diasporas have fostered nation-state formation; diasporas have also challenged the nation-state by their very existence as distinct political communities. The development of transnational political identities within the diasporas underscores the delineation of diasporas as political communities apart from host and home states, yet overlapping both. Depending on the case at hand, emigrant political activity can be a force for nation-state consolidation or for transnational identity formation that challenges the alignment of political identification with existing nation-states. Finally, as the information and communications environment moves from the print medium which enabled the rise of modern nation-states to the hyper-media environment (Diebert 1997), it may well be that the patterns of political identity formation typical of modernity will gradually give way to post-modern realignments toward transnationalism. The questions that remain, however, revolve around whether alternative transnational political identities can shape the mechanics of political power that have been organized around the nation-state or whether state-centric modern political institutions (e.g., democracy) can adapt to boundary-defying technologies and patterns of political identification.

Conclusion

Emigrant participation in home country politics is an underappreciated political phenomenon, and thinking of this phenomenon in terms of the globalization of domestic politics provides a conceptual framework that builds on previous analysis of transnational relations and is complementary to recent work in interdependence theory. The globalization of domestic politics is driven by three factors: increasing migration, which expands the number of potential political actors; the transportation and communications revolutions, which enable emigrants to maintain contact with their home states more easily; and increasing democratization, which creates not only a climate conducive to political activity in host states but also opportunities in home states. As the globalization of domestic politics expands, it establishes another dimension in which politics takes place – a dimension that is outside of the conceptual framework generated by the international anarchy–domestic hierarchy dichotomy of neorealism and the state-centric approach of neoliberal institutionalism and certain forms of constructivism.

The globalization of politics also has significant implications for comparative politics because it is both a product of democratization and a factor that may contribute to the democratization of certain home countries, as well as to revolutions and movements of national self-determination. Although researchers in comparative politics who are also area studies specialists tend to be much more cognizant of the impact that emigrants have on politics, more general comparative analysis of elections, political mobilization, political economy, etc., tends to focus on political actors located within the boundaries of the states being analyzed. In many examples discussed above, as well as in the case studies that follow, it is difficult to imagine comparative analysis of the practice of democracy and democratization in these countries without addressing the influence of emigrants, yet this is not uncommon in the field.

Finally, the globalization of domestic politics also raises normative questions usually reserved for political theorists and policy-makers. For example, what does this new dimension of politics mean for democracy? Given that democracy developed first within the confines of ancient city-states and then within the container of the modern nation-state, the globalization of domestic politics raises theoretical questions about bounding the *demos*: Should nationals residing outside the geographical jurisdiction over which a democracy rules be permitted to vote? If their remittances and investments support whole communities and contribute a significant share of the home country's GDP, would denying them the vote be tantamount to "taxation without representation"? If emigrants naturalize to their new state of residence, should they be permitted to keep their first citizenship? Ultimately, can democracy outgrow its nation-state container and be practiced on a transnational plane?

The following detailed examinations of various emigrant group experiences will establish a basis for informed consideration and debate over these crucial issues of contemporary and future politics. There are no easy answers to the questions raised or generalizations to the issues posed because, as the following cases studies reveal, there is great variety in the forms of emigrant political activity, the objectives of those activities and the impact they have. Depending on the case at hand, emigrants may be forces for liberal democracy in their homelands or supporters of authoritarian nationalists. Emigrant political activity may further the national interests of their host states or they may frustrate host-state foreign-policy objectives at every turn. Just because one cannot make easy generalizations across cases, however, does not mean that this political activity is without consequence on world politics as a whole. Indeed, analysts who fail to take emigrant political activity into account increasingly run the risk of misunderstanding the politics of a growing number of countries, as well as the relations of these countries with the rest of the world.

Notes

1 For a useful review, see Messina 1996.
2 For an overview, see Keohane and Nye 1971 and Mansbach *et al.* 1976. For more recent discussions, see Risse-Kappen 1995; Ferguson and Mansbach 1996; and Khagram *et al.* 2002.
3 For an overview and sampling of this transnationalism literature, see the special issue of *International Migration Review* (Levitt *et al.* 2003) and the website of the Economic and Social Research Council's Transnational Communities Programme, at www. transcomm.ox.ac.uk.
4 For an overview, see Sheffer 1986.
5 On the substitutability of mass migratory movements for revolutionary mass movements, see Turner 1920, chs 1–2; Hoffer 1951: 28–9; and Hirschman 1993.
6 For a broad systematic treatment of the political activity of political refugees and exiles, see Shain 1989.
7 On the history of the Chinese diaspora, particularly in South-East Asia, see Gungwu 1991. See chapters 7, 11 and 12 on the politics of the overseas Chinese.
8 Vesna Pusic is a member of the Faculty of Philosophy at the University of Zagreb; a co-founder and director of the Erasmus Guild, a non-governmental, non-partisan think tank; and publisher of the journal *Erasmus*.
9 For an overview and detailed discussions of the Armenian and Israeli cases, see Shain and Barth 2003.
10 From developed as well as developing countries.
11 For an example, see Weidenbaum and Hughes, 1996: 52–3, 56.
12 For a recent overview, see Sowell 1996.
13 The Czech émigré leader Tomás Masaryk drafted the Pittsburgh Agreement as a commitment to Slovak émigré groups that "Slovakia would have its own administration, its own Diet and its own courts." This agreement "brought the Slovaks in America, constituting about one third of the Slovak nation, into the ranks of the Czecho-Slovak independence movement," but it was subsequently repudiated by Masaryk after he became the first president of Czechoslovakia. See Kalvoda 1986.
14 To a much smaller extent, Syria and Armenia as well.

References

Abadan-Unat, N. (1997) "Ethnic Business, Ethnic Communities and 'Among Turks in Europe,'" in Uçarer, E. M., and Puchala, D. (eds) *Immigration into Western Societies: Implication and Policy Choices.* London: Pinter.

Adams, R. H., and Page, J. (2003) "International Migration, Remittances and Poverty in Developing Countries," World Bank Policy Research Working Paper 3179, December.

Appadurai, A. (1996) *Modernity at Large: Cultural Dimensions of Globalization*. Minneapolis: University of Minnesota Press.

Armstrong, J. A. (1976) "Mobilized and Proletarian Diasporas," *American Political Science Review*, vol. 20, no. 2, 393–408.

Artz, F. B. (1963) *Reaction and Revolution, 1814–1832*. New York: Harper & Row.

Bernstein, C. (1992) "The Holy Alliance," *Time*, February 24, pp. 28–35.

Birch, A. H. (1979) "Economic Models in Political Science: The Case of 'Exit, Voice, and Loyalty,'" *British Journal of Political Science*, vol. 5.

Black, P. W., and Avruch, K. (eds) (1993) "Culture in International Relations," *Millennium*, vol. 22 (winter) [special issue].

Blejwas, St. A. (1995) "Polonia and Politics," in Bukowczyk, J. J. (ed.) *Polish Americans and their History*. Pittsburgh: University of Pittsburgh Press.

Brooks, Karen (2003) "Mexicans in US May Soon Be Able to Cast Absentee Votes," Knight Ridder/Tribune News Service, October 30.

Brzezinski, Z. (1993) "The Great Transformation," *National Interest*, fall.

Burton, J. W. (1972) *World Society*. Cambridge: Cambridge University Press.

Callahan, W. A. (2003) "Beyond Cosmopolitanism and Nationalism: Diasporic Chinese and Neo-Nationalism in China and Thailand," *International Organization*, vol. 57, pp. 481–517.

Castles, S., and Miller, M. J. (1993) *The Age of Migration*. Basingstoke: Macmillan.

Cohen, R. (1997) *Global Diasporas: An Introduction*. London: UCL Press.

Cornelius, W. A., Martin, P. L., and Hollifield, J. F. (1994) *Controlling Immigration: A Global Perspective*. Stanford, CA: Stanford University Press.

Crawford, B. (1996) "Explaining Defection from International Cooperation: Germany's Unilateral Recognition of Croatia," *World Politics*, vol. 48, no. 4, pp. 482–521.

Dahl, R. A. (1989) *Democracy and its Critics*. New Haven, CT: Yale University Press.

Dessler, D. (1989) "What's at Stake in the Agent-Structure Debate," *International Organization*, vol. 43 (summer), pp. 441–73.

Deutsch, K., *et al.* (1957) *Political Community and the North Atlantic Area*. Princeton, NJ: Princeton University Press.

Diebert, R. J. (1997) *Parchment, Printing, and Hypermedia: Communication in World Order Transformation*. New York: Columbia University Press.

Dillon, S. (1996) "Mexico Is Near to Granting Expatriates Voting Rights," *New York Times*, June 16.

Drozdiak, W. (1998) "'Exiles' Donations Fund Kosovo Rebels," *Washington Post*, July 27.

El-Qorchi, M. (2002) "Hawala," *Finance and Development*, vol. 39, no. 4, pp. 31–3.

Ferguson, Y., and Mansbach, R. (1996) *Polities: Authority, Identities and Change*. Columbia: University of South Carolina Press.

Fisher, M. (1993) "Turkish Businesses, Offices Hit as Kurds Attack in 29 Cities," *Washington Post*, June 25.

Forrest, G. (1986) "Greece: The History of the Archaic Period," in Boardman, J., Griffin, J., and Murray, O. (eds) *The Oxford History of the Classical World*. Oxford: Oxford University Press.

Freeman, G. P., and Jupp, J. (eds) (1992) *Nations of Immigrants: Australia, the United States, and International Migration*. Melbourne and New York: Oxford University Press.

Glenny, M. (1992) *The Fall of Yugoslavia*. Harmondsworth: Penguin.

Glick Schiller, N., Basch, L., and Blanc-Szanton, C. (1992) *Toward a Transnational Perspective* on Migration: Race, Class, Ethnicity and Nationalism Reconsidered. *Annals of the New York Academy of Sciences*, vol. 465, July 6.

Gourevitch, P. (1978) "The Second Image Reversed: The International Sources of Domestic Politics," *International Organization*, vol. 32, no. 4, pp. 881–912.

Graham, M., and Khosravi, S. (2002) "Rebordering Public and Private in Iranian Cyberspace: Identity, Politics and Mobilization," *Identities: Global Studies in Culture and Power*, vol. 9, pp. 219–46.

Guelke, A. (1996) "The United States, Irish Americans and the Northern Ireland Peace Process," *International Affairs*, vol. 72, no. 3.

Gungwu, W. (1991) *China and the Overseas Chinese*. Singapore: Times Academic Press.

——(1995) "Greater China and the Overseas Chinese," in Shambaugh, D. (ed.) *Greater China: The Next Superpower?* Oxford: Oxford University Press.

Haas, E. B. (1968) *The Uniting of Europe: Political, Social and Economic Forces, 1950–1957*. 2nd edn, Stanford, CA: Stanford University Press.

Haas, P. M. (1992) "Knowledge Power, and International Policy Coordination," *International Organization*, vol. 46, no. 1 [special issue].

Hammar, T. (1990) *Democracy and the Nation-State: Aliens, Denizens and Citizens in a World of International Migration*. Aldershot: Avebury.

Hayek, F. A. (1945) "The Use of Knowledge in Society," *American Economic Review*, vol. 35, pp. 519–30.

Hedges, C. (1999) "Kosovo's Next Masters?," *Foreign Affairs*, vol. 78, no. 3, pp. 24–42.

Heisler, M. O. (1992) "Migration, International Relations and the New Europe: Theoretical Perspectives from Institutional Political Sociology," *International Migration Review*, vol. 26, no. 2, pp. 596–622.

Held, D. (1991) "Democracy, the Nation-State and the Global System," in Held, D. (ed.) *Political Theory Today*. Cambridge: Polity.

Hirschman, A. O. (1993) "Exit, Voice, and the Fate of the German Democratic Republic: An Essay in Conceptual History," *World Politics*, vol. 45, no. 2, pp. 173–202.

Hoffer, E. (1951) *The True Believer*. New York: Harper & Row.

Hoffmann-Novotny, H. J. (1997) "World Society and the Future of International Migration: A Theoretical Perspective," in Uçarer, E., and Puchala, D. J. (eds) *Immigration into Western Societies: Problems and Policies*. London: Pinter Press.

Hollifield, J. F. (1992) *Immigrants, Markets, and States: The Political Economy of Postwar Europe*. Cambridge, MA: Harvard University Press.

Hovannisain, R. G. (1993) "The Armenian Diaspora and the Narrative of Power," in Constas, D. C., and Platias, A. G. (eds) *Diasporas in World Politics: The Greeks in Comparative Perspective*. London: Macmillan.

Jepperson, R. L., Wendt, A., and Katzenstein, P. J. (1996) "Norms, Identity, and Culture in National Security," in Katzenstein, P. J. (ed.) *The Culture of National Security: Norms and Identity in World Politics*. New York: Columbia University Press.

Jones-Correa, M. (1998) *Between Two Nations: The Political Predicament of Latinos in New York City*. Ithaca, NY: Cornell University Press.

Kalvoda, J. (1986) *The Genesis of Czechoslovakia*. Boulder, CO: East European Monographs.

Katzenstein, P. J. (1996) "Introduction: Alternative Perspectives on national Security," in Katzenstein, P. J., *The Culture of National Security: Norms and Identity in World Politics*. New York: Columbia University Press.

Kearney, M. (1995) "The Local and the Global: The Anthropology of Globalization and Transnationalism," *Annual Review of Anthropology*, 24.

Keely, C. B. (1996) "How Nation-States Create and Respond to Refugee Flows," *International Migration Review*, vol. 30, no. 4, pp. 1046–66.

Keohane, R. O. (1984) *After Hegemony: Cooperation and Discord in the World Political Economy.* Princeton, NJ: Princeton University Press.

Keohane, R. O., and Milner, H. V. (1996) *Internationalization and Domestic Politics.* Cambridge: Cambridge University Press.

Keohane, R. O., and Nye, J. S., Jr. (eds) (1971) *Transnational Relations and World Politics.* Cambridge, MA: Harvard University Press.

——(1977) *Power and Interdependence.* Boston: Little, Brown.

Khagram, S., Riker, J. V., and Sikkink, K. (2002) *Restructuring World Politics: Transnational Social Movements, Networks, and Norms.* Minneapolis: University of Minnesota Press.

Kifner, J. (1994) "From Pizza Man in Canada to Croatian Kingmaker," *New York Times*, January 16.

Koslowski, R. (1998) "EU Migration Regimes: Established and Emergent," in Joppke, C. (ed.) *Challenge to the Nation-State: Immigration in Western Europe and the United States.* Oxford: Oxford University Press.

——(2000) *Migrants and Citizens: Demographic Change in the European States System.* Ithaca, NY: Cornell University Press.

——(2001) "Demographic Boundary Maintenance in World Politics: Of International Norms on Dual Nationality," in Albert, M., Jacobson, D., and Lapid,Y. (eds), *Identities, Borders, Orders: Rethinking International Relations Theory.* Minneapolis: University of Minnesota Press.

——(2002) "Human Migration and the Conceptualization of Pre-Modern World Politics," *International Studies Quarterly*, vol. 46, no. 3, pp. 375–99.

Kotkin, J. (1993) *Tribes: How Race, Religion and Identity Determine Success in the New Global Economy.* New York: Random House.

Kupchan, C. A. (1995) *Nationalism and Nationalities in the New Europe.* Ithaca, NY: Cornell University Press.

Kyle, D. (2000) *Transnational Peasants: Migrations, Networks, and Ethnicity in Andean Ecuador.* Baltimore: Johns Hopkins University Press.

Lapid, Y., and Kratochwil, F. (1996) *The Return of Culture and Identity in IR Theory.* Boulder, CO: Lynne Reinner.

League of Nations (1930a) "Hague Convention on Certain Questions relating to the Conflict of Nationality Laws," 179 *League of Nations Treaty Series*, 89.

——(1930b) "Military Obligations in Certain Cases of Double Nationality," 178 *League of Nations Treaty Series*, 227.

——(1930c) "Special Protocol Concerning Statelessness," *UK Treaty Series*, no. 112.

——(1930d) "Certain Case of Statelessness," 179 *League of Nations Treaty Series*, 116.

Levitt, P. (2001) *The Transnational Villagers.* Berkeley: University of California Press.

Levitt, P., DeWind, J., and Vertovec, S. (2003) *Transnational Migration: International Perspectives. International Migration Review*, vol. 37, no. 3 [special issue].

Loescher, G. (1989) "Introduction: Refugee Issues in International Relations," in Loescher, G., and Monahan, L. (eds) *Refugees and International Relations.* Oxford: Oxford University Press.

——(1993) *Beyond Charity: International Cooperation and the Global Refugee Crisis.* Oxford: Oxford University Press.

Mansbach, R. W., Ferguson, Y., and Lampert, D. E. (1976) *The Web of World Politics: Nonstate Actors in the Global System.* Englewood Cliffs, NJ: Prentice-Hall.

Marcus, A. (1995) "Kurdish TV from Britain is Nationalist Voice," *Reuters World Service*, May 15.

Martin, P. L. (1992) "Trade, Aid and Migration," *International Migration Review*, vol. 26, no. 1, pp. 162–72.

Mathias, C. (1981) "Ethnic Groups and Foreign Policy," *Foreign Affairs*, 95 (summer).

Messina, A. (1996) "The Not So Silent Revolution: Postwar Migration to Western Europe," *World Politics*, vol. 49, no. 1, pp. 130–54.

Miller, M. J. (1981) *Foreign Workers in Western Europe: An Emergent Political Force*. New York: Praeger.

——(1997) "International Migration and Security: Towards Transatlantic Convergence?," in Uçarer, E. M., and Puchala, D. (eds) *Immigration into Western Societies: Implication and Policy Choices*. London: Pinter.

Mitchell, C. (1989) "International Migration, International Relations and Foreign Policy," *International Migration Review*, vol. 23, no. 3, pp. 681–708.

Mitrany, D. (1946) *A Working Peace System*, London: Oxford University Press.

Money, J. (1997) "No Vacancy: The Political Geography of Immigration Control in Advanced Industrial Countries," *International Organization*, vol. 51, no. 4, pp. 685–720.

Money, J. (1999) *Fences and Neighbors: The Political Geography of Immigration Control*. Ithaca, NY: Cornell University Press.

Muenz, R., and Weiner, M. (1997) *Migrants, Refugees and Foreign Policy*. Oxford: Berghahn Books.

Murphy, B. (1998) "Kosovo Rebels Support Abroad," *Associated Press*, June 19.

Nash, M. (1989) "From Polonia with Love," *Time*, November 27, pp. 22–3.

O'Balance, E. (1996) *The Kurdish Struggle: 1920–94*. London: Macmillan.

Panagakos, A. N. (2003) "Downloading New Identities: Ethnicity, Technology, and Media in the Global Greek Village," *Identities: Global Studies in Culture and Power*, vol. 10, pp. 201–19.

Pattie, S. (1994) "At Home in Diaspora: Armenians in America," *Diaspora*, vol. 3, no. 2.

Portes, A. (1995) "Transnational Communites: Their Emergence and Significance in the Contemporary World System," Keynote address to the nineteenth Annual Conference on the Political Economy of the World System, University of Miami, April 21.

Posen, B. R. (1996) "Military Responses to Refugee Disasters," *International Security*, vol. 21, no. 1, pp. 72–111.

Pusic, V. (1996) author interview, September 9.

Putnam, R. D. (1988) "Diplomacy and Domestic Politics: The Logic of Two-Level Games," *International Organization*, vol. 42 (summer).

Risse-Kappen, T. (1995) *Bringing Transnational Relations Back In: Non-State Actors, Domestic Structures and International Institutions*. Cambridge: Cambridge University Press.

Roberts, J. M. (1978) *The French Revolution*. Oxford: Oxford University Press.

Rude, J. C. (1996) "Birth of a Nation in Cyberspace," *The Humanist*, vol. 56, no. 2.

Shain, Y. (1989) *The Frontier of Loyalty: Political Exiles in the Age of the Nation-State*. Middletown, CT: Wesleyan University Press.

——(1993) "US Diasporas as Regime Destabilizers," in Wiener, M. (ed.) *International Migration and Security*. Boulder, CO: Westview Press.

——(1999) *Marketing the American Creed Abroad: US Ethnic Diasporas and their Homelands in the Era of Multiculturalism*. Cambridge: Cambridge University Press.

Shain, Y., and Barth, A. (2003) "Diasporas and International Relations Theory," *International Organization*, vol. 57, pp. 449–79.

Sheffer, G. (ed.) (1986) *Modern Diasporas in International Politics*. New York: St. Martin's Press.

Sowell, T. (1996) *Migration and Cultures: A World View*. New York: Basic Books.

Stanton Russell, S. (1992) "Migrant Remittances and Development," *International Migration*, vol. 30, no. 3/4, pp. 267–87.

Stanton Russell, S., and Teitelbaum, M. S. (1992) *International Migration and International Trade*. Washington, DC: World Bank.

Swardson, A. (1993) "The Croats of Canada Prove their Hearts in the Homeland," *Washington Post*, March 8.

Sweeny, J. (1996) "High-Tech Execs March on Washington," *Computer Reseller News*, no. 672, February 26.

Teitelbaum, M. S., and Weiner, M. (eds) (1995) *Theatened Peoples, Threatened Borders: World Migration and US Policy*. New York: W. W. Norton.

Tucker, R. W., Keely, C. B., and Wrigley, L. (1990) *Immigration and US Foreign Policy*. Boulder, CO: Westview Press.

Turner, F. J. (1920) *The Frontier in American History*. New York: H. Holt.

Turner, P. (1991) *Capital Flows in the 1980s*. BIS Economic Papers, no. 30, Basel: Bank for International Settlements.

UNSTAT (1994) *Statistical Yearbook 1992*. Issue 39, New York: United Nations.

United Nations (1995) "United Nations, Population Division, Department for Economic and Social Information and Policy Analysis," *Trends in Total Migrant Stock, Revision 1*. New York: United Nations.

——(2002) *International Migration Report 2002*. New York: United Nations Population Division.

Waever, O., Buzan, B., Kelstrup, M., and Lemaitre, P. (1993) *Identity, Migration and the New Security Agenda in Europe*. New York: St. Martin's Press.

Walt, S. M. (1991) "The Renaissance of Security Studies," *International Studies Quarterly*, vol. 35, no. 2, pp. 211–39.

Waltz, K. N. (1959) *Man, the State, and War*. New York, Columbia University Press.

——(1979) *Theory of International Politics*. New York: Random House.

Watson, A. (1992) *The Evolution of International Society*. London: Routledge.

Wattenberg, B. J. (1991) *The First Universal Nation: Leading Indicators and Ideas about the Surge of America in the 1990s*. New York: Free Press.

Weidenbaum, M., and Hughes, S. (1996) *The Bamboo Network: How Expatriate Chinese Entrepreneurs Are Creating a New Economic Superpower in Asia*. New York: Free Press.

Weiner, M. (1989) "The Political Aspects of International Migration," paper presented at the March 30 meeting of the International Studies Association.

——(ed.) (1993) *International Migration and Security*. Boulder, CO: Westview Press.

——(1995) *The Global Migration Crisis: Challenge to States and to Human Rights*. New York: HarperCollins.

——(1996) "Bad Neighborhoods: An Inquiry into the Causes of Refugee Flows," *International Security*, vol. 21, no. 1, pp. 5–42.

Wendt, A. (1987) "The Agent-Structure Problem in International Relations Theory," *International Organization*, vol. 41 (summer), pp. 291–425.

——(1994) "Collective Identity Formation and the International State," *American Political Science Review*, vol. 88 (June), pp. 384–96.

——(1999) *Social Theory of International Politics*. Cambridge: Cambridge University Press.

Whelen, F. (1977) "Democratic Theory and the Boundary Problem," *Liberal Democracy*. *Nomos XXV*. New York: New York University Press.

World Bank (2003) *Global Development Finance 2003*. Washington, DC: World Bank.

Zolberg, A. R. (1992) Labour Migration and International Economic Regimes: Bretton Woods and After," in Kritz, M. M., Lim, L. L., and Zlotnik, H. (eds) *International Migration Systems: A Global Approach*. Oxford: Clarendon Press.

Zolberg, A. R., Suhrke, A., and Aguayo, S. (1989) *Escape from Violence*. New York: Oxford University Press.

2 Immigrant organizations and the globalization of Turkey's domestic politics

Nedim Ögelman

Associational life as a reflection of Turkish-origin political behavior

Scholars have defined the Turkish diaspora in many different ways (cf. Bainbridge 1993; Devlet 1991, 1992). Different definitions of this community have diverse geopolitical implications. The broadest construction is pan-ethnic. This conception envisions a loose community of people living in different nation-states primarily between Russia, the Balkans, and the north-west of China (Devlet 1991: 26). The narrowest construction focuses attention exclusively on Turkish citizens (ibid.). The following analysis defines Turkish-origin communities as something between the two extremes described above. The immigrant-origin communities under examination include all citizens and former citizens of Turkey living in a particular host country as well as their progeny. The Turkic people living in Central Asia or elsewhere who have no present or ancestral ties to the modern Turkish nation-state are beyond the scope of this study.

Have the Turkish-origin communities of Germany, the Netherlands, the United States, and Saudi Arabia established and maintained organizations engaging in homeland-oriented political activity? If so, how and why? These questions pertaining to the globalization of domestic politics frame the ensuing analysis. Scholars studying diaspora and immigrant politics provide some useful tools for approaching this topic. Ireland (1994: 24–7) identifies three general types of immigrant-origin political activity: homeland-oriented participation, institutional participation, and confrontational participation. The factors distinguishing these three types of participation are the homeland organizational networks in the host country, the legal status of immigrant-origin people, and the receiving society's cultural guidelines for political action. In focusing on homeland-oriented participation, this analysis considers all three of Ireland's determinant factors. Miller (1981) and Shain (1989) distinguish several types of organizations by their focus on homeland and host-country goals. Miller (1981: 34–44) describes the homeland-oriented activities of consular networks, surveillance-type homeland fraternal organizations, and pluralistic homeland fraternal organizations. Some of these associations try to reinforce the sending-country regime and others are clearly opposed to it. Ireland also cites the governmental, political, religious, civil-rights and labor organizations of the host country that enable immigrant-origin actors to exercise power (ibid.: 124–93). These typically focus on the host-country needs of the immigrant-origin actors. Focusing on diaspora politics, Shain (1989) conceives of immigrant-origin organizations that are moderately or extremely hostile to the sending-country regime as well as others that are staunch defenders of the home-land political system. The former two maintain reform or revolutionary exile agendas respectively, while loyalist immigrant-origin actors dictate the strategies of the latter (ibid.: 15–17, 162–5).

Building on these theoretical insights, my dissertation (Ögelman 2000: ch. 1) devises a four-cell typology of immigrant-origin associations based on the source of their founding ideas and resources, on one hand, and the focus of their goals on the other. This typology captures the essential elements of a broad variety of immigrant organizations. The four types of associations are: (1) exile organiza-tions, (2) sending-country leverage organizations, (3) host-country leverage organizations, and (4) integrationist organizations. The homeland is the primary source of founding ideas and resources instigating exile and sending-country leverage organizations. But they differ in the prevailing focus of their goals. Exile organizations are interested mainly in inducing change in the sending country, while sending-country leverage associations essentially work as lobby groups trying to influence host-country policies to favor the sending regime. The host country spawns the essential ideas and resources leading to the establishment of host-country leverage and integrationist associations. However, while the primary goals of host-country leverage associations focus on the sending country, those of integrationist organizations are directed toward the host country. Host-country leverage organizations contribute to the globalization of domestic politics, as do exile and sending-country leverage organizations. The ideas and culture generating the former, however, are clearly rooted in the host country. While these organiza-tions contribute to the globalization of domestic politics, they do not constitute cases of homeland politics transplanted into the host society. Whether an immigrant-origin organization is an exile or host-country leverage association is the common focus of politics between those supporting and those opposing its legitimacy. Opponents often try to show that it is an exile organization defying the national interest of the host country. In contrast, supporters try to show how well inte-grated into the host society and focused on the host country's national interest it is. The final type of organization, the integrationist association, does not contribute to the globalization of domestic politics because the ideas generating and goals sustaining it are firmly imbedded in the domestic political context of the host country. In sum, this typology posits that exile, sending-country leverage, and host-country leverage organizations are more likely to contribute to the global-ization of domestic politics than integrationist ones. The ensuing analysis will focus on explaining the existence or absence of the first two types of immigrant-origin organizations in Germany, the Netherlands, the United States, and Saudi Arabia.[1]

To determine if the sending country generated the ideas around which Turkish-origin organizations in the four host countries cohered, one must understand the primary political cleavages defining homeland conflicts. In the case of Turkey, these involve struggles between the Kemalist tenets of the modern Turkish nation-state and competing ethno-cultural forces rooted in the pre-twentieth-century history of the region and its people (Oehring 1984; *New York Times* 1990a). Prevailing conflicts pit Kemalists against Islamists as well as various ethnic minorities, such as Kurds[2] or Armenians.

Rapid and uneven economic development has also generated substantial conflict within Turkey's domestic political arena. Starting in the 1950s, rapid industrial development fueled by Marshall Plan aid and the Truman doctrine contributed to heightened tensions between wage earners and entrepreneurs with substantial capital holdings (Ahmad 1993; Yapp 1991: 309–29). These tensions climaxed in the late 1970s and were effectively subdued in the domestic context through a coup in September 1980.

While class-based conflicts dominated Turkish politics in the 1950s and 1960s, ethnic and cultural conflicts superseded them in the 1980s and 1990s. That conflicts based on these cleavages are spreading across national boundaries is substantiated by the Western nations' post-Cold War concerns with politicized Islam. NATO countries during the 1990s began to consider militant Islam one of the primary threats to the stability of Western Europe. In 1994, Western Europe expelled roughly 200 militant Islamic activists (*Migration News* 1995a; cf. *Jerusalem Post* 1990).

Many of Western Europe's Muslims are of Turkish origin. In the 1990s people of Turkish origin made up a particularly large proportion of Germany's 2 million[3] and a less significant portion of the Netherlands' 750,000[4] Muslim residents. Some of them supported militant movements to remove the sending country's prevailing Kemalist regime. According to one report, "older Muslims who arrived as guest workers reported that they did not think about their religion, and religious differences, until settled and they and their children suffered discrimination" (*Jerusalem Post* 1990). This report proceeds to say that economic deprivation also contributed to increasing support for militant Islamic organizations among ensuing generations of immigrant-origin actors.

The perception among the Turkish-origin communities in Germany and the Netherlands that they suffer discrimination and disadvantage due to the Islamic heritage of their homeland heightened in the late 1990s. Turkish governments became increasingly vocal in criticizing Germany and the Netherlands after a series of arson attacks took the lives of more than a dozen Turkish residents in those countries. The two host-country governments expressed alarm about the issue and took considerable investigative measures. However, violent interactions between Turkish-origin nationalists, Turkish-origin Kurds, and Turkish-origin Islamists made them more skeptical about whether the sources of conflict were at home or abroad (cf. Sayari 1986).[5] My analysis now describes Turkish-origin associational life in four different host countries to determine if and why immigrant organizations contributed to the globalization of Turkey's domestic politics.

Turkish-origin associations in Germany

In Germany, transplanted factions (exile and sending-country leverage organizations) seem to have thrived. All of the political conflicts indigenous to Turkey have manifested themselves in the organizational landscape of Germany's Turkish-origin community (Schmitter-Heisler 1986; Özcan 1992; Sezer and Thränhardt 1983), and no other country has been host to as many significant Turkish-origin federations with a global outreach as Germany. Table 2.1 shows some of the major exile and sending-country leverage organizations that maintained their headquarters in the country. This table provides the name of the association, the city in which it maintained its headquarters, whether its ideology focused on Turkey's ethno-cultural or socio-economic dimensions of conflict, and whether it constituted an exile or sending-country leverage organization.

The most prominent organizations headquartered in Germany until 1999 that contributed to the globalization of Turkish politics are exile organizations. This is primarily because the Turkish state endorsed the activities of sending-country leverage organizations but not of exile associations. The dominant sending-country leverage organizations coordinated their activities directly out of Turkey and simply maintained cells abroad because the sending state provided them with the best environment in which to do this. The exact opposite situation held for exile organizations. A hostile homeland environment severely limited their mobilizing capabilities, so they established their headquarters abroad in environments that gave them the greatest advantages and resources for successfully mobilizing constituents in various countries.

Table 2.1 Major exile and sending-country leverage federations headquartered in Germany

Organization (acronym – city of HQ)	Sending-country ideological orientation	Type (exile/sending-country leverage)
European Federation of Alevi Organizations (AABF – Cologne)	ethno-cultural	exile
Islamic Union of the National View (IGMG – Cologne)	ethno-cultural	exile
Federation of Islamic Clubs and Communities – Kaplanci (ICCB – Cologne)	ethno-cultural	exile
Turkish Islamic Union in Europe (ATIB – Cologne)	ethno-cultural	exile
Federation of Turkish Democratic Idealist Organizations in Europe – Grey Wolves (ADÜDTF – Frankfurt am Main)	ethno-cultural	exile
Federation of the People's Associations of Social Democrats (HDF – Duisburg)	socio-economic	sending-country leverage
European Association of Turkish Academics (EATA – Berlin)	ethno-cultural	sending-country leverage

While their nerve centers may not have been located in Germany, sending-country leverage associations were also quite successful in this host country. The German state favored and facilitated the activities of some sending-country leverage organizations over exile associations because it feared that the latter have a propensity to pursue violent strategies. The Federal Constitution Protection Agency (*Bundesamt für Verfassungsschutz* – BfV), the domestic bureau responsible for the sanctity of the basic law, placed many Islamic, Marxist, right-wing Turkish nationalist, and Kurdish exile organizations under heavy surveillance (BfV 1971–97). In 1993, the German state even banned one of the most extreme of the Turkish-origin Kurdish exile organizations – that associated with the Kurdistan Workers Party or PKK. The German state justified such actions precisely on fears that the sending country's domestic conflicts are penetrating its borders. In the late 1990s, the BfV considered immigrant-origin organizations introducing homeland conflicts into the host country to have replaced domestic class-based movements[6] as the primary threat to Germany's basic law and public order (Ögelman 2000: ch. 3).

In fact, the globalization of Turkey's domestic politics undermined effective Turkish-origin collective action in Germany. Interviews with the leaders of prominent umbrella organizations reveal that disagreements over the political direction of the sending country severely limited efforts to present a united front even on issues over which all of the organizations had a common position. Even the most prominent of Germany's Turkish-origin integrationist federations failed to overcome problems generated by the sending-country preferences of their prominent members (Ögelman 2000: ch. 4).

Turkish-origin associations in the Netherlands

Although slightly less conspicuous than in Germany, exile and sending-country leverage organizations also existed in the Netherlands and contributed to the same types of collective-action problems (Rath 1983; Rath and Saggar 1987: 39). The Kemalist, pan-Turkish nationalist, Islamic, Kurdish, Alevi, Armenian, and class cleavages manifested themselves in Dutch public space via immigrant-origin self-help organizations,[7] just as in Germany.

Perhaps one reason that exile organizations were less conspicuous in the Netherlands than in Germany is that the Dutch had gone further toward incorporating some of the exile organizations and thus somewhat undermined their homeland agendas. For example, as in Germany, Islamists in the Netherlands had to struggle to obtain rights and privileges. However, the Islamists in the Netherlands prevailed more quickly and comprehensively than their German counterparts in their efforts to obtain host-country support, such as state-sponsored Muslim schools and the right to broadcast publicly the call to prayer (Rath *et al.* 1997). Differences in the way German and Dutch societies have viewed religion contributes to the variation in how the German and Dutch governments interacted with Islamist exile organizations. The inconsistent manner in which Germany treated various religious confessions highlighted its cultural biases. In contrast, the Dutch state succeeded in cloaking its cultural biases by focusing on consistent rules with respect to religion (ibid.). Such concessions reduced barriers between the host society and immigrant-origin actors and induced Islamists in the Netherlands to focus on their role in the host society in lieu of their sending-country goals. This helps explain why Islamist exile organizations continued to locate their head-quarters in Germany.

On the other hand, a constituent base that continues to identify with the homeland is of no use, no matter how large it is, if the host country strictly forbids organizations around a particular cause. While Germany maintained a ban on organizations tied to the PKK, beginning in 1993, the Netherlands hosted the inaugural meeting of the Parliament of Kurdistan in Exile in its administrative capital, The Hague, on April 12, 1995. One PKK representative reflected on the Dutch accommodation of their efforts to organize outside Turkey as follows:

> The performance of the act proved to the world that the Dutch people and their government are democratic and fair relative to freedom of expression. This opportunity was also an act of tolerance. The Kurdish people will never forget such an act of understanding. It is obvious that the occasion will be remembered as an historic beginning in times to come.
>
> (*Irish Times* 1999)

Sporadically during the late 1990s, sending-country leverage associations responded to Dutch institutional support for Turkish-origin exile associations and their causes. Often, these responses involved letters to the authors or editors of articles who painted an unfavorable picture of the Turkish regime. Occasionally, the sending-country leverage organizations pursued more drastic measures to pro-test Dutch hospitality to exile associations. For example, the Turkish ambassador responded to the inaugural meeting of the Kurdish exile parliament by withdrawing from the Netherlands for a limited time (*Irish Times* 1999).

Turkish-origin associations in the United States of America

Although one finds both exile and sending-country leverage organizations at the micro level in particular communities (cf. *New York Times* 1996), Turkish-origin organizations in the United States did not enjoy the national or international exposure of those in Germany and the Netherlands. To the extent that they existed and operated in this host country, sending-country leverage organizations enjoyed greater success and support than exile associations. In addition to consular organizations, the most prominent sending-country leverage organi-zations included the Federation of Turkish American Associations, Inc., the Assembly of Turkish American Associations, the Turkish-American Council, and the Federation of Turkish American Cultural Associations. These were umbrella organizations with affiliates disbursed throughout the United States in areas with substantial Turkish-origin communities (*San Francisco Chronicle* 1997; *Hartford Courant* 1997; *Financial Times* 1997; *Times-Picayune* 1997a, 1997b; *New York Times* 1990b).

Regarding strategies, these organizations tried primarily to put out fires and promote Turkey's position in international affairs. They refuted questions of Turkey's integrity and generally supported the positions taken by the Turkish regime. They lobbied for Turkey's entry into the European Union and other Western European forums for cooperation (*New York Times* 1997; *Financial Times* 1997). They defended Turkish involvement in Cyprus. They refuted all the efforts of Armenian Americans to expose atrocities from the 1920s as well as their attempts to have the atrocities officially condemned (Assembly of Turkish American Associations 1987; *Los Angeles Times* 1987; *Boston Globe* 1990; *Wall Street Journal* 1992; *San Francisco Chronicle* 1998). They also promoted Turkish culture and expressed concern about the Greek lobby in the US undermining the typically good Turkish–American relations (*Columbus Dispatch* 1997; *Christian Science Monitor* 1985, 1988; *Wall Street Journal* 1988; *New York Times* 1987). In rare instances, Turkish Americans protested vigorously to the Greek lobby and clashed violently with Greek Americans (*New York Times* 1993). Turkish Americans also reacted strongly against criticism from the host-country media. For example, the television release of the film *Midnight Express* elicited strong responses from the Turkish-American community about how it had wrongfully tarnished their image and that of the Turkish state.[8] In short, the Turkish-American organizations pursued strategies typical for sending-country leverage organizations.

Turkish-origin associations in the Kingdom of Saudi Arabia

Research on politics in the Gulf States typically highlights the weakness of associational life (Stanton Russell 1988: 201). There were no opposition parties within Saudi Arabia, and those who wished to challenge its regime or government, such as Muhammad Massari's Committee for the Defence of Legitimate Rights, had to do so from abroad through exile organizations (*Saudi Arabia Index* 1999).

Within Saudi Arabia those trying to influence domestic politics were forced to do so through a variety of institutional channels typically considered apolitical. Such avenues included Islamic associations, civil service bureaus that give individuals some agency in the day-to-day process of governance,[9] and educational institutions (*Saudi Arabia Index* 1999). However, all of these avenues for political influence require considerable time and effort and yield subtle returns, if any.

Consequently, it is difficult to find any traces of Turkish-origin associational activity in Saudi Arabia. If such associational activity existed, it probably involved Islamic organizations. In the early 1980s, a Saudi Arabian association was sponsoring Islamic clerics that the Turkish state was sending to Western Europe. This arrangement, which caused a scandal and calls for the resignation of the Turkish government, shows Saudi Arabia's willingness to accommodate particular types of Turkish-origin associations, at least in theory. However, the missionary form of collective action is a double-edged sword. That Saudi Arabia wants to export Islam leaves it susceptible to foreign criticism based on this religion. Tensions with foreign powers such as Iraq and Yemen notwithstanding, the most organized and powerful threats to the Saudi regime have been domestic and foreign Muslim factions. In fact, citizen and non-citizen members of fanatical Islamist groups were the strongest critics of the Saudi regime and even tried to destabilize it by taking over or attacking the Grand Mosque of Mecca several times (*New York Times* 1979, 1980; *Christian Science Monitor* 1987; *Washington Post* 1989). But Saudi Arabia's willingness to respond to any challenges to its regime swiftly and with draconian measures dissuaded most immigrant-origin actors from pursuing politics within its territory. As evidenced by the reaction to the seizure of the Grand Mosque in November 1979, Saudi Arabia has been willing to intervene aggressively to stop even Islamic politics that threaten its regime.

The four cases above show that there has been substantial globalization of domestic politics, but this has not been an even outcome. The globalization of domestic politics has been more prevalent in democracies than in non-democracies. However, even non-democracies have become penetrated and are subject to political conflicts stemming from other countries. Additionally, even where Turkish domestic politics manifested itself in a very dramatic fashion, such as in Germany, organizations did not mold the diaspora community into an effective foreign lobbying force. Analysis now turns to three factors contributing to variation in the globalization of Turkish-origin politics in Germany, the Netherlands, the US, and Saudi Arabia. These are: (1) dimensions of migration, (2) developments in transportation and communications technology, and (3) democratization and immigrant rights and privileges.

Dimensions of migration

Clearly, the stock of immigrants plays a role in determining the extent of globalization of domestic politics. Table 2.2 provides data from the 1990s on the Turkish-origin populations of four different host countries. The Turkish-origin community in Germany was the largest among the four host countries under study, in terms of both stock and proportion of the total population. The Netherlands was third in terms of stock but second in terms of proportion. While the US was second in terms of stock of Turkish-origin inhabitants, its total population was large enough to make this community proportionally minute. Saudi Arabia had the smallest stock of Turkish-origin inhabitants, but they constituted a larger proportion of the entire population than in the United States.

The United States case provides a good example of how the relatively small size of a diaspora constituency can undermine strategies of sending-country leverage organizations. One article describes Turkish and Greek politics transplanted into the United States as follows:

> Over the years, the Washington end of the contest has been uneven, with Athens receiving the overwhelming balance of sympathy, especially in Congress. Greece has the natural advantage of more than two million Greek-Americans who comprise an effective lobby, as against an estimated 180,000 or so Americans of Turkish descent.
>
> (*New York Times* 1987)

Table 2.2 Demographic, economic, refugee, and absorption indicators for the Turkish-origin populations of four host countries

Host country	Turkish-origin population stock in 1,000s (% of total population)	Turkish-origin labor stock in 1,000s (% of Turkish-origin population)	Total inflow of refugees and asylum seekers from 1990 to 1996 in 1,000s (% of total inflow of Turkish-origin people)	Absorption	
				Naturalizations in 1996 (% of total Turkish-origin foreign population)	Right of birth (jus soli) citizenship acquisition
Germany	2,049.1 (2.5)[1]	759.1 (37.1)	161.0[2] (30.7)[3]	46,294 (2.3)[4]	Conditionally available
Netherlands	167.5[5] (1.1)[6]	33.0 (26.0)	5.0[7] (8.7)[8]	30,700 (24.2)[9]	Available in second generation[10]
United States	180.0–300.0[11] (≥0.1)	108.4–162.6[12] (54.2)	0.5[13] (1.9)[14]	1,885[15] (1.1–1.8)[16]	Available[17]
Saudi Arabia	160.0 (0.8)[18]	na[19]	na	33 (0.02)	Unavailable

Sources: SOPEMI 1998; US Bureau of the Census 1998; Birks and Sinclair 1980; Anani 1992; Statistical Abstract of the United States 1998; US Immigration and Naturalization Service 1997; AID 1995; Özkan 1997: 235.

Notes
 1 The numerator in this calculation is the Turkish-origin population and the denominator is the 1996 German population of 81,881.6 (in 1,000s), as reported by Germany's Federal Bureau of Statistics (*Statistisches Bundesamt*).
 2 The sum of annual inflows of asylum seekers and refugees from 1990 to 1996 (SOPEMI 1998: 244).
 3 This figure is the sum of annual inflows of asylum seekers and refugees from 1990 to 1996 divided by 524.6 (in 1000s), the sum of annual inflows of all Turkish-origin people entering between 1990 and 1996 (SOPEMI 1998: 231).
 4 Since Turkish-origin people in Germany remain foreigners unless they naturalize, the numerator of this figure is the stock in this cell and the denominator is the total Turkish-origin stock in 1996.
 5 Because the Netherlands officially absorbs Turkish-origin people relatively quickly, this figure may underrepresent the number of people under study. In particular, this figure may not account for the children of Turkish-origin people who were born with Dutch citizenship but who still maintain strong ties, possibly even citizenship, in the homeland of their parents and ancestors.
 6 The numerator in this calculation is the Turkish-origin population and the denominator is the 1996 Dutch population of 15,561 (in 1,000s), as published in the US Bureau of the Census, International Data Base.
 7 See note 1.
 8 This figure is the sum of annual inflows of asylum seekers and refugees from 1990 to 1996 divided by 57.4 (in 1,000s), the sum of annual inflows of all Turkish-origin people entering between 1990 and 1996 (SOPEMI 1998: 232).
 9 A considerable number of the Turkish-origin people in the Netherlands already have Dutch citizenship. Consequently, instead of the figure for Turkish-origin people in the Netherlands, the denominator for this calculation is only the Turkish citizens living in the Netherlands, or 127,000 (SOPEMI 1998: 254).
 10 If the parents of a child are foreigners who were born in the Netherlands and the child is also born in the Netherlands, then the child is born a Dutch citizen.
 11 The range here provides the highest and the lowest figures for the number of Turkish-origin

Table 2.2 notes *continued*

---

people living in the United States. The uncertainty of this figure results from the fact that Turkish-origin people are absorbed into the American polity within two generations.

12 The stock figures in this cell were obtained by taking the employed Turkish-origin people as estimated by the U.S. Census Bureau (54.2 percent) and multiplying this figure by the minimum and maximum number of Turkish-origin inhabitants of the United States as reported in the previous cell.

13 *Statistical Abstract of the United States* 1998: table 9, 12.

14 *INS Yearbook* 1997, 28.

15 *INS Yearbook* 1997, 148.

16 Since some Turkish-origin people in the United States are born citizens of the host country, this cell uses a US Census Bureau estimate of alien inhabitants of the US who have Turkish ancestry (104,400 to 174,000 people).

17 All children born on US soil are citizens of the United States irrespective of the citizenship status of their parents.

18 The numerator in this calculation is the Turkish-origin population and the denominator is the 1996 Saudi Arabian population of 19,409.0 (in 1,000s) as published in the US Bureau of the Census, International Data Base.

19 Although I have been unable to find data on the proportion of Saudi Arabia's Turkish-origin population in the labor market, it is safe to assume that the figure is exceptionally high. In Saudi Arabia, the immigrant-origin proportion of the labor force is higher than the native proportion (cf. Birks and Sinclair 1980; Anani 1992).

One of Turkey's foreign ministers emphasized the advantages that a substantial immigrant-origin community can provide when he said, "Unfortunately, we do not have Turkish-Americans in sufficient numbers in this country to counterbalance certain influences of ethnic politics" (ibid.).

Although Saudi Arabia's Turkish-origin community was proportionately larger than that of the US, it generated fewer organizations contributing to the globalization of domestic politics. In fact, although, according to official 1990 figures, over one-third (5,300,000) of Saudi Arabia's 14,870,000 inhabitants were foreigners, immigration produced only isolated instances of political activity, with which the Saudi regime dealt swiftly, decisively, and through draconian measures (*People* 1999). Saudi efforts to reduce the country's dependence on foreign labor and the regime's typical distortion of demographic statistics reflect its sensitivity to and awareness of the increasing difficulty of excluding such a proportionately large immigrant-origin population from the social exercise of domestic – or translocal – power. To the extent that Saudi Arabia controls the type of immigrants it attracts, it can reduce their propensity to introduce and pursue the domestic politics of their homelands. Clearly, Saudi Arabia has been most vulnerable where it has maintained the least amount of control over entries. Because much of the regime's legitimacy is based on its role as the custodian of Islam's holiest spots, in spite of its authoritarian traits Saudi Arabia exercises little control over the millions of pilgrims who arrive yearly and often remain longer than expected.

The host state's ability or inability to control the types of immigrants it receives also influenced the type of homeland political agendas, if any, that Turkish-origin actors pursued in Germany, the Netherlands, the United States, and Saudi Arabia (see Table 2.2). Germany and the Netherlands actively recruited Turkish-origin immigrants during the 1960s and 1970s to fuel their growing economies. These workers tended to be low- to semi-skilled, of a relatively low socio-economic status, and largely apolitical. Starting in the 1970s, however, both of these host countries began increasingly to view the Turkish-origin inhabitants as more than temporary labor. Both countries allowed workers to bring their families, incorporated them into the welfare state, and provided them with civil rights and limited political rights (Power 1979: 92; Rogers 1985; Weiner 1995: 81–2; *Irish Times* 1999). Following political turmoil in the homeland, networks established through labor migration, coupled with the generous asylum and refugee policies, insured a substantial additional influx of Turkish-origin refugees into Germany and the Netherlands.[10] However, a substantial post-Cold War asylum and refugee crisis convinced both host countries to alter their generous policies and establish more restrictive ones in compliance with institutional arrangements linked to the European Union (Widgren 1990; *Migration News* 1997, 1998a).

While economic advantage was also a primary concern of Turkish-origin immigrants moving to the United States,[11] this host country never recruited people from Turkey as guest workers. The United States also experienced the post-Cold War refugee crisis that affected Europe (Widgren 1990). However, the US version of the crisis never involved significant numbers of Turkish-origin actors. This helps explain the small size of the Turkish-origin diaspora in the United States, as well as its socio-economic characteristics – both of which served to distinguish this community from the analogous ones in Germany and the Netherlands. In fact, in contrast to the socio-economic composition of Turkish-origin communities in all three of the other host countries, the one in the United States included an exceptional proportion of scholars and businesspeople (Özkan 1997: 235).

Unlike the United States, but similar to Germany and the Netherlands, Saudi Arabia attracted a large number of low- and semi-skilled workers from Turkey. However, Saudi Arabia adhered strictly to the principles of a temporary labor relationship with its Turkish-origin guests (Weiner 1995: 80–1). Also, as with the United States, Saudi Arabia was not the magnet for refugees and asylum seekers from Turkey that Germany and the Netherlands were (see Table 2.2).

The final and perhaps most important type of diaspora actor that Turkey has spawned is the political migrant. De la Garza and Szekely (1997) distinguish political migrants from their economic and refugee counterparts by their relationship to the homeland political system. Political immigrants leave their homeland primarily because they are disenchanted with a political system that fails to integrate them effectively into the decision-making processes. In other words, political migrants are interested in exercising their voice, and they exit their homeland for social power reasons as opposed to economic ones or out of fear for their lives.

Interviews with leaders of prominent Turkish-origin organizations in Germany conducted in 1996–7 indicate that many of them were indeed political immigrants (Ögelman 2000: chs 3–4). These leaders typically arrived in Germany under the auspices of their studies or through family reunification, and quickly familiarized themselves with the less constrained parameters of politics that the country had to offer. The chief executive officer of the Turkish Community of Germany and SPD representative in the Hamburg parliament, Prof. Dr. Hakki Keskin, was perhaps the archetypal political immigrant. Having arrived in Germany as a student in the

1960s, Keskin quickly became involved in student politics and was a founding member of a prominent Turkish students' organization. He then became active as a member or founder of several immigrant-origin, host-country, and homeland political organizations. As a dual Turkish-German citizen, with agendas and ideas rooted in both host and sending country, and skilled and knowledgeable about the political opportunities and constraints of both, he was clearly an ideal agent for globalization of domestic politics (ibid.: chs 3–5). Interviews with the leaders of other Turkish-origin organizations yielded similar information, resulting in the conclusion that Turkey generated a substantial and consistent influx of political immigrants into Germany.

Lacking information from similar in-depth interviews with associational leaders in the other three host countries, this analysis provides hypotheses concerning the possible role of political immigrants in the globalization of Turkish politics within the Netherlands, the United States, and Saudi Arabia until 1999. Given that the Netherlands shares historical, institutional, and regional similarities with Germany, it is likely to have attracted substantial numbers of Turkish-origin political immigrants. The role of such immigrants within the Turkish-origin community in the United States is more ambiguous, though the political context probably appealed because it was not hostile toward them. Yet, the relatively small constituent base and the rapid rate at which this host country absorbs ensuing generations of immigrant-origin actors probably discouraged some Turkish-origin political immigrants from establishing themselves in the United States. Although it is close to the homeland, Saudi Arabia is the least likely destination: concerning translocal mobilization and pursuit of Turkish policy objectives from abroad, even Islamist political migrants probably found the Saudi environment unattractive. That transportation and communications technologies have reduced the role of proximity increases the likelihood that Turkish-origin political entrepreneurs would overcome obstacles to their homeland goals by moving to one of the advanced industrialized democracies as opposed to Saudi Arabia.

Transportation and communications technology in the globalization of domestic politics

Although transportation costs have come down considerably, reducing the distance barriers to the globalization of domestic politics, communications technology has provided the greater revolution facilitating translocal political activity. Homeland media and organizational materials remain inaccessible only in the most authoritarian of host countries. Even countries that put a premium on controlling sources of outside information have difficulties in keeping news from reaching interested consumers via email, satellite television, and the Internet.

Air and ground links between host and sending countries may play a substantial role in the globalization of domestic politics. If immigrants and their children retain strong links to – and networks with – the sending country, they are likely to retain an interest in the politics of the sending country. The number of daily flights connecting a host and sending country is one means of determining the possible strength of such networks. However, it is not the only means for assessing such links. In instances of close proximity, immigrants and their progeny often simply maintain contact with the homeland via ground transportation. That said, cheap air travel has given long-distance immigration some of the social and political traits typically associated with border commuting.

Considering flight links with major carriers between Istanbul and various locations in the four host countries on May 1, 1999 (see Table 2.3), host–homeland air links were strongest with Germany, followed by those with the United States, the Netherlands, and Saudi Arabia respectively. As a multitude of cheap charter

Table 2.3 Air links between host countries and Istanbul, Turkey, on May 1, 1999

Host country (total number of flights)	City in host country (total number of flights)	Direct and indirect flights to Istanbul	Direct and indirect flights from Istanbul
Germany (154)	Berlin (15)	8	7
	Cologne (12)	6	6
	Düsseldorf (23)	11	12
	Frankfurt (24)	13	11
	Hamburg (14)	7	7
	Hannover (16)	8	8
	Munich (22)	11	11
	Nuremberg (14)	7	7
	Stuttgart (14)	6	8
United States (75)	Chicago (12)	5	7
	Los Angeles (14)	8	6
	New York (22)	11	11
	San Francisco (14)	7	7
	Washington, DC (13)	6	7
The Netherlands (27)	Amsterdam (27)	14	13
Saudi Arabia (5)	Jeddah (4)	3	1
	Riyadh (1)	0	1

Sources: http://www.turkish-fltbooking.com/tks1e.htm; http://www.turkish-fltbooking.com/tks1.cgi

services and smaller airlines also exist,[12] Turkish-origin actors had tremendous access to short-term commutes between the homeland and all four host countries. Not surprisingly, the host country with the largest unabsorbed Turkish-origin community had the greatest number of flights linking it to the homeland. The country with the second greatest number of flights was the one furthest in physical distance from the homeland. One explanation for the relatively low number of flights between Saudi Arabia and Istanbul is that the immigrants could depend on cheaper land transportation and had fewer reasons for frequent short-term commutes.

While advances in transportation technology have facilitated physical contact between immigrant-origin actors and their homeland society, advances in communications technology have reduced the need for such interaction by improving the quality, accessibility, efficiency, and capacity of virtual connections with the sending country throughout the world.

Turkish newspapers and television channels of various homeland class or ethno-cultural political persuasions were widely available in 1999 in Germany, the Netherlands, and larger cities in the United States. While Saudi Arabia was relatively successful at censoring foreign-language newspapers, it had greater difficulties with satellite television from abroad.

Evidence on the consumer tendencies of Turkish-origin actors in Germany and the Netherlands indicate that these communities preferred homeland to host-country media. According to one survey in the mid-1990s, while 87 percent of the Turkish-origin respondents regularly read Turkish newspapers, only 76 percent of them consumed German-language print media (Mehrländer *et al.* 1996: 296–7). Turkish-origin people consumed almost as much Turkish as German radio and television: of the survey respondents, 90 percent consumed Turkish and 93 percent German radio and television (ibid.: 299–300). According to the *Hilversummary* (1996), the Turkish-origin inhabitants in the Netherlands made "more use of the available media (television and newspapers) from their own country or in their own language, than of the available Dutch media products." Although there is less evidence on the consumption habits of Turkish-origin people in the United States, Turkish media were available there as well.

Saudi Arabia constitutes a clear deviation concerning immigrant access to printed media and was struggling to remain an equally strong exception to the situation in advanced democracies regarding foreign television. The 1998 *World Press Freedom Review* described general access to media in Saudi Arabia as follows:

> All domestic radio and television stations are state owned and directed. The privately owned print media is closely monitored, and tightly controlled by, the Minister of Information. Foreign newspapers, periodicals and books are screened at point of entry and often censored or banned.
>
> (*Saudi Arabia* 1999)

Saudi Arabia was struggling in its attempts to control satellite television consumption. In particular it tried to ban satellite dishes and censor foreign press reports criticizing the Saudi royal family and government (*IPI Report* 1996). However, advances in satellite television technology undermined these efforts to eliminate potential outside influences on Saudi domestic politics (*MEED Middle East Economic Digest* 1994).

Email and the Internet have proven themselves even less susceptible to government censorship. Table 2.4 provides a list of the Internet addresses maintained by various Turkish-origin organizations by association type and location of the website. This list indicates that virtually all of the exile and sending-country leverage organizations maintained home pages. Turkey was the base of most of the sending-country leverage association web pages, or else these types of organizations were electronically linked to ones that were located in the sending country. Germany was home to most of the web servers run by exile organizations. In some cases it is difficult to determine where the web page was located. This further illustrates the powerful way in which electronic media contribute to the globalization of domestic politics. In addition to the home pages maintained by exile and sending-country leverage organizations, most of the Turkish-origin newspapers, journals, television, and radio stations also maintained home pages providing online versions of their products.

Given that information about Turkey's domestic politics was readily available on the Internet and through email, what if anything did host countries do to limit this electronic contact with the homeland? The short answer is, in advanced industrialized democracies they did very little. Internet and email censorship was not a dominant issue in Germany, the Netherlands, and the United States. These new media were widely available in all three countries. Islamists who used the Internet to circumvent Turkish policies provide a good example of how this media indeed contributed to the globalization of Turkey's domestic politics. The Islamist factions in Turkey responded to the 1997 ban on religious schools by providing education from abroad via the Internet.[13] They used this tactic because it is difficult to regulate. The web pages could be administered in Germany or the Netherlands where the organizations were not subject to Turkish rules but read in Turkey where the government had a difficult time monitoring and regulating consumption. In a similar fashion, Turkish-origin associations in the United States used email list-servers to elicit financial support, make announcements about meetings and events, and rally support for specific strategic actions. Among other things, the associations distributed messages through local branches, which provided form letters that the email recipient could send to his or her representatives in the US Congress.[14] Typically, these emails tried to elicit action against efforts to condemn Turkey's historical relations with Armenians and Kurds.

According to a report by management consultant Arthur D. Little, in 1999 the United States[15] led the world in Internet use and sophistication, followed by Germany[16] (*Internet Activity – Domain.de* 1999). The third strongest country for Internet use out of our four host countries was the Netherlands.[17] Saudi Arabia constitutes the host country in which the Internet facilitated globalization of domestic politics the least.

Table 2.4 Internet home pages of Turkish-origin organizations in Germany, the Netherlands, the United States, Saudi Arabia, and elsewhere

Host country	Organization	Political orientation	Web address
Germany	Federation of Turkish Student Clubs in Germany	Pro-regime	http://wwwrzstud.rz.uni-karlsruhe.de/~uh9x/vstk/bts
	Turkish Community in Germany	Pro-regime	http://www.tgd.de/
	Turkish Embassy of Germany	Pro-regime	http://www.tcbonnbe.de/tr/index.htm
	European Association of Turkish Academics	Pro-regime	http://ourworld.compuserve.com/homepages/eata
	Kurdish Student's Association of Germany	Anti-regime	http://www.uni-kassel.de/ssv/asta/inter/kurd/kurd.html
	Kurdistan Web	Anti-regime	http://www.humanrights.de/~kurdweb/
	Kurdistan Information Center	Anti-regime	http://www.nadir.org/nadir/initiativ/kiz/
	Islamic Union of the National View	Anti-regime	http://www.igmg.de/
	European Federation of Alevi Organizations	Anti-regime	http://www.alevi.com/
	Federation of Islamic Cultural Centers	Anti-regime	http://www.vikz.de/
Netherlands	Kurdish Information Network	Anti-regime	http://www.xs4all.nl/~tank/kurdish/htdocs/
US	Assembly of Turkish American Associations	Pro-regime	http://www.ataa.org/
	Federation of Turkish American Associations, Inc.	Pro-regime	http://www.ftaa.org/
	Intercollegiate Turkish Students Society	Pro-regime	http://www.itss.org/
	Atatürk Society of America	Pro-regime	http://www.jnpcs.com/selanik/
	American-Turkish Association of Southern California	NA	http://www.turkiye.net/ata-sc/
	Turkish Embassy to the United States	Pro-regime	http://www.turkey.org:80/turkey/
	Washington Kurdish Institute	Anti-regime	http://www.clark.net/kurd/
	American Kurdish Information Network	Anti-regime	http://www.kurdistan.org/
	The Virtual Kurdish Consulate in Los Angeles	Anti-regime	http://www-rcf.usc.edu/~madjdsad/kurdish.html
	Islamic Union of the National View	Anti-regime	http://www.milligorus.com/
Saudi Arabia	NONE OBSERVED		

Table 2.4 Continued

Host country	Organization	Political orientation	Web address
Organizations related to Turkey's domestic politics that are outside of the four host countries but are accessible through the Internet	Motherland Party	Pro-regime	http://www.anap.org.tr/
	Great Unity Party (Nationalist)	Pro-regime	http://www.bbp.org.tr/
	Republican People's Party	Pro-regime	http://www.chp.org.tr/
	Virtue Party	Anti-regime	http://www.fp.org.tr/
	True Path Party	Pro-regime	http://www.dyp.org.tr/
	Nationalist Movement Party	Pro-regime	http://www.mhp.org.tr/
	Democratic Turkey Party	Pro-regime	http://www.dtp.org.tr/
	The Parliament of Kurdistan in Exile	Anti-regime	http://www.ariga.com/peacebiz/peacelnk/kurd.htm
	Kurdish Library and Documentation Center	Anti-regime	http://www.marebalticum.se/kurd/index.htm
	Kurdistan Workers' Party (PKK)	Anti-regime	http://burn.ucsd.edu/~ats/PKK/pkk.html
	National Liberation Front of Kurdistan Balkan Representation	Anti-regime	http://www.kurd.gr/kurd-en/index.html
	Islamic Kurdish League	Anti-regime	http://www.ite.mh.se/~abdsu97/ikl/english/index.html
	Kurdistan Liberation	Anti-regime	http://guerilla.hypermart.net/
	People's Liberation Party-Front of Turkey/Peoples Revolutionary Vanguard	Anti-regime	http://www.kurtuluscephesi.com/
	Communist Labour Party of Turkey/Leninist	Anti-regime	http://www.devrim.org/
	Marxist-Leninist Communist Party	Anti-regime	http://members.aol.com/ilkbirlik/index.htm
	Revolutionary Workers' Party	Anti-regime	http://www.geocities.com/CapitolHill/Senate/5060/
	United Communist Party of Turkey	Anti-regime	http://www.geocities.com/CapitolHill/5817/
	Republic of Turkey Ministry of Religious Affairs	Pro-regime	http://www.diyanet.gov.tr
	Republic of Turkey Ministry of Foreign Affairs	Pro-regime	http://www.mfa.gov.tr

Saudi Arabia provided Internet access to a very limited audience, mostly researchers. However, many more people living within Saudi Arabia's borders could and did access the Internet simply by calling providers in Bahrain. In mid-1997, Saudi Arabia announced that it would make the Internet available locally. However, as was discussed in connection with newspapers and television, it has been very important to the Saudi regime that it controls information entering its borders. In order to filter out undesirable material, in the 1990s the government tried to funnel all international websites through a system designed to prevent users from establishing links to prohibited ones. The interior ministry determined what was permissible and the system was to be updated daily (*Internet Activity* 1999; *Saudi Arabia* 1999). The Internet is clearly a communications medium that concerned the Saudi regime precisely because it is difficult for any modern state to insulate its people from outside information and political influences that may undermine its strength (*Business Week* 1995, 1996). It appears that their efforts at controlling this powerful new medium were not entirely successful.

Up to now, analysis of Turkish-origin actors in the four host countries until 1999 supports the following generalizations. Although the dimensions of immigration clearly play a role in the globalization of domestic politics, countries with a lower proportion of Turkish-origin immigrants (the United States) may generate more political activity based on homeland issues than ones with a greater percentage (Saudi Arabia). Likewise, Turkey's domestic politics influences immigrant-origin associational activity in countries with a smaller stock of Turkish-origin people (the Netherlands) about as much as it affects the politics of a host country in which this community entails more people (Germany). Instead of helping differentiate host country contexts, advances in transportation and communications technology function as great equalizers, reducing the role of proximity in the globalization of domestic politics.

Understanding the stock, proportion, and type of immigrants entering the host country, together with knowledge of its technological links to the sending country, does not suffice for explaining the globalization of domestic politics. One also needs to understand a host country's capability and strategy for absorbing and controlling immigrants.

Democratization and the political rights of immigrants

Democratization, the political rights of foreigners, and the latter's experiences with formal as well as informal discrimination in the host country all affect the absorption of an immigrant-origin community. Absorption is the ability to take in and incorporate something. Some environments are highly absorbent, capable of integrating or assimilating large numbers and types of things without disintegrating. Others are less able to incorporate fully substantial quantities and kinds. That which remains unabsorbed is more likely to retain some of its old characteristics. At a minimum, what remains unabsorbed will remain distinct from the medium with which it has come into contact.

The relationship between immigrant political behavior and the globalization of domestic politics is analogous to the description of absorption above. Those whom the host society does not properly absorb are more likely to retain homeland attributes, more likely to maintain and remain sensitive to the boundaries between them and the environment in which they exist, and less likely to assimilate. Under such conditions, unabsorbed immigrants are naturally more susceptible to long-term homeland-oriented mobilization that contributes to the globalization of domestic politics (cf. Miller 1981: 42–4; Weiner 1995: 75–92).

Two of the clearest manifestations of a country's absorptive capacity are its citizenship laws and the prevalence of formal and informal discrimination against foreigners.

Access to citizenship

One important distinction in studying diaspora politics involves the status of immigrant-origin actors in the host country. Are they full members of the host society? What do they have to sacrifice in order to become full members of the host society? Can they be full members of both host society and homeland? Germany, the Netherlands, the United States, and Saudi Arabia have maintained diverse policies regarding incorporation of their respective Turkish-origin inhabitants (see Table 2.2).

German citizenship law has been based on the principle of ancestral lineage (*jus sanguinis*), whereby children born in Germany to Turkish nationals did not receive German citizenship. Germany's Social Democratic–Green government in late 1999 adopted citizenship legislation that added the principle of birthplace (*jus soli*) to the laws governing ascription of German citizenship. Those born to foreign parents in Germany after December 31, 1999, are German citizens, but only if one of their parents has been a legal resident in Germany for at least eight years. In addition, at least one parent must have an unlimited residence permit (*unbefristete Aufenthaltserlaubnis*) or a residence entitlement (*Aufenthaltsberechtigung*) at the time of the child's birth. Concerning naturalization, Germany required applicants "to prove that they have given up their old citizenship, that is, they have been 'released' from – most commonly – Turkish citizenship" (*Migration News* 1999). The 1999 citizenship reforms increased the number of exemptions to this requirement, for example, in cases of political refugees whose home country may not easily release them from their previous citizenship; however, dual nationality is tolerated only temporarily for children of Turks who become German and Turkish citizens at birth. Those who obtain German and another citizenship by birth have to give up one citizenship between ages 18 and 23.

In contrast, the Netherlands permitted foreigners born on its soil to naturalize at 18 "without proving that they have given up their old citizenship" (*Migration News* 1999). It also allowed foreigners who have lived in the Netherlands for five years to naturalize without having to give up their old citizenship and ascribed Dutch nationality to the children of foreign parents at least one of whom was born within its territory (*Migration News* 1999; AID 1995: 19). Clearly, Dutch policies were better for absorbing immigrant-origin people than those of Germany. However,

Germany's 1999 citizenship reforms made its design for absorbing immigrant-origin actors similar to that of the Netherlands. After this legislation passed, the largest remaining distinction was that the Netherlands remained more tolerant of dual citizenship than Germany.

A country that uses birthright citizenship to absorb immigrant-origin actors more than the Netherlands is the United States. All children born within US territory are citizens of this host country irrespective of the status of their parents. This may explain the low naturalization rate for Turkish-origin actors in the United States. In this host country, all alien residents know that their children will become full members even if they themselves take no deliberate actions to naturalize. The naturalization process itself has been no more of a deterrent in the United States than in Germany and perhaps more difficult than in the Netherlands. That the United States requires those naturalizing to relinquish their former citizenship makes its process very similar to that of Germany. One crucial difference, however, is that the United States has, as a rule, tolerated dual citizenship.[18]

Of the four host countries under investigation, Saudi Arabia is the one with naturalization rules that were least conducive to the absorption of immigrant-origin actors. Saudi Arabian citizenship was exclusively a function of ancestry. The extreme *jus sanguinis* conception of citizenship not only excluded the option of naturalization but also dictated that foreigners born in Saudi Arabia could not obtain citizenship. Moreover, foreigners and their progeny could not obtain citizenship through marriage and childbearing except in rare exceptions because non-citizens generally were not allowed to marry Saudi Arabians (*Texas Lawyer* 1994). Between 1984 and 1988, thirty-three Turkish-origin actors became Saudi nationals. Of these, twenty-five were women and eight men (see Table 2.2).

In sum, while the United States has incorporated immigrant-origin actors within two generations and the Netherlands within three, Germany and Saudi Arabia have not been as absorbent and have maintained substantial and growing immigrant-origin foreign populations even in the absence of new inflows. However, because Germany adopted citizenship laws similar to those in the Netherlands during May 1999, its absorptive capacity probably has increased. Analysis now turns to the rights and privileges that non-citizens enjoy and which facilitate or hinder their abilities to pursue homeland politics within the host country.

Rights and privileges of non-citizens

Germany's Turkish-origin population has had the same social rights and privileges and more or less the same civil rights as anyone else in the host polity in fact if not by law (cf. Ögelman 2000, ch. 3). For example, Germany and the Netherlands provided bilingual education for Turkish-origin children (*Los Angeles Times* 1998). However, Germany's Turkish-origin population did not enjoy the same political rights as the rest of the host polity. In fact, after the Maastricht Treaty came into force, Germany developed a tiered system of rights and privileges concerning political rights. Ethnic Germans and German citizens had the greatest access to political rights, European Union citizens were slightly inhibited in their access to political participation, and third-country nationals were the most disadvantaged. Germany's Turkish-origin inhabitants became frustrated over the fact that the Maastricht Treaty endowed European Union citizens but not third-country nationals with local voting rights (*Migration News* 1995c).

Informal discrimination further served to keep the Turkish-origin inhabitants of Germany from becoming fully absorbed by the host country. During the 1980s, Turkish-origin people were one of the least liked communities in Germany (Thränhardt 1989). Incidents of racist violence, such as the arson attacks in Sollingen and Mölln in the early 1990s, as well as the more subtle forms of negative discrimination experienced by Turkish-origin individuals, contributed to the maintenance of homeland identity. This, in turn, provided exile and sending-country leverage organizations with strong constituent support in Germany.

Of the four host countries, the Netherlands provided non-citizens with the most comprehensive set of social, civil, and political rights. Long-resident foreigners in the Netherlands acquired all of the rights of Dutch citizens with the exception of the right to vote in national elections. However, non-citizens in the Netherlands always lived under the fear deportation, as in all other host countries (cf. *Migration News* 1995b). Additionally, the communal obligations of the Netherlands as a member of the European Union contributed to a revaluation of Dutch citizenship as non-citizen rights became more restrictive (*Migration News* 1994; *Irish Times* 1999). Moreover, like the Germans, the Dutch during the 1980s and 1990s had less sympathy for the Turkish-origin members of their society than most of their other minorities (Ögelman 2000, ch. 5).

Similarly, increasing civil and social rights for foreigners were devaluing United States citizenship. Until the late 1990s, legal permanent residents had all of the same rights as citizens with the exception of voting rights and the right to hold public office. Legislation in the late 1990s, however, revalued citizenship as it threatened to exclude non-citizens from certain social rights. Yet, as mentioned earlier, non-citizens' rights is only an issue for the first generation of immigrant-origin actors, because ensuing generations born in the United States are full citizens.

The issue of access to citizenship is less relevant in the Saudi Arabian case because both citizens and non-citizens were severely limited in their ability to influence governmental decision-making. According to the 1998 *World Press Freedom Review*, "[t]he government of Saudi Arabia – an absolute monarchy – does not tolerate criticism in any shape or form" (*Saudi Arabia* 1999). However, the Saudi regime did differentiate between citizens and non-citizens with respect to access to education, property, residence, and many aspects of the welfare state. Only Saudi citizens had a right to higher education, property ownership, and permanent residence. Foreigners only remained in this host country if a citizen sponsored them or they were the children of employed aliens (*Texas Lawyer* 1994). These exceptions notwithstanding, societal rules were equally restrictive for citizens and non-citizens (*Washington Post* 1997).

Moreover, the costs were quite high for trying quickly and visibly to mobilize support for causes rooted in another country's domestic politics. The Saudi

Arabian government took draconian measures to constrain and limit foreigner involvement in its domestic political processes. Foreigners in Saudi Arabia were subject to the same rules as citizens. On August 11, 1995, the Saudi Arabian state beheaded two Turks along with six other foreigners. Three days later, on August 14, 1995, two more Turkish immigrants were beheaded. Turkey's efforts to keep Saudi Arabia from beheading twenty additional Turkish citizens by applying diplomatic pressure on the host country were unsuccessful.[19] Although all of these men were beheaded for smuggling drugs, Saudi Arabia clearly reserved the right to try and punish all immigrants found guilty of a capital crime under its Islamic laws.[20] In many cases this constituted a more rigorous and severe punishment than that which the immigrants would have faced in the homeland (*The Independent* 1995). The relatively higher costs for violating host-country rules or even putting oneself in potential conflict with the host state made Saudi Arabia a hostile environment for homeland political activity.

Conclusion

Analysis of the Turkish-origin organizational landscape in Germany, the Netherlands, the United States, and Saudi Arabia reveals substantial variation between the activity in these host countries. As of 1999, Turkish-origin organizations had become highly visible in Germany and slightly less so in the Netherlands. Exile and sending-country leverage organizations located in these states enjoyed the support of a substantial constituent base, received considerable attention in the local press, and directly or indirectly influenced host-country policy-making. Yet, the existence of opposing exile and sending-country leverage organizations clearly undermined each community's ability to lobby. While relatively united in their objectives, the Turkish-origin organizations in the United States did not command attention or receive exposure comparable to those in Germany and the Netherlands. Turkish-origin organizations in Saudi Arabia were virtually non-existent. Some Turkish-origin actors, Islamists in particular, may have engaged in subtle forms of political activity based on their homeland ideology. Nevertheless, Saudi Arabia, the only clearly non-democratic host country under study, also provides the least evidence of immigrant organizations contributing to the globalization of Turkey's domestic politics.

Four components have contributed to variation in the extent to which Turkish-origin associations in different host countries contributed to the globalization of domestic politics. The first is modern means of transportation and communication. Cheap and accessible air travel, satellite television, email, and the Internet have fundamentally altered geopolitics by reducing the role of proximity and distance in distinguishing international from domestic affairs. All societies, even non-democratic ones, are finding it difficult to remain isolated. Information on all aspects of Turkish domestic politics was as available in Germany, the Netherlands, and the United States as in the homeland itself. Even in Saudi Arabia, modern information technology was making it increasingly difficult for the authoritarian regime to resist the globalization of domestic politics.

The second element influencing the ability of Turkish-origin organizations to pursue Turkey's politics abroad is the relative size of the diaspora community in a given host country. By this, I mean the size of the immigrant-origin community that identifies with the homeland as a proportion of the entire host-country population. Germany, which had the largest Turkish-origin community in terms of stock and proportion of total population, also had the associational landscape that most clearly contributed to the globalization of domestic politics. The Netherlands had the second greatest proportion of Turkish-origin inhabitants, and its Turkish-origin associations clearly contributed to the globalization of homeland politics as well. Although the proportion of Turkish-origin people in Saudi Arabia was larger than in the United States, the latter generated organizations contributing to the globalization of Turkish politics more than the former. The next element contributing to the globalization of domestic politics helps explain this.

As evidenced by the discussion of Saudi Arabia and the United States above, size and proportion of diaspora community is not sufficient to explain the globalization of domestic politics. In order for organizations to contribute to this process, a third element must also exist. The host country must be at least marginally, but not completely, willing and capable of absorbing immigrants. Absorption involves access to rights, privileges, and duties enjoyed by host-country citizens as well as the absence of formal and informal discrimination. If immigrant-origin actors are not absorbed, then they may exist in the host country with such limited social, civil, and political mobility that they cannot establish organizations or pursue any kind of collective action. Conversely, if the host country absorbs immigrant-origin actors quickly and fully, then these new members will be more likely to sever ties with the homeland. In short, there is a curvilinear relationship between absorption of immigrant-origin actors and the propensity of these people to establish and support organizations contributing to the globalization of homeland politics. When the host society absorbs immigrant-origin actors enough for them to be able effectively to pursue collective action within its borders, but not enough that they become secure in their affiliation with the receiving country, their organizations are likely to contribute to the globalization of homeland politics. None of the four countries under study was completely absorbent. Even countries that maintained highly absorptive formal rules often had a native population that maintained informal barriers against immigrant-origin actors. That said, the United States was the most absorbent of the four countries under study, followed by the Netherlands and Germany. Saudi Arabia was the least absorbent, coming close to the extreme at which immigrant-origin actors are not even incorporated enough to exercise marginal social power. Germany, and to a lesser extent the Netherlands, provided enough rights and privileges to Turkish-origin actors while maintaining strong informal barriers to complete incorporation to encourage them to establish organizations contributing to the globalization of homeland politics.

The final component facilitating the globalization of domestic politics is democratization. While three of the countries under study had democratized, one of them clearly did not depend on popular representation in its decision-making processes. Countries that fail to provide their own citizens with mobilizing opportunities are unlikely to attract immigrant-origin actors looking for a better environment in which to organize. In fact, such countries are more likely to become sources of exile organizations. This was the case with Saudi Arabia. Unlike the three democracies under study, the globalization of homeland politics was unlikely to manifest itself as associational activity in Saudi Arabia irrespective of how large and unabsorbed its Turkish-origin community was. Instead, political emigrants dissatisfied with their mobilizing opportunities in Turkey pursued their goals by establishing exile organizations in Germany, the Netherlands and the United States. The Turkish state and its supporters responded to these political emigrants by establishing their own organizations and competing with exile associations on foreign shores over issues that generate struggle and conflict within the sending country.

Notes

1 Analysis of these organizations covers the period up until 1999.
2 Although no host country under study maintains accurate statistics on Turkish-origin Kurds, estimates indicate that a sizeable proportion of the Turkish-origin communities in Germany and the Netherlands identifies with this ethnic sub-group. The *Irish Times* (1999) claims that "the Kurdish population in the Netherlands stands at about 46,000. Ironically, given the present situation, many Kurdish families originally from southern Turkey, are classed as Turkish in official Dutch statistics." The estimate implies that more than one of every five of the Netherlands' Turkish-origin inhabitants is, actually, Kurdish. In 1995, Germany's Federal Bureau of Statistics estimated that 400,000 to 500,000, or 21 to 24 percent, of its Turkish-origin inhabitants are Kurds. This analysis does not focus on Turkey's Kurdish diaspora, though some of the conflicts that it generates among Turkish-origin communities warrant attention here. In summer 1991, Kurdish nationalists assaulted a Turkish consulate in the Netherlands (*Atlanta Constitution* 1991). In March 1992, Kurdish nationalists attacked Turkish businesses or embassies in Germany and the Netherlands among other Western European countries (*Ottawa Citizen* 1992). In 1999, the Turkish government capture of the PKK leader Abdullah Öcalan generated a series of protest actions throughout Western Europe.
3 Roughly, 80 percent of Germany's Muslims are of Turkish origin. Germany has a total population of roughly 81 million. Consequently, Muslims constitute about 2.5 percent and Turkish-origin Muslims about 2 percent of the population.
4 Roughly 22 percent of the Netherlands' Muslims are of Turkish origin. The Netherlands has a total population of roughly 15 million. Muslims constitute 5 percent and Turkish-origin Muslims slightly more than 1 percent of the entire Dutch population.
5 One article describes Turkish-origin infighting throughout Western Europe as follows.

> While some Turks living in [W]estern Europe have been the targets of native right-wing extremists in recent years, other incidents of anti-Turkish violence have been attributed to Kurdish activists involved in the 13-year-old war against the Turkish armed forces in south-eastern Turkey. Some Kurdish fighters see violence in European cities as a way of attracting attention to their cause.
>
> (*The Independent* 1997)

6 The BfV used to consider Marxist revolutionary movements that emerged from within Germany's domestic political context, such as the Red Army Faction, to be the most threatening organizations.
7 Organizations such as National View, the PKK, the Turkish Consulates, the Atatürk

Society of the Netherlands, the Grey Wolves, the Suleymanists, the Kaplanci, the Diyanet, and others, which clearly developed around ideas rooted in Turkey's domestic political environment (http://www.xs4all.nl/~hisnieuw/dossier/allochtoon/tur.html).

8 "A group of Turkish Americans has filed a $300 million discrimination suit against ABC and Columbia Pictures over the showing of the movie 'Midnight Express' . . . The class-action suit contends that ABC and Columbia presented the film as a 'true' dramatization of the harrowing ordeal of a convicted American drug dealer in a Turkish prison . . . As a result, the suit claims, the showing of the film 'served to aid and incite' discrimination against the 300,000 Turkish Americans living in the United States . . . 'Midnight Express' is 'an attempt to insult and dehumanize the Turkish people as dirty, inferior, sexually perverse and morally corrupt,' the suit alleges" (*Washington Post* 1984).

9 In 1985 there were 100,000 foreigners employed in civil service jobs and expatriates held 22 percent of all public sector appointments (Stanton Russell 1988: 203).

10 "In 1997, some 250,880 foreigners applied for asylum in the EU, up from 231,610 in 1996. Germany had 104,400 asylum applicants or 42 percent of the total; . . . Netherlands with 34,400 or 14 percent . . . The leading countries of origin were ex-Yugoslavia (15 percent), Iraq (12 percent) and Turkey (11 percent)" (*Migration News* 1998b).

11 A recent report on New York's Turkish-origin immigrant community illustrates the economic push factors driving the population movement in the absence of formal recruitment from the host country. The report states, "There were 9,500 Turks enumerated in the 1990 Census in New York, mostly in Sunnyside, Queens, and, as economic conditions in Turkey deteriorate, their number may now top 25,000" (*Migration News* 1996a).

12 Small private airlines and charter groups, such as Onur Air, operate in particularly high numbers in and out of Germany.

13 "German-born Mehmet Sabri Erbakan, the nephew of former Prime Minister and Welfare Party leader Necmettin Erbakan, said courses would be offered on the Internet for students in Turkey wishing to fill the three-year gap left by the closure of the *imam hatip* schools at the secondary level. . . . Last year, half a million pupils, boys and girls, were being educated in imam hatips. Although the schools were under the control of the Ministry of National Education, Turkey's secular elite feared their graduates would infiltrate the bureaucracy and influence it. Under the new rules, students can only attend these schools after the age of 14, when they have completed eight years of secular education. . . . The 'Milli Görüs,' which is the biggest Islamic group in Germany, where 2.7 million Turkish workers live, is currently negotiating with computer companies and hopes to make 10,000 PCs available to students by the start of the academic year. Hosted on a German server, the course will effectively be out of reach of the Turkish judicial authorities. The curriculum, Mr Erbakan said, will include Arabic and Koranic lessons but will not differ much from the one that had been offered in the imam hatips in Turkey" (*Turkey Update* 1998).

14 One such form letter from 1998 ends as follows, "As a Turkish-American, I strongly urge you not to support H.Con.Res.55, an unfair piece of legislation that serves a biased ethnic agenda, does not reflect the truth, insults Turkish-Americans and Turks all around the world, and will unnecessarily damage US–Turkish relations." From: ATAAOFFICE <ATAAOFFICE@aol.com> Date: Wed, 15 Apr 1998 17:33:50 EDT Subject: ATAA ACTION ALERT: GENOCIDE RESOLUTION.

15 "In April 1999, Cyberatlas reported that there are 83 million adults 16 years and older using the Internet in the US. This number is according to Intelliquest Research and makes up over 40 percent of the US population age 16 and older" (http://www. headcount.com/count/datafind.htm?search=&choice=country&id=6).

16 "In March 1999, Nua Internet Surveys reported that there are 8.4 million with Internet access in Germany" (http://www.headcount.com/count/datafind.htm?search=&choice =country&id=199).

17 "In January 1998, IDC Research reported that there are 1.39 million people accessing the Internet in Netherlands" (http://www.headcount.com/count/datafind.htm?search= &choice=country&id=77).

18 "Dual nationality is not now a political issue in the US, even though it is estimated that perhaps 500,000 of the four million children born in the US each year are or could be dual nationals – those born in the US do not have to choose a nationality, since they are automatically US citizens, and the country of one parent may also consider them citizens. One difference between the US and Germany is that the US requires foreigners who become naturalized US citizens to renounce their former citizenship, but demands no proof that they have had their passport canceled" (*Migration News* 1999).

19 See http://www.access.ch/tuerkei/GRUPH/Chronology/C8.htm.

20 "Under Saudi Arabia's Sharia law, rapists, murderers and violent armed robbers are sentenced to public beheading by the sword. The death sentence was introduced for drug traffickers in 1987. More than 140 people have been beheaded in Saudi Arabia this year, a record figure. Fewer than 60 of them were Saudi nationals, with Somalis and Pakistanis forming the largest groups of foreigners" (*The Guardian* 1995).

References

Ahmad, F. (1993) "Turkey," in Krieg, J. (ed.) *The Oxford Companion to Politics of the World.* Oxford: Oxford University Press, pp. 926–8.

AID (*Ausländer in Deutschland*) (1995) vol. 3.

Anani, J. (1992) "Policies and Labour Demand in GCC Countries," Support to Arab Migration Policies: An ILO/UNDP Project. Seminar on Migration Policies in Arab Labor-Sending Countries, Cairo, May 2–4.

Assembly of Turkish American Associations (1987) *Armenian Allegations – Myth and Reality: A Handbook of Facts and Documents.* 2nd rev. edn, Washington, DC: The Assembly.

Atlanta Constitution (1991) "Kurds protest alleged Turkish brutality," July 13, Foreign News, p. A10.

Bainbridge, M. (ed.) (1993) *The Turkic Peoples of the World.* New York: Kegan Paul International.

BfV (Bundesamt für Verfassungsschutz) (1971–97) *Verfassungsschutzbericht.* Bonn: Bundesministerium des Innern, Bundesdruckerei GmbH.

Birks, J. S. and Sinclair, C. A. (1980) *International Migration and Development in the Arab Region.* Geneva: International Labor Organization.

Boston Globe (1990) "Author Defends Book on Armenia Killings," April 18, p. 4.

Business Week (1995) "An Intruder in the Kingdom: Saudi Officials Try to Police Taboo Subjects on the Internet," August 21, p. 40.

——(1996) "Cybersurfers of Arabia," June 3, p. 108.

Christian Science Monitor (1985) "As Congress Considers Tribute to Armenians, Reagan Assures Key Ally, Turkey," April 24, p. 3.

——(1987) "Mecca Violence Threatens to Widen Conflict," August 3, p. 1.

——(1988) "A Turkish View of Dukakis," August 10, p. 13.

Columbus Dispatch (1997) "Close Turkish Community Worries about its Reputation," December 14, p. 1D.

de al Garza, R. O., and Seckely, G. (1997) "Policy, Politics and Emigration: Reexamining the Mexican Experience," in F. D. Bean, R. O. de la Garza, B. R. Roberts and S. Weintraub (eds) *At the Crossroads: Mexican Migration and US Policy.* Lanham, MD: Rowman & Littlefield.

Devlet, N. (1991) "Türkiye ve Dis Türkler," *Türk Yurdu*, May, pp. 26–32.

——(1992) "Türk Dünyasinin Demografik ve Ekonomik Yapisina Toplu Bir Bakis," *Türk Dünyasi El Kitabi*, vol. 121, no. A-23, pp. 55–91.

Financial Times (1997) "Turkey Tries to Promote US Ties," February 19, p. 3.

Hartford Courant (1997) "World Affairs Dinner to Spotlight Turkey," March 25, p. B5.

Hilversummary (1996) "Mass Media Use by Immigrants in the Netherlands," online http://www.omroep.nl/nos/rtv/voorlichting/hsumm/hs4_5.html.

Internet Activity (1999) online http://GURUKUL.AMERICAN.EDU/CARMEL/FB9122A/Internet.htm (December 31).

Internet Activity – Domain .de (1999) online: http://gurukul.american.edu/initeb/es0939a/Internet.htm.

IPI Report (1996) "World Press Freedom Review: Saudi Arabia," Dec–Jan, p. 80.

Ireland, P. (1994) *The Policy Challenge of Ethnic Diversity: Immigrant Politics in France and Switzerland.* Cambridge, MA: Harvard University Press.

Irish Times (1999) "Kurdish Rebel Leader Hoped to Take Refuge in the Netherlands after Long Association," February 18, p. 13.

Jerusalem Post (1990) "Holland's Salman Rushdie," October 31.

Los Angeles Times (1987) "Turks Act to Kill Bill Adding Discussion of Armenian Genocide to School Studies," August 29, p. 3.

——(1998) "Education in First Languages," May 12, p. B6.

MEED Middle East Economic Digest (1994) "Dish Ban Challenge for Saudi Television," March 25, pp. 2–4.

Mehrländer, U., Ascheberg, C., and Ueltzhöffer, J. (1996) *Situation der ausländischen Arbeitnehmer und ihrer Familienangehörigen in der Bundesrepublik Deutschland.* Bonn: Bundesministerium für Arbeit und Sozialordnung.

Migration News (1994) "Border Controls and Foreign Workers in the EU," vol. 1, no. 7.

——(1995a) "Over 10 Million Muslim Immigrants in Europe," vol. 2, no. 6.

——(1995b) "Alien Smuggling," vol. 2, no. 7.

——(1995c) "Germany: Asylum, Construction, Voting, and Vietnamese," vol. 2, no. 12.

——(1996a) "Immigrants and US Business," vol. 3, no. 6.

——(1997) "Netherlands: Tighten," vol. 4, no. 12.

——(1998a) "EU Promotes Intra-EU Mobility," vol. 5, no. 1

——(1998b) "EU: Asylum Seekers up in 1997," vol. 5, no. 7.

——(1999) "Germany: Dual Nationality," vol. 6, no. 2.

Miller, M. (1981) *Foreign Workers in Western Europe: An Emerging Political Force.* New York: Praeger.

New York Times (1979) November 23, p. 16.

——(1980) "Saudis, a Year after Mecca Raid, Proceed with Care," December 24, p. A2.

——(1987) "Greece and Turkey, the Local War," March 26, p. B8.

——(1990a) "Turkey Sensitive about its Identity," February 6, p. A7.

——(1990b) "Parading for Causes," May 18, p. C4.

——(1993) "2 Police Officers are Injured During Greek Parade," March 29, p. B1.

——(1996) "In the Queens Mosaic, a Turkish Inlay: Community Takes Root in Sunnyside," April 2, p. B1.

——(1997) "U.S. Should Help Turkey Enter Europe," December 22, p. A26.

Oehring, O. (1984) *Türkei im Spannungsfeld Extremer Ideologien (1973–1980).* Berlin: Klaus Schwartz.

Ögelman, N. (2000) *Transplanted Factions and Local Action: The Development of Germany's Turkish-Origin Associations*, dissertation, University of Texas at Austin.

Ottawa Citizen (1992) "Turkey: Nine More Die in Clashes between Troops, Kurds," March 24, p. A6.

Özcan, E. (1992) *Türkische Immigrantenorganizationen in der Bundesrepublik Deutschland.* Berlin: Hitit Verlag.

Özkan, N. (1997) *Türk Dünyasi: Nüfus, Sosyal Yapi, Dil, Edebiyat.* Kayseri, Turkey: Gecit Yapilari.

People (1999) online http://unlhrfsls.unl.edu/hrfs865/SAUDI/PEOPLE.HTM (December 31).

Power, J. (1979) *Migrant Workers in Western Europe and the United States.* Oxford: Pergamon Press.

Rath, J. (1983) "The Enfranchisement of Immigrants in Practice: Turkish and Moroccan Islands in the Fairway of Dutch Politics," *Netherlands Journal of Sociology*, vol. 19, no. 2: pp. 151–80.

Rath, J., and Saggar, S. (1987) "Ethnicity as a Political Tool: The British and Dutch Cases," Paper presented at the Conference on Ethnic and Racial Minorities in Advanced Industrial Societies, University of Notre Dame, Southbend, Indiana, December 3–5.

Rath, J., Meyer, A., and Sunier, T. (1997) "The Establishment of Islamic Institutions in a De-Pillarizing Society," *Tijdschrift voor economische en sociale geografie*, vol. 88, no. 4, pp. 389–95.

Rogers, R. (ed.) (1985) *Guests Come to Stay: The Effects of European Labor Migration on Sending and Receiving Countries.* Boulder, CO: Westview Press.

San Francisco Chronicle (1997) "Mt. Davidson Cross Sale Measure Ignites Ethnic Feud," October 23, p. A21.

——(1998) "Armenians to Dedicate Cross on Mt. Davidson," April 24, p. A1.

Saudi Arabia (1999) online: http://www.freemedia.at/archive97/saudiara.htm (December 31).

Saudi Arabia Index (1999) online: http://www.uni-wuerzburg.de/law/sa__indx.html (December 31).

Sayari, S. (1986) "Migration Policies of Sending Countries: Perspectives on the Turkish Experience," in Heisler, M. O., and Schmitter-Heisler, B. (eds) *From Foreign Workers to Settlers? Transnational Migration and the Emergence of New Minorities. Annals of the American Academy of Political and Social Science*, 485, pp. 87–97 [special issue].

Schmitter-Heisler, B. (1986) "Immigrant Settlement and the Structure of Emergent Immigrant Communities in Western Europe," in Heisler, M. O., and Schmitter-Heisler, B. (eds) *From Foreign Workers to Settlers? Transnational Migration and the Emergence of New Minorities. Annals of the American Academy of Political and Social Science*, 485, pp. 76–86 [special issue].

Sezer, A., and Thränhardt, D. (1983) "Türkische Organizationen in der Bundesrepublik," in Meier-Braun, K., and Pazarkaya, Y. (eds) *Die Türken.* Frankfurt am Main: Ullstein.

Shain, Y. (1989) *The Frontier of Loyalty: Political Exiles in the Age of the Nation-State.* Middletown, CT: Wesleyan University Press.

SOPEMI (1998) *Trends in International Migration.* Paris: OECD.

Stanton Russell, S. (1988) "Migration and Political Integration in the Arab World," in Luciani, G., and Salame, G. (eds) *The Politics of Arab Integration.* London: Croom Helm, ch. 8.

Texas Lawyer (1994) "Weekly Case Sumaries; 5th US Circuit; Administrative Procedure. Faddoul v. INS, No. 93–4303, 10/25/94, 16 pp.," November 7, p. 5.

The Guardian (1995) "Saudis Spurn Clemency Plea," August 22, p. 10.

The Independent (1995) "Turkey Pins Hopes on Saudi Courts," August 24, p. 16.

——(1997) "Turks Fear Anti-Islamic Hate Behind Murders," April 3, International Section, p. 17.

Thränhardt, D. (1989) "Patterns of Organization among Different Ethnic Minorities," *New German Critique*, vol. 46, winter, pp. 10–26 [special edn].

Times-Picayune (1997a) January 2, p. 4C.

——(1997b) January 5, p. 3F2.

Turkey Update (1998) "Islamists Plan to Use the Internet to Bypass Ban," online: http://www.turkeyupdate.com/imam.htm (December 31).

U.S. Bureau of the Census (1998) *International Data Base*. Washington, DC: US Census Bureau.

Wall Street Journal (1988) "U.S. Turks Worry about a Dukakis Presidency, and their Alarm Stirs their Political Activism," July 26, p. 62.

——(1992) "Anti-Turk Diatribe Twists Recent History," February 21, p. A15.

Washington Post (1984) "The TV Column," August 15, p. B14.

——(1989) "Explosions in Mecca Kill 1, Hurt 16 on Hajj," July 11, p. A17.

——(1997) "Saudis Set Tougher Rules for Ramadan," December 26, p. A32.

Weiner, M. (1995) *The Global Migration Crisis: Challenge to States and to Human Rights*. New York: HarperCollins.

Widgren, J. (1990) "The Asylum Crisis in the OECD Region." Paper commissioned by The Fletcher School Program on International and U.S. Refugee Policy.

Yapp, M. (1991) *The Near East Since the First World War*. London: Longman.

3 Mobilizing ethnic conflict

Kurdish separatism in Germany and the PKK

Alynna J. Lyon and Emek M. Uçarer

A world cleanly divided into nation-states does not correspond with the contemporary reality of political identity and territory. Many ethnic groups straddle borders and reside within several countries. The Kurds are but one example of this lack of fit and the tensions that emerge with multi-state ethnicities. Kurds also have established enclaves in states outside Kurdish homelands. Interestingly, the struggle for statehood has recently moved into the countries of the European Union, with specific intensity in Germany, which is home to some 500,000 Kurds (Van Voorst 1996). The Kurdish separatist movement has become internationalized and has taken root on German soil, which subtly confronts German sovereignty. The consequences are significant not only for Kurdish nationalism, but also for the maintenance of democracy in Germany, as well as Turkey's relations with Germany and other European countries. Furthermore, while the internationalization of ethnic conflict creates challenges for both home and host countries, it also creates theoretical challenges for understanding this phenomenon.

This study examines the diffusion of Kurdish separatist contention in light of the Kurdish separatist movement in Germany, coordinated by the *Partiya Karkeren Kurdistan* (Workers' Party of Kurdistan), or PKK. It seeks primarily to explore the modalities of political mobilization by an ethnic group, in this case the Kurds, in a host country. At the same time, it implies that such mobilization also affects the home country. The study proceeds in three stages. First, it reviews the theoretical tools available to facilitate analysis of the diffusion of ethnic and national conflict across state borders. It then briefly traces the origin of Kurdish discontent in Turkey and the spilling of Kurdish activism into Germany through migration, diffusion and deliberate activism (Suhrke and Noble 1977). Next, the study examines the presence of Kurdish separatist organizations in Germany, with specific focus on the activities of the PKK and its efforts to mobilize the Kurdish population there. An overview of PKK activities in Germany and the German response suggest favorable conditions for Kurdish extremist activities in the country during the 1980s and the early 1990s.

We suggest a model with which Kurdish mobilization in Germany can be explained. The model draws on Doug McAdam's work (1982) on political mobilization and argues that Kurdish nationalism was exported from Turkey to

Germany through existing migration links between the two countries. It explores the relative ease with which political opportunity and organizational resources could be capitalized on in a liberal democratic state such as Germany, which was initially tolerant to Kurdish dissent. Such exportation of Kurdish nationalism, fostered and maintained by the PKK, embroiled Germany and Turkey in a multi-faceted political dilemma, both domestically and bilaterally. While the study does not cover the full range of transnational linkages, it begins to set the groundwork for more research in that direction by focusing on the effects of exported nationalism on the host country. Finally, it outlines some of the consequences of such activism for Germany, Turkey and the Kurdish activists in Germany.

The international diffusion of ethnic and national conflict

Kurds reside in at least six countries (Iran, Iraq, Syria, Armenia, Azerbaijan and Turkey). Their case is intriguing – the discontent of certain segments of these separatist movements has splashed into the political pools of other states where Kurds do not constitute a sizeable minority. This presents a challenge for the conventional understanding of ethnicity. Traditional studies on ethnic conflict considered separatist movements and ethnic conflict within the *internal* dynamics of the state in which the dissenting groups reside. These studies rendered detailed descriptions of cultural traits, myths and language. Although descriptively thick, most provide few conceptual tools to apply to the transnational spillover of ethnic contention (Horowitz 1985: xi).

Examining diaspora politics provides an opportunity to overcome this pitfall by considering what Benedict Anderson identifies as "long-distance nationalism" (Anderson 1991). Understanding transnational ethnic conflict begins by establishing how an ethnic diaspora emerges, and Sidney Tarrow (1994), who examines social protest, contributes a framework for this. He maintains that social contention is the product of popular responses to state policies and argues that social movements often represent a backlash against a consolidation of power by the state that seeks to "standardize discourse among groups of citizens and between them and their rulers" (Tarrow 1994: 196). Separatist movements are a type of social movement and provide the context in which to understand the contentious dialogue between a state and a distinct ethnic group.

Many groups that are dissatisfied with the political climate in their home state can opt to migrate to other countries, especially if they conclude that they cannot find viable avenues for dissent in their homelands. Furthermore, the choice of destination is often informed by the political opportunities available in the host countries. Current technological innovations, the rapid growth of communications and transportation, provide a conduit for the international diffusion of contention through which dissent is sent abroad. Ted Gurr identifies diffusion as the "processes by which conflict in one country directly affects political action in adjoining countries" (Gurr 1993: 133). As those affected by the conflict look for protection elsewhere, refugees and asylum seekers become the most obvious conduits of diffusion. Furthermore, external kin-groups can become mobilized around claims for increased political access based on distinct identities. With advanced communication networks, international demands for labor supplies and free movement of people, the components in homeland societies that are conducive to mobilization are easily transferred from one country to another, and ethnic kin already in another country can be enlisted in the pursuit. Gurr posits that disadvantaged groups might be able to increase their potential for mobilization and rebellion at home by drawing on their kinship ties across borders and attempting to recruit and mobilize others (ibid.).

This supplies a partial explanation why Kurds travelled from Turkey to Germany. However, the Kurdish presence in Germany goes beyond simple migration that connects Germany, Turkey and the Kurds in a triad. The PKK, which was highly organized and mounted a protest campaign within Germany, capitalized on the fledgling Kurdish communities in Germany to expand its separatist front. As a result of this phenomenon, German soil became a setting from which to wage a battle for a Kurdish state. For the most part, this battle is being waged only by a faction within the Kurdish migrant population, effectively launching a "second front" for the PKK (Leggewie 1996: 79).

The relationship of Kurdish separatism to its home and host countries is illustrated in Figure 3.1. The solid line portrays the traditional understanding of ethnic conflict and separatism as a relationship between a minority population and its government. The broken line indicates common interstate relationships and the dotted lines show the dynamics of bilateral and transnational ethnic conflict. The internationalization of ethnic conflict adds five new dimensions to the traditional portrayal of ethnic conflict (shown in line 1) as between the ethnic minority and the home country. Diffusion of contention becomes relevant for third-party governments. Ethnic groups in both the host and the home country can interact, indirectly with the host and home governments (lines 3 and 4), or directly with other ethnic groups in various countries (line 5). Finally, the host and home governments engage in a political exchange as well (line 2), typical of bilateral diplomacy.

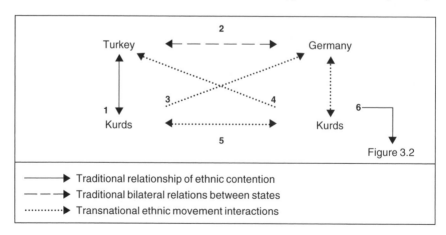

Figure 3.1 Transnational interactions of Kurdish separatism.

There are six possible dyads to examine in order to gain a full understanding of the international dimensions of ethnic conflict. We begin with a discussion of linkage 1 and trace the origins of Kurdish ethnic discontent in Turkey. We then explore linkage 3, capturing diffusion through the migratory path of Kurds from Turkey to Germany. In this context, we explore linkage 6, illustrated by the organization of the Kurdish population in Germany as the PKK extended its battle into Germany. Within linkage 6, we can also document the consequences of the mobilization for both the German policy process and Kurdish activism in Germany. While these are the main concerns of this chapter, the analysis will briefly explore linkage 2, highlighting German efforts to elicit policy change in Turkey and the Turkish resistance to such preludes. Linkage 4, one that suggests that Kurdish activists in Germany have some impact on the Turkish government, can be inferred from Turkish attention to the developments in Germany, even though policy change that can directly be linked to the mobilization in Germany cannot as yet be documented. Finally, linkage 5, while indispensable to a thorough review of transnationalization, is left out of this discussion because the existing data do not yet shed light on the dynamics of that dyad.

The origins of Kurdish ethnic discontent in Turkey

Kurds are the fourth largest ethnic group in the Middle East. Within each state the Kurdish minority has faced considerable oppression. The Kurds' quest for expression of their culture and language has been denied by all the states in which they reside and Kurdish access to political representation has been quelled by policies of assimilation and repression, leading to the discontent which not only fuelled resistance to such policies in Turkey, but was also instrumental in setting the stage for the discussion of discontent to Germany. As such, this section briefly reviews the ethnic contention between Kurds and the Turkish government, highlighted in linkage 1.

Half of the Kurdish community worldwide lives within the borders of the Turkish Republic and most are concentrated in south-eastern Turkey. Statehood has eluded the Kurds in Turkey, partially as a result of historical developments and more recently because of the politics surrounding the territory in which they live.[1] Eager to maintain the country's territorial integrity after the demise of the Ottoman Empire, Turkish policy towards the Kurds has been one of "assimilating" them as Turks. Since the 1920s, when the republic was created out of the ashes of an empire, Turkey has rejected the notion that separate ethnic identities exist within its borders. The only "minorities" that were acknowledged were the non-Muslim minorities, mainly Greeks, Jews and Armenians. There was no mention of Kurds, a Muslim group, as constituting a minority. Furthermore, the claim to the ethnic unity of Turkey has been incorporated into various constitutions, which, beginning in 1924, forbade the use of all languages except Turkish, prohibited Kurds from taking Kurdish names and proscribed the instruction of Kurdish in Turkish schools.[2] These measures incited the Sheik Said rebellion in 1925, which was put down forcefully. While many Kurds have since then been successfully integrated into Turkish society, there remain those who adamantly demand their ethnic, linguistic and cultural autonomy, despite some progress on cultural rights in the 1990s – including the legalization of the Kurdish language on 12 April 1991 and the sprouting of Kurdish newspapers, TV and radio programmes during the latter half of the 1990s. It is in this vein that they seek to create and maintain an allegiance to a Kurdish identity, at home and abroad, which is a relatively new phenomenon.[3]

In the late 1950s and early 1960s, Kurds in Turkey began to protest against the Turkish denial of Kurdish cultural and political identity. This activism was quickly crushed and many of its organizers were imprisoned or killed. During the 1970s and early 1980s, protests grew and the Turkish regime increased its repression. In 1984, separatist Kurds in Turkey began a series of violent protests, the result of which was thirteen years of civil war, which claimed the lives of some 30,000 people (Cohen 1999). Soon afterwards, in 1987, the Turkish government adopted an Emergency Decree, which covered the ten south-eastern provinces with large Kurdish populations. Accordingly, the regional governor could censor news, ban strikes or lockouts, and impose internal exile (US Department of State 1995). Governmental response to dissent included imprisonment, torture, raids on Kurdish communities, and a complete ban on freedom of speech and expression.

Such restrictions and the stepping up of assimilationist policies elicited resistance by segments of the Kurdish population in Turkey, paving the way for political and military efforts ranging from calls for autonomy to cessation in the late 1970s. Perhaps the most radical of these was the PKK, which emerged in Turkey in the late 1970s and was headed by Abdullah Öcalan. In 1984 the organization launched a guerrilla war in Turkey using acts of violence against Turkish authorities to voice its separatist claims (German Interior Ministry 1997). The PKK's platform consisted of a mixture of communist and nationalist ideologies, and it fought for the establishment of a "Free Kurdistan."

The first act that brought the PKK into the limelight was its attack against a Turkish military post on August 15, 1984, after which the organization became classified as a "separatist terrorist organization" by Turkish authorities. Not long after that, the organization "exported" some of its activities to Germany, where it found a democratic society unwilling to clamp down on dissent and a population of some 500,000 who could potentially be mobilized. From then on, the PKK continued its activities in Turkey and strove to flourish in Germany.

Diffusion of discontent to Germany: migration and international activism

Linkages 3 and 6 in Figure 3.1 seek to explore the interaction between the ethnic group and a country that is not the traditional homeland. This section begins to explore that dynamic in the light of the migration of first workers and then refugees who carried their homeland politics to Germany. In many cases, Kurds chose to flee the repression in Turkey, first to the west of the country and then abroad. In line with Tarrow's predictions, Turkish policies focusing on assimilation resulted in the uprooting of Kurdish people as they fled intrusive state policies (US Department of State 1995: sect. 1). Germany became a favorite destination of the Kurdish exodus from Turkey, though the origins of these migratory trends predate the escalation of Kurdish dissent in Turkey. Kurds went to Germany as Turkish nationals in the 1960s. The guest workers who were welcomed into Germany in those years became the first trickle of Kurdish immigrants from Turkey. These early immigrants were limited by Article 10 of the 1965 Aliens Act, which established that residence and working permits could be suspended if a foreign resident impaired "significant interests of the Federal Republic of Germany."[4]

After the recruitment halt in 1973 as a result of sluggish economies and the oil crisis, Kurdish migratory flows took on a different form. Kurds, who could no longer be recruited as workers, opted to apply for political asylum in Germany. Given the situation in Turkey, German officials were willing to offer them protection, and Kurdish asylum seekers soon came to account for 90 percent of asylum applications lodged by Turkish nationals. During those years, Germany continued to attract Kurdish asylum seekers who, in addition to being able to hook into existing ethnic networks, could also receive generous social security benefits (Uzulis 1998). Compared to other countries with an influx of Kurds, such as France and Italy, Germany, with its recognition process as well as its reception and support infrastructure, was a superior destination.

Soon, there was a Kurdish diaspora in Germany which could be mobilized to protest against activity directed at calling attention to the plight of Kurds in Turkey, forcing the German government to put pressure on Turkey to reconsider or recant its forced assimilation of its Kurdish minority, and indirectly force Turkey's hand into a redirection of its policies. Such mobilization occurred as a result of the activities of the Kurdish cultural organizations that mushroomed in Germany in the 1980s and 1990s, some of which developed close ties to and facilitated the strengthening of the PKK in Germany. The PKK could thus complement its domestic efforts by opening a second front in Europe in general and Germany in particular.

Mobilization of ethnic dissent in Germany

This section explores further linkage 6 by reviewing the political activities of some Kurds in Germany after the emergence of the diaspora. Although there was a hint of anti-immigrant sentiment in the 1980s, the presence of the Kurdish diaspora within Germany by and large did not interfere with the domestic political environment until an extremist separatist faction exported its activities from Turkey on to German soil. One way of explaining why the Kurdish separatist movement, specifically the PKK, has targeted Germany as a base of operations is by applying a model of group mobilization. This chapter operates on the premise that "ethnopolitical rebellion is primarily driven by grievances among an ethnic group and by how well an ethnic group is mobilized and, hence, in a position to take collective action" (Gurr and Moore 1997: 1083) and attempts to portray the interaction of the domestic and international dimensions of ethnic conflict. The model is depicted in Figure 3.2.

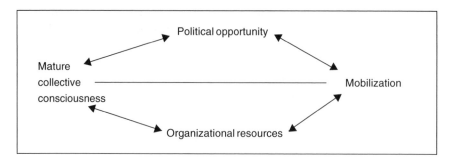

Figure 3.2 Process of PKK mobilization in Germany.
Source: Lyon 1999.

Separatist movement mobilization is the product of three general forces: a consolidated and politicized identity, operational resources and political opportunity. This process of mobilization is an extension of Doug McAdam's "political process model," in which he presents three streams that lead to mobilization (cognitive liberation, organizational resources, political opportunity structures). He argues that, when these converge, they produce the fertile ground for the mobilization of people (McAdam 1982: 51). This chapter alters the model slightly by adapting the first tier, cognitive liberation, to discuss the framing of Kurdish political identity. The formation and politicization of an identity group establishes the foundation for ethno-nationalism. Second, the building of resources, financial and organizational, is paramount for the movement's viability. And, finally, political opportunity must be present to lend both support and optimism to the movement's formation and potential success. The following section highlights the confluence of these variables and traces the components of mobilization that were present in Germany but absent in Turkey.

Expression of Kurdish identity

One of the most significant aspects that contributed to the transnational diffusion of Kurdish separatism was the development of the collective insurgent consciousness. Many Kurds have not been able to express their "Kurdishness" in any of their traditional homelands. Of these countries, the Turkish state has been the most emphatic in denying cultural and linguistic autonomy. Thus, when they came to Germany in the 1960s and 1970s, the barriers to the expression of their identity were lifted in the territory of a liberal democratic state and it became possible to explore and express Kurdish cultural and linguistic identity.

The expression of ethnic, linguistic and cultural traits provides a foundation for developing community ties and awareness. Unlike Turkey, Germany has a liberal democracy which allows the expression of otherness, as long as the means are in line with German laws on associations and public manifestations, making it possible for Turkish citizens to discover and, more importantly, express their Kurdish identity (Leggewie 1996). The formation of cultural associations, typical in migrant communities in host countries and possibly prohibited in the homelands, further led to the consolidation of this Kurdish identity in Germany. The drive to experience, express and share the Kurdish identity can be observed in the dramatic proliferation of Kurdish cultural organizations in Western Europe as well as an increase in their print and Internet publications.

These associations played an important identity-forming and -maintaining role by celebrating Kurdish national holidays such as Nawroz, the Kurdish new year, fostering the use and informal teaching of the Kurdish language, and providing a gathering point where those who identified themselves as Kurds could convene. Preliminary observations suggest that these cultural organizations took on the dual role of maintaining an allegiance to the Kurdish identity and recruiting other migrants to follow suit. Initial evidence of this dynamic is documented by Östen Wahlbeck's study of Kurdish cultural associations (Wahlbeck 1999). The PKK was not indifferent to these developments and actively sought to penetrate the cultural organizations in an effort to recruit activists and secure funding.

Political opportunities for mobilization of the PKK in Germany

Although identity is an important aspect of mobilization, it does not alone explain the timing and methods of PKK contention. A group with cognitive awareness of itself as politically relevant also needs to perceive the attainment of political gains and have optimism concerning successful realization of increased political power. Understanding the political space that needs to be present for mobilization to occur is facilitated by the idea of political opportunity. Tarrow sees opportunity structures as "consistent – but not necessarily formal or permanent – dimensions of the political environment that provides incentives for people to undertake collective action by affecting their expectations for success or failure" (Tarrow 1994: 82). Democratic institutional structures tend to benefit insurgent groups. In fact, the strategic position of all challengers appears to be enhanced when political structures encourage debate and political dialogue.

There were multiple efforts at mobilization within Turkey. However, state sanctions became so powerful that optimism concerning success as well as fear of retaliation discouraged most types of Kurdish political dissent. The lack of access to Turkish political institutions and the lack of significant allies seem to have thwarted successful mobilization within the Kurdish minority in Turkey. By contrast, Germany, guided by the principles of liberal democracy, which protects freedom of expression and association, offered a political climate within which mobilization carried considerably fewer risks. In fact, during the late 1970s and early 1980s when the PKK began to organize within Germany, the German government was acquiescent towards protest activity. What is key in this discussion is that the political institutional structures of Germany provided access to political dialogue without the fear of repression. In this climate, the PKK was able effectively to marshal its organizational cadres and resources towards its multiple goals.

The PKK's organization and resources

In addition to the freedom to manoeuvre and a sense of Kurdish group cohesiveness, resources, ranging from leadership to communications channels, are key to realizing protest activities and mobilizing dissent (McAdam, cited in Smith and Pagnucco 1992: 176). Beginning shortly after its inception, the PKK was quick to cast its organizational net, which consisted of various governance levels, in Germany. The PKK divided Germany into eight "regions," about thirty "subregions" and numerous "lodges" or boroughs. YEK-KOM, the Federation of Kurdish Associations in Germany, is the umbrella organization that brings together the Kurdish associations that work closely with the PKK. In Germany, the PKK tried to expand its sphere of influence by establishing close links with associations that cater to special groups, such as Alewites, youth and women. It has welcomed, if not supported, the mushrooming of various NGOs that bring together journalists, writers and legal experts who support the Kurds' struggle for independence.

One of the most important objectives for the organization has been to spread awareness in Germany, as well as other places in Europe, about the plight of Kurds. To that end, the organization published a newspaper, *Serxwebun* (Freedom), which continues to serve as the PKK's propaganda organ (German Interior Ministry 1996). Until 1996, the PKK also used MED TV, the organization's official TV channel, for political means.[5] Until that time, it had been a venue of choice for the PKK leader, who made frequent appearances to announce actions to be taken against the German government – a subject to which we shall return later.

The activities of the PKK and its related organizations are financed through the contributions of members, the sale of publications, and donations, which were used for the PKK's operations in Europe and Turkey (German Interior Ministry 1996: 5). The organization has been able to collect an impressive amount of contributions, part of which was allegedly procured through forced donations. In 1994 the PKK was found to extort money from Kurdish asylum seekers (*Tageszeitung* 1994b) and Kurdish business owners brought charges against individuals who extorted money from them in the name of the organization (*Tageszeitung* 1994c). Some who refused to pay the "protection money" or "contributions" were even assaulted (*Tageszeitung* 1994d). Furthermore, the German Ministry of the Interior argues that the organization actively encouraged some of its members to get involved in the lucrative narcotics trade.

When speaking of the PKK as an organization, one must also highlight the role of its entrepreneurial leadership. Abdullah Öcalan, the long-time uncontested leader and one-time student of political science, founded the PKK in 1978 and subsequently ran it with an iron fist, sometimes being likened to Stalin in his leadership style. He was supremely in charge of an outfit that trained some 30,000 guerrillas to stage a war in what the PKK claimed to be the Kurdish homeland in Turkey. With his capture in Kenya in 1999, the PKK lost a charismatic and ruthless leader, raising questions about its future viability as an organization. Until then, however, he was instrumental in strategizing PKK activities both in Turkey and in Europe.

The contentious politics of the PKK in Germany

There were three general groups of activities that involved the PKK in Germany. First, the PKK seized every opportunity to bring the conflict in Turkey to the attention of the German and European public. This was done by staging demonstrations decrying Turkish military engagement in south-eastern Turkey, organizing hunger strikes, holding large-scale protests to promote visibility and solidarity, and engaging in highway blocks. A second set of activities that brought the PKK into the limelight were the attacks against Turks, Turkish businesses and Turkish associations in Germany. Later on, a new kind of protest activity emerged as PKK sympathizers began to protest against German actions taken against the organization. Though PKK activities in Germany go back to the late 1980s, they gathered steam in the early 1990s. As a result of a series of events we shall discuss below, the PKK was banned in Germany in 1993. Instead of stopping the protests and the violence associated with the party, this ban was followed by an additional three years of protests and escalating violence until mid-1996, when the PKK changed its course and opted to tone down both its rhetoric and its violent activities.

Late 1980s to 1993: setting the stage for PKK activism

The PKK was instrumental in staging large-scale demonstrations in various urban centres in Germany to protest against the political situation in Turkey. Large-scale demonstrations would be mounted on anniversaries or landmark days (such as Nawroz) or soon after heightened Turkish military activity in south-eastern Turkey. These types of demonstrations initially ended without incident. For example, in April 1990, 10,000 Kurds assembled in front of Cologne Cathedral in a demonstration that was supported by the PKK. They protested against the military course pursued by Turkey in relation to its Kurdish minority and called for Kurdish autonomy in Turkey (*Tageszeitung* 1990). Likewise, the PKK's thirteenth birthday was celebrated in a peaceful gathering by 8,000 in Bremen on December 9, 1991 (*Tageszeitung* 1991). In many of these cases, either large urban centres were selected as places to gather, helping visibility, or the protests were staged in front of the various Turkish consulates in the country.

Hunger strikes were a frequent form of public demonstration for the PKK as well as a sign of solidarity. Staged in places with high visibility in major German cities, they were supplemented with propaganda material to mobilize Kurdish and German support for the aims of the PKK. They were often organized with numerous participants and were sometimes coordinated with other demonstrations in other European countries. For example, a 120-person hunger strike was begun simultaneously in Hamburg and Kiel. This event was coordinated with a 700-person affair in Brussels, protesting against the forced migration of Kurds out of some 300 villages in south-eastern Turkey.[6]

Beginning in 1992 and continuing with increased intensity until 1996, Turks and Turkish businesses became the targets of what was now developing into a violent struggle on the part of the PKK. On March 22, 1992, a Turkish bank and travel agency were severely vandalized in Bremen and an estimated 150 demonstrators blocked the entrance of the Bremen local government for several hours (*Tageszeitung* 1992). During this event, eighteen demonstrators, all of whom had PKK propaganda materials, were arrested. During the early 1990s, Turkish cultural and sports associations as well as businesses were the targets of such attacks (Asendorpf 1994).

Violence in Germany involving Kurds also presented itself in the form of attacks that targeted other Kurds. As early as 1987 there were growing tensions between several competing Kurdish organizations in Germany, most notably KOMKAR (the Association for Kurdish Workers for Kurdistan). Tensions between the PKK and KOMKAR occasionally broke out in violence in the late 1980s and early 1990s and some PKK members were later sentenced for the murder of several KOMKAR members.[7] In addition to its turf war with challengers, the PKK has not been accommodating of dissent among its own cadres. As early as 1984 ex-PKK members who had either fallen from grace or decided to leave the organization were dealt with firmly by the PKK, often being killed execution style (*Tageszeitung* 1995a).[8] This suggests an effort on the part of the PKK to maintain its organizational upper hand.

Consequence of PKK activism in Germany and the German response

In 1985, soon after the PKK began mobilizing protest movements in Germany, the *Bundesverfassungsschutz* (the Office for the Protection of the German Constitution) started monitoring its activities and began recording these in its annual report (Lavel 1987). What followed was mounting tension between the German authorities concerned with violence and the PKK seeking to gain ground in Germany. As early as 1987 the German Ministry of the Interior, as well as the Office of the Federal Prosecutor, were concerned about the escalating PKK violence in Germany. The PKK was increasingly perceived as a criminal organization, and this began to erode Germany's willingness to tolerate Kurdish expressions of dissent in general. The violence that caused headaches for German administrators was mostly related to the turf war between the PKK and KOMKAR, which had claimed the lives of some and left others injured. It was during this time, and apparently as a direct consequence of the turf-war-related killings, that the German authorities first began to consider a ban of the organization.[9]

The German authorities had a difficult time shaping the idea of a ban, partly because the federal prosecutor could not find sufficient evidence that the PKK had an established military wing in Germany or that other individuals were being flown in to commit acts of terrorism (Lavel 1987). While there was evidence that there was some chain of command in the PKK, it did not have a formal structure that was easy to identify. Rather, it was organized as a thick net of Kurdish workers' organizations, sports clubs, cultural centres, and Kurdish migrants' associations. Each of these appeared to function under the direction of governing boards which, the organizations claimed, were completely autonomous.

Uncomfortable about proceeding directly to a ban which could be seen as an excessive curtailment of the freedom of association and opinion, the German authorities first tried to respond by engaging the legal system. As early as 1988, charges were brought against Kurds by the federal prosecutor.[10] Perhaps the biggest legal offensive against the PKK began in 1989. The Federal Prosecutor's Office charged nineteen PKK members in a "mammoth court case against the PKK in Düsseldorf" and used Article 129a of the Federal German Penal Code, which sanctions "membership in a terrorist organization" (Markmeyer 1989). The PKK and other Kurds and Turks responded by demonstrating in front of the court-house.[11] Because Article 129a was *not* applicable to foreign organizations, the prosecution chose to adopt a line that called the PKK a "terrorist organization," paving the way for the 1993 ban that was put in place exactly on the same premises. After beginning to monitor the PKK in 1987, German police also began surprise raids and searches on PKK premises. These search-and-seizure operations were continued, and the PKK responded with further demonstrations protesting against them (von Appen 1993).

1993: Germany bans the PKK – political opportunity structures in jeopardy

As a result of mounting political pressure – ostensibly both from the domestic politi-cal process and from Turkey, which was extremely unhappy about Germany's lenience towards the PKK – Germany outlawed the PKK in 1993, almost a decade after it started monitoring the organization. In June 1993 several coordinated events were staged in three European countries that served as the long-awaited opportunity for Germany to justify a ban. The ban came after Kurds occupied the Turkish consulate in Munich and took several people hostage in a standoff. Interestingly, the protests were not confined to Germany. On June 24, 1993, several individuals who identified themselves as Kurds stormed into Turkish consulates in Munich, Marseilles and Bern and took personnel hostage. Simul-taneously, many Turkish businesses, banks and travel agencies were attacked in almost all the major German cities, causing significant material damage. The PKK was initially quiet on the issue. The Kurdistan Committee, the unofficial mouthpiece for the PKK in Europe, argued that these acts were not orchestrated and that the Kurds involved had "spontaneously" engaged in this wave of events, an explanation that did not hold much water (Hahn 1993a). Others argued that the PKK was behind these actions, and that only the PKK could organize such a widespread outbreak of events that seemed to be coordinated not only in Germany but across borders.

The goal of the Munich occupation was clearly to put pressure on the German government to assume a mediating position in the resolution of the Kurdish problem in Turkey: the occupiers wanted Chancellor Helmut Kohl to make a public appearance on TV in which he was to ask the Turkish government to stop "the war against the Kurds" immediately (*Tageszeitung* 1993b). This, of course, was an indirect attempt to impact policy in the home country by trying to draw the host country into the conflict and urging it to use bilateral diplomacy to secure a desired outcome. Meanwhile, there was unrest unfolding in other cities in Germany during the same day. After a sit-in in front of the Turkish consulate in Karlsruhe, demonstrators attempted to raid the consulate and clashed with the police (*Tageszeitung* 1993c). In other words, the dynamics of linkage 6 in Figure 3.1 were set in motion to cause the dynamics captured in linkage 2 as Kurds in Germany sought to pressure the German government to influence Turkish domestic policy. Hostilities escalated until November 1993, when one person died and several others were seriously injured during attacks against Turkish businesses. This was apparently the last straw. The immediate reaction from Bonn was to intensify calls for banning the PKK and its affiliated organizations (Hahn 1993b). The politicians in Bonn were not necessarily clear about what the ban could achieve or, worse still, trigger. However, they were able to agree that such acts could no longer be tolerated in Germany.

The episode had further domestic political consequences for Germany and highlighted the differences of opinion across the political spectrum. This wave of violence against Turkish businesses allowed the Christian Democratic federal minister of the interior, Manfred Kanther, the opportunity to adopt an even harder line against the PKK, calling for the full implementation of the ban (*Tageszeitung* 1995c). His opponents, mainly the Greens, argued that any such response would not only not stop the attacks, but also drive a larger number of individuals, who through such acts would feel singled out and cornered, towards even more violence. By contrast, the Social Democrats, the second largest party in the country, supported Kanther's position.[12]

In the end, the hardliners won over the sceptics. In November 1993, four months after the Munich episode and immediately after the latest hostilities, Kanther placed the PKK and thirty-five of its affiliated organizations in eleven *Länder* under a federal ban.[13] Not surprisingly, demonstrations followed the announcement of the decision. In Frankfurt, 300 Kurds occupied a Kurdish cultural centre that was closed as a result of the ban. In defiance of the announcement, in November 1993, one day *after* the Kurdistan Committee was banned along with the PKK, 3,000 celebrated the fifteenth anniversary of the founding of the PKK (Rabinbach 1993). A leading PKK figure, Kani Yilmaz, the PKK's spokesman in Europe, warned that 1994 would be a very dangerous year for tourists in Turkey. Another leading figure from the ranks, Beyram Aslan of the Kurdistan Committee, argued that the real loser was the German minister of the interior because the German government "made itself a party to the war through its decision [to ban the PKK]" (*Tageszeitung* 1993d). Several solidarity demonstrations were staged during the following days in various German urban centres, apparently unhindered by the German police, who initially took a "wait and see" approach.

The PKK after the ban: 1993–6

Just as the sceptics feared, taking restrictive action against the PKK initially did little to stem the violence. On the contrary, contention escalated between 1993 and 1996. The individual *Länder* also took their own steps to outlaw other organizations that were suspected of being front operations for the PKK.[14] The bans on these various organizations were subsequently upheld in German courts.[15] After the ban, arrests of suspected PKK members and leaders accelerated. The federal attorney-general litigated against thirty-two people in leadership positions within the PKK, charging them with membership of a terrorist organization.

After the ban on the PKK, German police had ample grounds to intervene in Kurdish demonstrations and occasionally to use force in dispersing them. They refrained from issuing permits to non-PKK demonstrations for fear that they would turn violent, a move that, in the interest of caution, restricted the freedom of expression for those persons and organizations that were not affiliated to the PKK (*Tageszeitung* 1996b). However, on several occasions protesters sought to stage their demonstrations anyway, clashing with the intervening police in the process (*Tageszeitung* 1996a).

The German Ministry of the Interior was first to acknowledge that, despite the ban, "the PKK had nonetheless remained active" (*Tageszeitung* 1996a). Its members and sympathizers disregarded the laws against PKK demonstrations, continued to collect donations on behalf of the organization, and distributed propaganda material. Demonstrations, authorized or not, were organized that decried the outlawing of the PKK, sometimes resulting in hostilities between the police and demonstrators who had propaganda material for the PKK (*Tageszeitung* 1995e). On June 17, 1995, 200,000 supporters of the PKK staged the largest demonstration up until that time in Bonn. (German Federal Solicitor 1995).

In March 1996, the Free Kurdish Women's Association (associated with the PKK) staged a demonstration on International Women's Day. The demonstration in Bonn, 1,200 people strong, broke out into hostilities during which the German police officers were attacked (German Interior Ministry 1996: 4). It appeared that, despite the ban and perhaps because of it, Germany's control of the situation dwindled alongside mounting domestic criticism that the principles of liberal democracy were being trampled upon.

Unhappy that the windows of political opportunity were rapidly closing on the organization in Germany, Öcalan engaged in harsh rhetoric, accusing Germany of condoning violent activities both in Germany and in Turkey in 1995 and 1996. In January 1996, Öcalan threatened massive uprisings in Europe with many casualties, particularly in Germany, if the Turkish government did not respond to the PKK ceasefire in south-eastern Turkey. He then threatened to attack Turkish vacation resorts – favorites for German travellers – which would cause bloodshed, especially around Nawroz, arguing that Kurds should protect "their democratic rights in Germany with utmost determination." His threatening tone reached its climax in March 1996, when he claimed in a MED TV interview that "Germany has launched a war against the PKK . . . Should Germany decide to stick to this policy, we can return the damage. Each and every Kurd can become a suicide bomber."[16]

In subsequent interviews, Öcalan continued to blame Germany for being an accomplice in genocide and announced that there would be suicide bombings, particularly on the coastline of Turkey. On another occasion, he lashed out at the German government, accusing it of siding with Turkey and clamping down on

Kurdish freedom of expression in Germany (Lüders 1996). Surprisingly, his harsh tone and threats came to an abrupt end in mid-1996, marking a change in PKK strategy. Cognizant that his tone and the violence staged by the PKK were costing the organization the sympathy it had slowly mustered over the years, Öcalan opted for a new strategy. This time, he toned down the threats and attempted to gain legitimacy as the spokesperson for *all* Kurds. He began publicly to denounce the violence of the past as a mistake and to argue that a non-violent political dialogue was needed between the PKK and Germany. This shift in his tone can be interpreted as an effort to regain lost ground in Germany and to unclog the political opportunity structures.

The PKK's about-face: a new strategy?

Beginning in mid-1996, Öcalan began to preach moderation to his followers. He now claimed that what he in fact wanted was a political dialogue with Germany, which would lead to a political solution. To facilitate such dialogue, he promised an end to PKK-led violence in Germany (German Interior Ministry 1997: 3). Öcalan repeated his plea for moderation at every opportunity, and PKK members, by and large, abided by his call. As expected, with the decline of criminal incidents, it became unfeasible for Germany to justify a continued ban on an organization that was keeping a low profile and steering clear of violence. In early 1997, there were increasing pleas for the lifting of the ban, from the left as well as the right of the political spectrum. CDU officials began pushing for a lifting of the ban in early 1997. Heinrich Lummer, a CDU representative from Berlin, proclaimed at the Bundestag: "We have had relative peace with the PKK in Germany during the last year. Should it continue to act responsibly, I don't see why the ban should be continued" (quoted in Krump 1997).

Also in 1997, two high-level German officials met with Öcalan in Damascus, Syria, in an effort to persuade him to call off attacks against Turks and Turkish businesses in Germany. Following this meeting, Lummer had a similar meeting with Öcalan during which he repeated the German government's plea. In the face of the growing public unpopularity of the PKK's attacks in Germany, as well as insistent German officials, Öcalan guaranteed an end to violence, and on January 13, 1998, based on the decrease in PKK violence, the Federal Prosecutor's Office announced that the PKK was no longer regarded as a terrorist organization but rather as a criminal organization.[17] This represented a reward for the PKK and meant that its members, if sued, would no longer be charged with membership of a terrorist organization (Article 129a); rather, they would be charged with crimes such as extortion, manslaughter, and possession of unregistered weapons (*Tageszeitung* 1997). Shortly after, an article appeared in Istanbul in the Turkish unofficial PKK periodical *Özgür Halk*, signed by the PKK leader's pen name Ali Firat, in which Öcalan conceded defeat against the Turkish army (Koydl 1998). Moreover, he seemed to be trying to distance himself from a war that the PKK was losing, as well as to reformulate his strategy towards striving for political recognition in Europe along the lines of the PLO. Currently, the PKK claims that, after meeting in January 2000, it reached a decision to lay down its arms and will now seek political solutions (Kinzer 2000). In turn, Germany now fully recognizes that the presence of the Kurdish diaspora influences its relations with Turkey and its politics at the *Land*, regional, and federal levels. German authorities thus face a dual challenge: international criticism if they extradite PKK members back to Turkey, where they may be in danger; or accusations by Turkey of harbouring a terrorist organization.

The situation took a new turn as Turkish commando forces captured Öcalan in Kenya on February 15, 1999. The arrest spurred massive protests across Germany, including the occupation of the Greek consulate in Berlin. After a highly publicized trial in Turkey, Öcalan was found guilty of treason and sentenced to death. In response to the conviction, Kurds in Germany again voiced their displeasure as thousands of protestors took to the streets. A few months later, a similar scenario was played out in Cologne in response to a Turkish appeals court upholding the death sentence. The German interior minister, Otto Schily, issued appeals for calm from the large Kurdish minority and repeatedly reminded protestors that Turkey will not carry out the sentence until the European Court of Human Rights hears Öcalan's case. At the same time, Germany also placed Turkey under intense diplomatic pressure. Germany's foreign minister, Joschka Fischer, travelled to Turkey and requested that the death penalty be lifted against Öcalan. Here again we see linkage 2 indicated in Figure 3.1, as the Kurdish presence in Germany has influenced Germany's bilateral relations with Turkey. In addition, the EU enlargement commissioner has warned Turkey that, if the death penalty *is* carried out, Turkey's chances of becoming a future EU member would be slim. Öcalan's lawyers are appealing to the Strasbourg-based European Court of Human Rights, a process that could last up to two years. Turkey is very aware that the "Kurdish situation" has grown beyond the borders of traditional Kurdish homelands and now threatens the long-term Turkish goal of integrating economically and politically into Western Europe.

Conclusion

This chapter has documented why and how Kurdish separatism was exported from traditional homelands to Western liberal democracies and highlighted factors that contribute to the diffusion of ethnic conflict. Firstly, countries with established migration links to countries of origin are more likely to be confronted with the consequences of the mobilization of ethnic separatism. These countries, like Germany, which at one time had favourable immigration and asylum policies, unintentionally facilitated the diffusion of contention, which resulted in established Kurdish enclaves. The political opportunity structures provided by the liberal democratic German state allowed for the consolidation of political identity, the aggregation of resources and the sprouting of protest activities through both institutional and non-institutional means. This process affected the domestic politics of Germany as the country sought to come to terms with migrant activism. It also contributed to mounting domestic turmoil in Turkey.

Second, this model of international mobilization provides some insight into why the Kurds – specifically the PKK – were successful in their efforts within the liberal democratic structures of Germany. In terms of the consolidation of identity the model helps illuminate that the measures taken to outlaw the PKK and prosecute its members may actually have contributed to a further building of cohesiveness within the Kurdish diaspora population (Henkel 1996). Furthermore, the PKK was able to take advantage of the opportunities for dissent that is, within the parameters of the law, guarded by liberal democracies. While Germany ultimately outlawed radical expressions of Kurdish separatism, specifically PKK activities, this was the product of a lengthy domestic debate, and the legal measures used by the German government to bridle PKK activities were gentle compared to those taken in Turkey.

The concept of political opportunity helps to explain why the PKK and Öcalan had their recent about-face in terms of the tactics they employ and their rhetoric concerning the use of violence. It can be argued that the windows of opportunity closed after 1993 and the use of violence became counterproductive. Thus, after the ban, the PKK sought an alternative method of protest that was more suited to the current political milieu, distancing the PKK from violence and expressing the struggle in political, not military, terms within a democratic setting (*Tageszeitung* 1996a).

While this chapter is concerned primarily with the bilateral diffusion of ethnic conflict, it implies that these developments also have regional implications, especially in Western Europe. Not surprisingly, the diffusion of Kurdish separatism does not stop at Germany's doors but is as much a regional phenomenon as it is domestic and international. The Kurdish question has become a thorny issue between the EU and Turkey, especially because it figures prominently in the EU's refusal to consider Turkey's application for membership on human-rights grounds. It is quite clear that "the internal Turkish conflict has also become international: a steady stream of refugees, military assistance to Turkey from NATO countries and the presence of the PKK in European countries: this has embroiled European governments in Turkish affairs" (Ansay 1991: 831). One would also have to add that the Turkish government is now embroiled in the affairs of European governments too, as it seeks to put pressure on many EU members to discontinue their acquiescence vis-à-vis Kurdish separatist groups.

The German case suggests that the model of mobilization adapted from Doug McAdam is a useful tool in understanding ethnic conflict in host countries. However, the model needs to be supplemented by an analysis of the responses to mobilization in other host countries. Mobilization is not the end of the dynamic political struggle that lies beneath separatist efforts. The voicing of dissent elicits responses from the host countries which force the dissenting factions to rethink their options in the host country and, at the same time, search for other venues to further their cause.

Notes

1 These issues concern access to natural resources such as water and the commercially important infrastructure such as the Turkish–Iraqi oil pipeline, which runs through the region.

2 The constraints placed on the expression of Kurdish identity continued through other constitutions that were drafted subsequently. More recently, the 1982 Turkish Constitution stated that "no political party may concern itself with the defense, development, or diffusion of any non-Turkish language or culture; nor may they seek to create minorities within our frontiers or to destroy our national unity" (Article 89 of the Constitution of the Turkish Republic). In another effort to clamp down on separatist activities, in 1991 Turkey adopted an Anti-Terror Law which allowed for a very broad definition of terrorism, giving the government *carte blanche* to prosecute separatist activities.

3 Beginning with the first organized resistance to assimilation, which dates back to the mid-1920s, we see sporadic efforts to create a collective Kurdish consciousness. These efforts have intensified during the last forty years. See Kirisci and Winrow 1997.

4 Article 10, Para. 1, Nr. 11, of the 1961 Aliens Act. This clause left extensive leeway for interpretation because it could be applied so broadly, and "a foreign worker could be deported for insignificant offences, such as a traffic accident or disobeying a traffic rule" (Ansay 1991).

5 MED TV was shut down in 1996 after the contract to use a satellite to broadcast was terminated. The station struck a deal with a Polish company after a French company would not renew the PKK's contract. In 1996, the Polish company also cancelled MED TV's contract, putting an end to its broadcasts (*Tageszeitung* 1995b).

6 One poignant episode concerned Gülnaz Dagistanli, a Kurdish woman living in Germany, who died during a hunger strike in 1995. Her death unleashed a series of protest marches that gathered some 15,000 people, some of whom travelled from all over Germany to Berlin for the memorial ceremony (Kugler 1995).

7 For example, in 1987 a 37-year-old recognized refugee, apparently a KOMKAR member, was murdered in Hannover as he was on his way to a KOMKAR meeting. KOMKAR charged the PKK with the murder, arguing that the deceased had been continually harassed and threatened by PKK functionaries in the weeks preceding his murder. It was argued that this act of the PKK was in revenge for the death of one of its members during a Nawroz celebration in Munich (Voges 1987).

8 Before the first ex-PKK member was killed at the hands of the PKK, there were reports that the organization had been threatening critics, dissidents, and other groups for at least three years. The individual charged with the murder, Ali Tas, was a leading figure in both the PKK and BIRKOM, another Kurdish separatist organization that was founded by close supporters of Öcalan who left Turkey for Germany in 1980 (Lavel 1987). See also Abadan-Unat 1997.

9 These concerns were voiced after the PKK attacked KOMKAR members during a Nawroz celebration. Two KOMKAR members were seriously injured and one subsequently died (Lavel 1987).

10 Two of these individuals, Mehmet Bingöl, who was killed in May 1984, and Murat Bayrakli, who was killed in June 1984, were ex-PKK members who appeared to be prosecuted by the organization (*Tageszeitung* 1988). Six years later, one of those individuals was found guilty of carrying out murders under the PKK's orders (*Tageszeitung* 1994a).

11 As another example of how the movements are closely linked across borders, Kurdish women occupied the garden of the German embassy in Paris in protest against the case that began in Düsseldorf (*Tageszeitung* 1994a).

12 See *Tageszeitung* 1995d. In highway blocks that occurred some time after the ban, the police became increasingly obstructive, dispersing the demonstrators with water cannons.

The blocks provided ample ammunition for law-and-order politicians, who had begun calling for stricter laws which would deal firmly with those foreigners, even those with permanent resident status, who were abusing Germany's welcome through acts that disrupted public safety (Gottschlich 1994).

13 Among the other organizations to be banned were ERNK (Kurdistan National Liberation Front), the Berxwedan Publishers, the Kurdish news agency Kurd-Ha, the Federation of the Patriotic Kurdish Worker and Cultural Association, and the Kurdistan Committee (Hahn 1993c). See also *Tageszeitung* 1993a.

14 For example, the land minister of the interior for Baden-Württemberg banned the German–Kurdish Friendship Association in Stuttgart on May 13, 1996, arguing that the association was working as a central hub for the PKK and that it had taken part in violent acts. In an act of defiance, some 200 demonstrators gathered in Stuttgart on May 18 to condemn the decision (German Interior Ministry 1997).

15 On April 9, 1996, the Upper Administrative Court (*Oberverwaltungsgericht*) in Bremen ruled against the appeal of the HEVALTI-Kurdish-German Association for the Friendship of Peoples that the ban on its activities be lifted. Similarly, on May 29 the Upper Administrative Court in Münster ruled against the appeal of the Agri publishing company, which was ordered to shut down earlier. The company was found guilty of having distributed PKK/ERNK propaganda material (German Interior Ministry 1997).

16 Interview with MED TV on March 24, 1996. Quoted in German Interior Ministry 1997.

17 The Turkish government immediately responded with a protest. Ismail Cem, the foreign minister, claimed that the federal prosecutor had no reliable basis for taking such action. See Yilmaz 1998.

References

Abadan-Unat, N. (1997) "Ethnic Business, Ethnic Communities, and Ethno-Politics among Turks in Europe", in Uçarer, E. M., and Puchala, D. J. (eds) *Immigration into Western Societies: Problems and Policies*. London: Pinter Publishers, pp. 229–51.

Anderson, B. (1991) *Imagined Communities*. London: Verso.

Ansay, T. (1991) "The New UN Convention in Light of the German and Turkish Experience", *International Migration Review*, vol. 25, no. 5, pp. 831–46.

Asendorpf, D. (1994) "Menschenverachtende Anschläge: Brandschläge auf türkische Einrichtungen in Bremen", *Tageszeitung*, November 29, p. 4.

Cohen, R. (1999) "Arrest Uniting Europe's Kurds in Indignation", *New York Times*, February 19, p. A1.

German Federal Solicitor (1995) *Der Generalbundesanwalt beim Bundesgerichtshof-Pressemitteilung*. Karlsruhe: German Federal Solicitor.

German Interior Ministry (1996) *Verfassungsschutzbericht 1995*. Bonn: Bundesministerium des Innern.

——(1997) *Verfassungsschutzbericht 1996*. Bonn: Bundesministerium des Innern.

Gottschlich, J. (1994) "Im Gleichklang mit Volkes Stimmen", *Tageszeitung*, March 24, p. 3.

Gurr, T. R. (1993) *Minorities at Risk*. Washington, DC: United States Institute of Peace Press.

Gurr, T. R., and Moore, W. H. (1997) "Ethnopolitical Rebellion: a Cross-Sectional Analysis of the 1980s and Risk Assessments for the 1990s", *American Journal of Political Science*, vol. 41, no. 4, pp. 1079–103.

Hahn, D. (1993a) "Kurden nehmen Europa in die Pflicht", *Tageszeitung*, June 25, p. 3.

——(1993b) "Am Tag danach ist Bonn sich einig: Verbietet die kurdische Arbeiterpartei!", *Tageszeitung*, November 6, p. 3.

——(1993c) "Nach dem Verbot der Arbeiterpartei Kurdistans (PKK) und 35 weiterer Vereine befürchten kurdische ImmigrantInnen Hetze, Kriminalisierung und Massenabschiebung in die Türkei", *Tageszeitung*, November 27, p. 3.

Henkel, K (1996) Interview with Dr. Norman Paech, "Why is Germany's Ban on the PKK Illegal?", *Junge Welt*, November 22, http://burn.ucsd.edu/archives/ats-l/1996.Dec/ 0017.html.

Horowitz, D. L. (1985) *Ethnic Groups in Conflict*. Berkeley: University of California Press.

Kinzer, S. (2000) "Kurdish Rebels Tell Turkey They are Ending their War", *New York Times*, February 10, p. A14.

Kirisci, K., and Windrow, G. (1997) *The Kurdish Question and Turkey: An Example of a Transstate Ethnic Conflict*. London: Frank Cass.

Koydl, W. (1998) "Warum PKK-Chef Öcalan von der bevorstehenden Niederlage seiner Kurden-Guerilla spricht", *Süddeutsche Zeitung*, January 28, p. 4.

Krump, H. (1997) "Ist die PKK manierlich, soll sie erlaubt sein", *Berliner Morgenpost*, January 24, http://www.berliner-morgenpost.de/bm/bm_archiv/970124/politik/story06.html.

Kugler, A. (1995) "Trauermarsch in Berlin", *Tageszeitung*, August 1, p. 3.

Lavel, K. (1987) "Deutsche Sicherheitsorgane schuren das Feuer", *Tageszeitung*, July 2, pp. 8–9.

Leggewie, C. (1996) "How Turks Became Kurds, not Germans", *Dissent*, vol. 43, summer, pp. 79–83.

Lüders, M. (1996) "Interview with Abdullah Öcalan, Leader of the Workers Party of Kurdistan PKK", *Die Zeit*, April 5, p. 7.

Lyon, A. (1999) "International Contributions to the Mobilization of Ethnic Conflict: Sri Lanka, Iraq, and Rwanda", PhD dissertation, Department of Government and International Studies, University of South Carolina, Columbia.

Markmeyer, B. (1989) "Tumulte im Monsterprozeß: Proteste von Angeklagten und VerteigerInnen zum Auftakt des 129a-Verfahrens gegen neunzehn Kurden und Kurdinnen", *Tageszeitung*, October 25, pp. 1–2.

McAdam, D. (1982) *Political Process and the Development of Black Insurgency*. Chicago: University of Chicago Press.

Rabinbach, A. (1993) "Fire and Blood in Germany", *Dissent*, vol. 40, autumn, pp. 416–18.

Smith, J., and Pagnucco, R. (1992) "Political Process and the 1989 Chinese Student Movement", *Studies in Conflict and Terrorism*, vol. 15, pp. 169–84.

Suhrke, A., and Noble, L. G. (1977) *Ethnic Conflict in International Relations*. New York: Praeger.

Tageszeitung (1988) "Rebmann klagt 16 Kurden an", November 9, p. 5.

——(1990) "Kurden demonstrieren: Protest gegen Ausnahmezustand in Türkisch-Kurdistan", April 23, p. 7.

——(1991) "8,000 Kurden bei PKK-Geburtstag", December 9, p. 21.

——(1992) "Bank verwüstet, Bürgerschaft blockiert", March 24, p. 21.

——(1993a) "Kurden demonstrierten: Festnahmen, CDU für PKK-Verbot", June 28, p. 2.

——(1993b) "Kurden starten Kamikaze-Aktionen: Geiselnahme in München, Anschläge in vielen Städten, ein Toter bei Schiesserei in Bern", June 25, p. 1.

——(1993c) "Seiters prüft Verbot der kurdischen Arbeiterpartei: Unblutiges Ende der Konsulatbesetzung", June 26, p. 1.

——(1993d) "Kurdischer Kulturverein wieder besetzt, BRD zum Kriegsgebiet erklärt", November 30, p. 17.

——(1994a) "Lebenslang für Kurden: Kiliç tötete im Auftrag der PKK", January 14, p. 4.

——(1994b) "PKK Drohung: Kurde gegen Kurde", April 16, p. 4.

——(1994c) "Für die PKK gespendet? Prozeß: Kurden bestreiten Erpressung", April 22, p. 22.

——(1994d) "Schutzgeld: Türke überfallen", July 23, p. 4.

——(1995a) "Hinrichtung: PKK nahm Rache", January 10, p. 5.

——(1995b) "PKK droht mit Kamikaze-Anschlägen: Touristen sollen die Türkei meiden", January 20, p. 2.

——(1995c) "Neue Verbotsoffensive gegen kurdische Vereine: Innenminister Kanther hält nach Anschlägen auf türkische Reisebüros den 'konsequenten Vollzug' des PKK-Verbots für Notwendig", March 3, p. 2.

——(1995d) "Die SPD ist für Kanther", March 4, p. 4.

——(1995e) "Kurden-Demo: 400 Festnahmen", June 6, p. 4.

——(1996a) "PKK-Demo endet mit verletzten", March 11, p. 4.

——(1996b) "Kurden-Demo in Bonn polizeilich verboten", December 6, p. 5.

——(1997) "45,000 Kurden für Ende des Krieges", April 28, p. 4.

Tarrow, S. (1994) *Power in Movement*. Cambridge: Cambridge University Press.

US Department of State (1995) *Human Rights in Turkey: Briefing of the Commission on Security and Cooperation in Europe*. Washington, DC: Commission on Security and Cooperation in Europe.

Uzulis, A. (1998) "Border Police Expects 10,000 Kurds", *Welt am Sonntag*, January 4, p. 1.

Van Voorst, B. (1996) "Europe: Embittered Guests", *Time International*, April 4, p. 27.

Voges, J. (1987) "Linker Kurde ermordet", *Tageszeitung*, May 5, p. 2.

von Appen, K. (1993) "Kurden-Protest: Bücherrazia als Auslöser", *Tageszeitung*, January 13, p. 17.

Wahlbeck, O. (1999) *Kurdish Diasporas: A Comparative Study of Kurdish Refugee Communities*. London: Macmillan.

Yilmaz, I. (1998) "Cem: Yanlis sahibini üzer", *Milliyet*, January 15, p. 1.

4 Israelis in a Jewish diaspora

The dilemmas of a globalized group

Gallya Lahav and Asher Arian

Introduction

The boundaries of Israel's political system are difficult to identify. At one level this reflects the protracted conflict between Israel and its Arab neighbors. But no less a difficulty in setting these boundaries is the spiritual and material influence on Israeli policy of Jews who are not Israelis and the large number of Israelis who have migrated abroad and live in the Jewish diaspora. While more than a third of the world's Jews live in Israel at the beginning of the twenty-first century, Israel has been a point of identity, pride, and purpose for much of world Jewry during the last half of the twentieth century.

The evolution of the complex relationship between Israelis and Jews poses a number of issues for the relations within and between the two communities, and for Israeli domestic politics. The relationship between Israeli émigrés and the Jewish diaspora is an intricate one in Jewish history and is riddled with a series of conundrums tied to the preservation of the Jewish people, to the democratic nature of the state that gives great weight to religion in defining its "demos," and to larger questions of Jewish national and religious identity.

The Jewish diaspora plays a critical role as forces of globalization impact Israeli domestic politics. The role of the state of Israel for Jews who do not live there has enormous potential importance because of the 1951 Law of Return, which in effect provides immediate citizenship for every Jew upon request. This policy has been the concrete expression of the Zionist prophetic vision of the "ingathering of the exiles," and has given the Jewish diaspora a unique role in Israel. Since its establishment in 1948, the Israeli state has encouraged diaspora Jews to settle in the "Holy Land" and has sought to facilitate their absorption. This has been part of a broader demographic strategy to create a strong, democratic state through population-building, while simultaneously discouraging Jewish emigration and supporting Arab emigration. How the Israeli state has managed in this sea of conflicting currents while adapting to forces of increasing globalization may be measured by migration patterns and attitudinal preferences of Israeli and American Jews.

In attempting to gauge the effects and challenges of globalization on Israeli domestic politics, two sets of questions are addressed here. First, how do the dynamics of globalization and migration affect the relations between Israeli and

Jewish diasporas, and their participation and political impact inside and outside of Israel? Second, how is the Israeli state affected by, and how does it react to these dynamics? Put differently, with an estimated 10 to 15 percent of Israelis living abroad, what patterns of interaction can we observe at the beginning of the twenty-first century between the emerging Israeli diaspora (including modern Israeli transnationals) and the larger co-ethnic community of the Jewish diaspora? What evidence exists of coalescence or community-building between the center and this diaspora as a result of global changes?

Globalization, migration and the state

The extent to which developments subsumed under the term "globalization" have eroded national sovereignty has engaged international relations and comparative politics scholars alike (Evans 1998; Keohane and Milner 1996). International migration lies at the crossroads of these debates, not only because it is associated with transnational flows, but precisely because it involves human beings with wills and norms. In this context, the globalization of domestic politics via diaspora groups which may be at the nexus of transnational spaces would thus be expected to constrain states.[1] How does globalization affect the Israeli state through diaspora politics abroad?

Migration policies are intricately related to population structures and nation-state formation (Zolberg 1981). Demographic changes can be seen largely as a result of structural and ideological factors that relate to the evolution of nation-states in the world system. Therefore, the impact of globalization by increasing the mobility of people, capital, trade and information poses to reorganize boundaries, and therefore challenges the traditional notion of the nation-state (Bauman 1998). The increased opportunities for emigrants and diasporas to influence both their host and their homeland politics transcend the locus of boundary-maintenance activity, and challenge the state's exclusive role in pursuing its national interests.

According to network migration theories, former migrants and non-migrants in origin are connected to newer migrants through ties of kinship, friendship and shared community origin, thereby constituting a form of social capital that reduces the costs and risks of migration and increases the expected net returns to movement (Massey *et al.* 1993; Basch *et al.* 1994). In this sense, both receiving and sending countries may be envisaged as having limited impact in regulating migration and its consequences. Indeed, as Israeli immigrants are rapidly becoming one of the largest new migrant groups in some of America's major cities such as Los Angeles and New York, they join the ranks of their Jewish co-ethnics in the United States, the second largest Jewish community in the world. Together, they constitute a potentially powerful voice for Israeli politics abroad.

Theoretically speaking, the confluence of globalization and international migration dynamics would lead us to expect the emergence of a unified and cohesive Jewish diaspora – a homogenizing effect, rather than a community of divisions. However, the empirical findings here suggest that the Israeli case fits less well the notion of globalization and networks as both linking and unifying social groups and constraining nation-states. The effects of globalization with regard to diaspora participation have been limited on the Israeli state, and they have surprisingly not served to overcome the divisions between Jewish and Israeli communities abroad. As we will see in the subsequent sections, this Israeli anomaly must be seen as a function of the Israeli state.

Israelis and Jews as a diaspora: a demographic portrait

Since the separation of church and state in nineteenth-century France, issues of identity, belonging, and loyalty of diaspora Jews have been questioned. The notorious Dreyfus affair in fact spurred Zionist thinkers such as Theodore Herzl to convene the World Zionist Congress (1897) that ultimately led to the call for the creation of a Jewish homeland. By the turn of the twenty-first century, the Zionist movement had successfully reached its goal of changing the place of residence of the world's Jews from the diaspora to Zion (see Table 4.1). In 1882, there were 24,000 Jews in *Eretz* (the Land of) *Israel*, or 0.31 percent of the world's Jews. By 1995, Israel's 4.4 million Jews constituted 34.2 percent of the 13 million world Jewish population (DellaPergola 1998; Goldscheider 1996). By 2002, Israel reported more than 5 million Jews, comprising nearly 40 percent of world Jewry and more than three-quarters of the state's citizens (CBS 2003).

Israel's Zionist ideological goals were extraordinarily successful, as evidenced by its demographic structure and its absorption of more immigrants, per base

Table 4.1 Population of Jews in Israel and the world, 1882–2002

Year	Size of population (in thousands)	Number of Jews in Israel (in thousands)	Percentage of Jews in Israel's population	Number of Jews in world (in millions)	Percentage of Jews of world in Israel
1882	600	24	4.0	7.7	0.31
1922	752	84	11.2	8.0	1.1
1939	1,545	464	30.0	16.6	2.8
1948	806	650	80.6	11.5	5.7
1954	1,718	1,526	88.8	11.9	12.8
1967	2,777	2,384	85.8	13.6	17.5
1986	4,331	3,561	82.2	13.0	27.4
1996	5,619	4,550	81.0	13.0	35.0
2002	6,631	5,094	76.8	13.0	39.0
Including the territories:					
1967	3,744	2,384	63.7		
1986	5,712	3,561	62.3		
1996	7,489	4,550	60.8		
2002	9,800	5,094	52.0		

Sources: Friedlander and Goldscheider 1979; Horowitz and Lissak 1978; and various volumes of the *Statistical Abstract of Israel* and the *American Jewish Yearbook*. Population figures up to 1939 are for *Eretz Israel*. The 1948 through 2002 figures above the line relate to the pre-1967 borders; population figures that include the territories are shown below the line.

population, than any other country in the world. With the exception of the 1950s, when the government attempted to reduce the number of people through a "rules of selection" policy, mass immigration of Jews to Israel has been actively encouraged. Between 1948 and 1951, Israel admitted 666,000 Jewish immigrants, mostly people from Mediterranean countries and survivors of the Holocaust from Europe, who joined a base population of only 600,000. Since 1989, more than 1 million immigrants have arrived in Israel, mostly from the former USSR. Thus, Israel's demographic structure today consists mainly of first- or second-generation immigrants (Meyers 1998: 2).

While Zionism provided a ready ideology for immigration to *Eretz Israel*, most Jews who moved and who had other options chose not to go to Israel. That was especially true of the mass migration from Russia and Poland to the United States at the beginning of the twentieth century, and it was equally true of those Jews allowed to leave the Soviet Union near the end of that century. Thus, while Zionism was successful in reversing the 2,000-year diaspora characterized by the dispersion of many sizeable Jewish communities throughout the world (particularly in Europe, the lands of the Middle East and North Africa), by the late 1990s, a shift from Zion to the diaspora – from the center to the periphery – may be seen to have taken place with the consolidation of two sizeable diverging Jewish communities (*Israelis in the US* 1999).

A trend toward a concentration of Jews in two free and democratic countries seems inevitable. Compared to the 32 percent of Israel's world Jews in 1995, the 5.7 million Jews in the United States made up 44 percent of the Jewish people. The next largest community of Jews in the world is much smaller than the 5.7 million Jews who live in the US and the 4.4 million in Israel. Only two other countries (France and Russia) have communities larger than a half million, and an additional four (Argentina, Canada, Ukraine, and the United Kingdom) have Jewish communities between a quarter and a half million people. The changing demographics of the two co-ethnic communities pose a competitive potential between "Jews from the Promised Land" and those from "the Land of Promise" (Shokeid 1988: x). With only two major communities, friction between them will have immediate significance, since the stakes will get higher from crisis to crisis.

While figures vary because the Jewish community tends to use high estimates for political purposes and the Jewish federations take low estimates for fundraising strategies, the numbers of Jews in the US in 2000 totaled approximately 5.2 million people, according to the National Jewish Population Survey of the United Jewish Federations (National Jewish Population Survey 2000–2001). In that survey there were 2.9 million Jewish households, defined as a household with at least one Jewish adult, with a total of 6.7 million people residing in them. Of all people in Jewish households, 76 percent were Jews and 24 percent were not Jews.

Among the American Jewish diaspora, there has been a dramatic increase in the intermarriage rate over the past decades; from 9 percent in 1965 to 47 percent in 2000. The intermarriage rate for Jews who married before 1970 stood at 13 percent, rose to 28 percent for those whose marriages started in the 1970s, and then increased again to 38 percent for Jews married in the first half of the 1980s.

Since 1985, the rate of increase in intermarriages has slowed as intermarriage levels have stabilized in the mid-40 percent range. Among Jews whose marriages started in 1985–90, the intermarriage rate is 43 percent. The intermarriage rate is also 43 percent for Jews whose marriages began in 1991–5. Jews who have married since 1996 had an intermarriage rate of 47 percent.[2]

Studies have also indicated a strong tendency for children of intermarriages not to be raised as Jews, to marry outside of the religion, and to abandon Judaism within one generation (*Jerusalem Post* 1991). Such realizations have been met by intensified drives of Jewish organizations and the Israeli government to attract young American Jews to Israel, as well as to sponsor immersion programs which tap into second-generation Israelis abroad.

Within the Zionist context, two demographic developments are of notable concern to the Israeli state. The rate of Israeli emigration and the rapid demographic decline of Jewish survival in general are at the core of national preservation. Thus, added to the potential conflict of polarized communities, the diminution of the Israeli state as a center of Jewish life has become a matter of considerable concern.

Jewish emigration from Israel

A key demographic concern that has engaged Zionist thinkers and Israeli policy-makers has been Israeli emigration patterns and the emergence of a diaspora of Israeli Jews. The role and impact of this diaspora group on the Israeli state is beset with measurement problems. First, the identification of an Israeli is difficult to operationalize because it raises the "Who is a Jew?" question, including the status of those converted to Judaism by its Conservative and Reform (as opposed to the Orthodox) branches, those born of Jewish fathers (the religious law stipulates mothers), etc. Then there is the problematic status of, to name a few, those who consider themselves Jews, those brought up in Jewish homes, and those of Jewish descent who do not consider themselves Jewish.

Second, reliable emigration data are beset with these definitional problems and other technical difficulties that stem from the fact that democratic countries do not collect data on "returns." Third, as Gold and Phillips (1996) aptly note, "The problem of 'Who is an Israeli' is no less, and probably quite more, complex than the issue of 'Who is a Jew.'" While someone who was born in Israel but now lives in the US is a clear-cut case, that of a person who lived a significant portion of their life in Israel but was born in another country is less obvious. Finally, it is also likely that a considerable number of US residents who were born in Israel are not Jewish, but Arabs (Kosmin 1993).

Even if we accept the rough estimate of 10 to 15 percent of Israelis to be living abroad, the question of impact remains unclear for political analysts. In an age of globalization of domestic politics, however, emigrant and diaspora groups have rapidly changed the impact of even small fractions of a population. In the Israeli case, the challenges faced by the democratic state at a time of rapid demographic change and the lack of growth of the total world Jewish population make this a very important datum.

The role of Israelis in a Jewish diaspora introduces complex variations on the important theme of diasporas in globalized politics. Jews have often been regarded as the best example of a diaspora society – what John Armstrong calls an "archetypical diaspora" (1976: 394). The use of the term diaspora (derived from the Greek words *dia* – over and *speiro* – sow) itself can be traced back to the Old Testament and the experiences of the ancient Jews, and has loosely come to be associated with experiences of victimization by a dispossessed people. In the case of Israeli emigrants as a subset of a larger Jewish diaspora, the theme is different since there seems to be little in common between the contemporary emigration of Israelis and the mass emigration of Jews to America at the turn of the century. Those who left Israel (estimated in 1990 at between 110,000 and 135,000; Cohen and Haberfeld 1997) often had professional skills and financial resources, seemingly ready to surrender their status as members of the dominant majority in Israel in exchange for the status of hopeful immigrants in the US (Shokeid 1988: 5), while the mass immigration entailed the exodus of approximately 2 million impoverished, persecuted refugees from Eastern Europe. Since the basis of Zionism is an "ingathering of exiles," the notion of a diaspora in the Israeli case seems antithetical to the founding principles of the Israeli nation-state.

Demography is always linked to politics and public policy, and Israel is no exception, especially in terms of two key items on the Israeli agenda – security and national identity (Meyers 1998). Indeed, Israel's relationship with neighboring Arab states and with resident Arabs has been central to its national interest. Israeli national identity as a Jewish and democratic state has also been closely linked to questions of immigration and the definition of Jewishness. The result of these concerns has been a permanent immigration policy, extremely liberal for Jews, a reflection of early state consolidation of a homogenous cultural population. The institutionalization of Zionist ideology in the newly independent Israeli state reflected these ambitions. The Declaration of Independence stated that "the State of Israel is open to Jewish immigration and the ingathering of Exiles." According to Israel's first prime minister, David Ben-Gurion, upon his presentation of the Law of Return and the Nationality Law to the Israeli *Knesset* (Parliament), "these laws reflect the central mission of our State, namely to fulfill the vision of the redemption of Israel . . . by the ingathering of the exiles" (*Divrei Ha'Knesset* 1950; see also Zucker 1989: 120). These Zionist goals were further institutionalized with the creation of a Ministry of Immigration, and ideologically buttressed by references to Jewish immigrants as "*olim*" (the ascending) and the stigma attached to emigrants as "*yordim*" (the descending).

In the light of national goals, demographic trends have been oriented toward the "ingathering" of Jews because of the importance of population growth for security and ideological reasons. In this context, the concurrent emigration of Israelis (a natural phenomenon for any country) has been particularly problematic for a liberal democracy that cannot prohibit emigration. While precise figures are impossible to obtain, a substantial number of Israeli Jews left the country between the 1950s and 1990s. The early 1950s and mid-1970s witnessed the highest rate of outflow in Israeli history. The proportion of emigrants to immigrants was higher (although the absolute number was lower) in the 1950s than in the late 1970s, a period in which problems of emigration concerned the public (Arian 1998: 31). While the newly established liberal democracy could not treat emigration as a crime, as in Europe's early mercantilist period described by Zolberg (1981), Israeli emigrants had been generally stigmatized, both officially and indirectly. By the late 1970s, the then prime minister, Yitzhak Rabin, denounced this emigration, calling Israeli emigrants "the fallen among the weaklings" (in Hebrew, *nefolet shel nemushot*), and the government admitted that this large demographic loss was a matter of serious national concern.

Initial government plans to encourage residents to return were fairly unsuccessful (Friedberg and Kfir 1988). These packages, granted to those *yordim* who returned to Israel after being abroad for at least two to five years, included benefits identical to those granted to new immigrants (mainly customs rebates and housing benefits). In 1980, the Israeli government charged the then deputy prime minister, Simcha Ehrlich, and the director-general of the Jewish Agency, Shmuel Lahis, with the task of investigating the matter. Ehrlich and Lahis were concerned only with *yerida* (emigration) to the United States, since it was clear that it was the major destination for *yordim*. The Lahis Report, published in 1980, divulged between 300,000 and 500,000 *yordim* in the United States (with the majority of them in New York and Los Angeles). That report suggested that the loss to Israel of many citizens, most of whom were young and skilled, was bound to have disturbing implications for the demography, economy, morale and defense of the country. It pointed out that the *yordim* themselves were greatly attached to Israel and that this feeling should be nurtured. The Israel Government Yearbooks after 1981 declared that measures would be taken to discourage emigration and to persuade the *yordim* to return to Israel, as well as to increase immigration from both Eastern and Western countries. The finding of the Lahis Report alarmed the Israeli Jewish public when they were publicized by the media, and the reaction of the government was evidenced by the transfer of activities to the prime minister's office to deter emigration (Arian 1998: 6). By the mid-1980s, the prime minister's office, along with a special appointed committee consisting of the directors-general of the Ministries of Defense, Education and Culture, Finance, Housing, and Labor and Welfare, and chaired by the director-general of the Ministry of Immigrant Absorption, adopted recommendations to deter emigration, which aimed at young persons nearing the age of military service, recommending intensification of education in Zionist values. Despite the repeated government declarations that the problem of Jewish emigration was viewed as a deplorable trend, turn-around was fairly ineffective.

The government tried to target that part of the population most likely to emigrate: young persons in their twenties who had completed their period of military service, and were experiencing difficulties in securing independent adequate housing and/or in supporting themselves while pursuing their studies in institutions of higher learning. Nonetheless, the bureaucratic complexity involving the Ministries of Defense, Labour and Welfare, Education and Culture, and Construction and Housing, not to mention the Ministry of Finance for implementation, made access to special entitlements such as housing, employment, higher studies and income tax rebates for demobilized soldiers fairly remote (Friedberg and Kfir 1988: 9).

Israeli government sources report that the number of Israelis returning home has increased substantially since 1992, the year of the election of the Labor Party in Israel and a major economic recession in the United States. During the years 1985–91, the annual average number of returnees was 5,500; during 1992–4, 10,500 returnees; and in 1993 and in 1994, 14,000 (*Israel Shelanu* 1995). Moreover, in the 1990s, those returning to Israel were of higher educational level than those staying in the United States (Cohen 2002: 54; Cohen and Haberfeld 1997). In great part, this return migration has been reinforced by an intensified official outreach policy toward expatriates, and a booming economy in Israel which has encouraged increased return migration (Gold and Phillips 1996: 64).

As the Israeli state matured, the cultural meaning of emigration began to change. In an age of globalization, the question of whether *yordim* in fact lacked Zionist values or patriotism became more tenuous. *Yerida* (emigration) became increasingly related to ideological shifts and social changes in Israeli society that included the decline of the pioneering spirit and the growing ideals of a consumption society, which have produced an identity crisis among Israelis (Shokeid 1988: 7). Moreover, the majority of Israeli emigrants could no longer be described as marginal members of society or "weaklings." By the mid-1980s, it had become clear that Israelis who were acquiring rights of permanent residence in the United States were not only from the upper socio-economic strata of Israeli society, but also more numerous comparatively than nationals of other countries whose total population was far larger than that of Israel. An example of this for the 1982–5 period is the comparison of Israeli government officials and other Western officials on category A visas in the US who altered their status to permanent residents of the US (see Table 4.2). The number of Israeli academics and professionals who had settled abroad ("the brain drain") posed an important concern for Israeli policy-makers. They included senior scientists, medical personnel, engineers, technicians, and computer specialists who sought abroad professional advancement and increased earnings, not to mention Israeli students who, after studying abroad and graduating, found greater rewards abroad (Arian 1998: 11).

Several demographic trends were evident by the early 1990s: a continuing stream of Israeli immigrants to the US; a rise in the number of Israelis returning to Israel to live; and the emergence of a new "transnationals" category of individuals with footholds in both the United States and Israel (see Gold 2000a).[3] In the social and political sphere, Israeli émigrés showed signs of growing self-acceptance, albeit distinct from American-Jewish communal life. These changes must be seen more as a function of developments in Israel than experiences prompted by their residence in the United States.

Israeli emigration patterns over the last fifty years constitute notable demographic shifts that may be roughly correlated to the evolution of the Israeli state and its reaction to globalization. First, the official Israeli view of *yordim* began to

Table 4.2 Total number of foreigners altering their status in the United States from category A (government official) and category H (temporary workers and trainees) visas to permanent residents, 1982–5

	Israel	Austria	Belgium	Denmark	France	Greece	Ireland	Italy
A-visas	127	11	11	11	28	13	3	37
H-visas	504	77	148	83	351	127	166	214

Source: *Statistical Yearbook of the United States Immigration and Naturalization Service*, 1982–5; see Friedberg and Kfir 1988.

change in the early 1990s to a more symbolically favorable strategy of encouraging "re-*aliyah*" (return to ascension). In a 1991 interview, Yitzhak Rabin retracted his earlier statement, and embraced Israelis living abroad as "an integral part of the Jewish community and there is no point talking about ostracism" (Golan 1992; Gold and Phillips 1996: 52). Government incentives to reverse the flow by encouraging residents to return appeared to be partially successful; those who returned under this plan increased from 8,000 in 1991 to 14,000 residents in 1995 (Arian 1998: 31). Indeed, the stigma attached to emigration decreased considerably over the 1990s. One result of the trend toward a more open and competitive society spurred by globalization has been a growing acceptance of the fact that where one lives is a private decision as well as a public one. When asked whether they were considering emigration, approximately 14 percent of the adult Jewish population in Israel, and about a quarter of those in their twenties, reported that they were.[4] The other side of this acceptance is the decline of feeling that *aliyah* is essential to the country's future. In the 1970s, 85 to 90 percent agreed with that statement; in the 1988 and 1990 surveys, the number fell to 82 percent, in 1992 to 71 percent, and in the 1994 and 1995 surveys to 64 and 67 percent (Ministry of Immigrant Absorption 1996: 57). This trend has particular significance for the relations of the Israeli and American co-ethnic communities, as will be discussed in the next section.

Second, initiatives to reverse the "brain-drain" phenomenon were embraced by technological and scientific industries that reinforced the state's interests to make Israel a competitive market. The impetus, for example, behind the establishment of the Center for Submicron Semiconductor Science as part of the Weizmann Institute was intended to stimulate new high-tech local industry by bringing Israeli emigrants back home and inducing young graduates not to leave (*Jerusalem Post* 1989). According to Professor Yoseph Imry, one of the chief nuclear physicists involved with this program:

> I feel uncomfortable when I remember how many of my friends have left. I see them go one by one, first to study and then to stay. It gets harder and harder to hold on. The lack of jobs in academia and in industry, the poorly-equipped labs that do exist, as well as low salaries, push these bright people away. Native-born Americans are a minority in places like California's Silicon

Valley. There are Israelis, Asiatics and even Arabs from various countries . . .
Science is stagnating here. In half a generation, the damage will be irreversible
unless we act now.

To compete in a globalized economy, Israel adopted a pluralist style rather than
the traditional heavy-handed centralist form, but the goal of increasing the number
of Jews in Israel was the same.

Third, Israel's remarkable economic achievements in the 1990s in the global
market impacted significantly on emigration trends. By the early 1990s, Israel
attained the highest gross domestic product (GDP) growth rate among Western
(OECD) economies (6.2 percent in 1991; 6.7 percent in 1992). A 1994 World Bank
report of the standard of living of the nations of the world listed Israel in eighteenth
place (*Ha-Aretz* 1994). Israel provided an attractive option for foreign investors in
the 1990s. This was due to the partial lifting of the Arab boycott as a result of the
Oslo accords with the PLO, the successful spin-off of technologies developed in
military and defense-related industries, the influx of educated professionals from
the former Soviet Union, and government subsidies for investors. Some spectators
have gone so far as to place Israel's potential as comparable to that of Hong Kong
or Singapore (Barnett 1996: 107–40). In 1995, a total of $2.3 billion was invested in
Israel – a twentyfold increase from 1992. Most opportunities were seen in high-
tech industries, which included corporations such as Intel, IBM, Digital Equip-
ment, Motorola, and National Semiconductor. The Intel Corporation, one of the
world's major producers of integrated security and chips for microprocessors, for
example, accepted a Ministry of Industry and Trade offer of a $380 million grant,
conditional on Israel being the site of a $1 billion Intel expansion project. Venture
capital in Israeli industry as well soared from $55 million in 1991 to $480 million in
1995 (Sher 1996: 36–9). More significant to the individual Israeli have been
government reforms on strict foreign-exchange controls introduced on the eve of
the fiftieth Independence Day celebrations in April 1998. These reforms permitted
Israelis freely to invest abroad an unlimited amount of foreign currency (in
contrast to the previous $7,000 limit). The reforms represented an effort to make
the Israeli shekel a fully convertible currency on world markets and to integrate
Israel into the global financial community, by attracting both foreign banks to
Israel and investors to more open Israeli markets. In the aftermath, Merrill Lynch
launched a bond offering valued at $47 million, while the International Finance
Corporation issued an offering through the Deutsche Bank of Germany worth $54
million (Machlis 1998).

These trends underscore the importance of return immigration to Israel, as well
as the emergence of a "transnational" Israeli community, which maintains social,
cultural, economic and political links to both home and host country. Indeed, a
number of factors make the movement of Israelis to the United States fit the
general description of a "transnational" group (Glick Schiller *et al.* 1992; Gold
2000b). These include education level, occupational and cultural skills that are
useful in both countries, and access to networks that provide a broad range of
services (Gold and Phillips 1996: 96). In addition, Israelis are more likely to

become naturalized, and are among a select few groups to be allowed to have dual citizenship in both countries (Jasso and Rosenzweig 1990), further linking the two.

The rate of Israeli "returns" has increased both on a temporary basis (i.e., children on summer vacations) and on a more permanent basis. Since there is no legal definition of a "*yored*" it is impossible to know who has left permanently and who is traveling as a tourist, as a student, or on business. An unobtrusive measure of emigration adopted here is generated by the Israeli Border Police and the Israel Central Bureau of Statistics, which record the exits and entrances of Israeli residents. Extrapolated data suggest that, in the period 1985–96, there was a significant rise in Israeli returns after one year or more abroad (the OECD definition of "immigrant") over time. In fact, while the conventional logic is that most immigrants who return to their home countries do so within one or two years after migration (Cohen and Haberfeld 1997: 207), the rate of return migration of Israeli-born persons residing in the US was between 2.5 and 5 years, a high rate compared with those experienced by other immigrant groups in the United States (Jasso and Rosenzweig 1990).

For all of these reasons, one might argue that the responses of the Israeli state to globalization probably account more for Israel's demographic trends than any external change beyond Israel's influence or borders. When economic disparities narrow between the two "homes," ideological and national factors related to the Israeli nation-state itself seem to attract Israelis to return, to stay, or to create transnational spaces. Their assimilation into a wider Jewish diaspora remains limited, as is borne out and explained by significant attitudinal distances between the Israeli and American-Jewish communities in general. The next section provides an attitudinal portrait that accompanies these demographic changes.

Israelis and Jews: an attitudinal profile

The relationship between Israelis and Jews in America has raised a novel situation in the process of network migration. While American Jews have a strong record of supporting the Israeli state, they have long viewed Israelis coming to settle in the United States with ambivalence. While most American Jews have chosen not to participate personally in the "ingathering of the exiles," they have seen themselves playing a vital role by contributing money and insuring political support for the Israeli state. The converse role of Israelis, in this view, was to inhabit and develop the country and defend it. Leaving the Jewish state, therefore, has been perceived as negatively to American Jews as to the Israeli state – a betrayal to the "unspoken compact between American and Israeli Jews" (Gold and Phillips 1996: 52). If the American-Jewish community denounces this type of migration, the typical Israeli retorts sound like these:

> Listen, I lived 25 years in Israel. Served in the army. I've paid my dues. Why don't you Americans go pay yours while I stay here for a while and send money to Israel every year?
>
> (*Israelis in America* 1999)

> It's much easier to give away money than blood. You offer money and expect in exchange that my children and I defend the Jewish state. You should understand that Israel is yours as much as it is mine. Now I've decided to change places with you. I'm going to make money and give some of it to Israel, while you and your children make aliya to Israel.
>
> (Israeli single woman in her early thirties who emigrated to America in her teens, cited in Shokeid 1988: 36)

These tensions have generated a social and an official division between the two communities. Organized American-Jewish federations have been very unreceptive to Israeli immigrants, as has been illustrated by the distinctions made between Soviet Jews and Israeli emigrants for assistance eligibility (Cohen 1986: 155–65). The ambivalent status of diaspora Israelis for Jews and Jewish organizations has become problematic as the demographic profile of Israeli emigrants has appeared less and less like "the wretched refuse" and consisted increasingly of highly mobile and highly successful professionals. Israelis are generally not included in organizations concerning Jewish charities or social service, despite their growing presence in American-Jewish communities.

Although the relationship between the two groups has become warmer, partly as a result of the changing attitude of the Israeli government noted above, processes inherent in the different experiences of the two groups have kept them separated. Studies and polls conducted by the Council of Jewish Federations in the 1990s have revealed a dramatic shift in loyalty among American Jews to the Israeli state. Two major reasons include the role of religion, which has become more pluralistic in the United States, and, most interestingly, the role of the Israeli state itself. Ironically, American Jews seemed to loosen their bonds with Israel precisely because they were so sure of its success with a globalized economy and a powerful army (*Boston Globe* 1998).

It is very significant that, as Israel has experienced rapid economic growth and military strength, its traditional economic support from the Jewish diaspora, particularly in the United States, has declined. Israel's import of capital from Jewish organizations in the United States has undergone a notable decline as a result of a shift in priorities. This has coincided with the passing of the older generation of American-Jewish community leaders, whose formative years were spent during the Holocaust and the establishment of the state of Israel, in contrast to a younger generation of leaders, to whom Israel has been a fact of life (Arian 1998: 64). Assuming Israel continues to thrive economically, and American Jews remain fully integrated and increasingly assimilated (as evidenced by the unprecedented "outmarrying" rate of marriages), the impact of demography and the different roles of religion and identity will inexorably lead the two communities down two different paths.

The differentiation among Israelis and diaspora Jews often rests on the distinction between religious and national identifications. Israeli emigrants introduce a revision to the usual categories of Jews in the diaspora. They often repudiate Jewish tradition, assuming instead a greater Hebrew culture, while they abandon the Jewish homeland and cradle of the culture which they claim to represent

(Shokeid 1988: 51). Many Israelis – even those young able-bodied migrants who arrive in the US in the aftermath of their military service – continue to perceive their national undertaking as providing a refuge for the world's Jews.[5] Similarly, many Jews in the world show pride, concern, and anxiety (or other emotions) toward Israel in a manner unusual for citizens of foreign countries. Regardless of the distribution of opinion about Israel among diaspora Jews, the question of identity is always near the surface. If Jews were persecuted in the Middle Ages for having a distinct religion, in modern times this dilemma is compounded by the existence of the state of Israel, and the difficulties this raises regarding both religious and national loyalties (Arian 1998: 10).

The major arena of conflict, though rarely expressed explicitly, is in the field of personal and national identity (see also Gold 2000a). Of those who described themselves as Jews by religion in the United States, 80 percent expressed a denominational preference for the Conservative and Reform synagogue movements, while only some 6 percent identified themselves as strictly religious, Orthodox Jews (Council of Jewish Federations 1990). In Israel, secular Israelis consider themselves Orthodox regardless of their alienation from any form of Orthodoxy. They are usually unaware of the religious traditions (i.e., Conservative and Reform movements) of the majority of organized American Jewry, and which are often very different from those represented by Israeli Orthodoxy (Shokeid 1988: 40). This religious pluralism fits in the American mainstream culture of denominational and communal association (Glazer 1957), and is simultaneously alien to Israelis' perception of Jewish identity, which is an elementary component in the Israeli definition of citizenship and nationality. Israelis arriving in America discover the central role of the synagogue in the life of American Jews, while American Jews are stunned by the ignorance and complete withdrawal of Israelis from Jewish tradition and organizations (Shokeid 1988: 40).

These religious and national conceptual differences are reinforced institutionally and culturally. The role of synagogues and community organizations in each country varies considerably and reflects the social and political differences of the Israeli and American systems more generally. While American Jewry is considered to be one of the most viable and resourceful ethnic communities in America, Israeli immigrants have been shown to dissociate themselves from active participation in Jewish communal and national organizations in the US and not to initiate formal institutions of their own (Shokeid 1988: 44; Gold 2000a: 415).[6] This could be interpreted as a reflection of de Tocqueville's early claim of American associations as a way of life contrasted with the Israeli political culture, with its habitual dependency on governmental agencies, while communal action is based on shared security problems (Shokeid 1988: 44).[7]

These cleavages between Israeli emigrants and their American-Jewish counterparts are reinforced by larger attitudinal distances between the two communities. These differences can be seen from the results of simultaneous polls of Jews in the United States and in Israel undertaken by the *Los Angeles Times* and *Yediot Aharonot* in spring 1998 on the occasion of Israel's fiftieth anniversary. Answers to questions of mutual interaction are indicative of the direction of affinity and/or familiarity between the two co-ethnic groups (see Table 4.3).

Table 4.3 Interactions: American and Israeli Jewish samples

Topic	Responses	United States	Israel
Visit	Israel/	37%	–
	United States	–	41%
Willing to live in the other country	No	90%	82%
Friends or relatives in the other country	Yes	42%	73%
1) The US should have a sizeable Jewish population	(1)	66%	47%
or			
2) All Jews should live in Israel	(2)	15%	42%

Source: Roper Center for Public Opinion Reseach, polls 407 and 408, sponsored by *Yediot Aharonot* and the *Los Angeles Times*, March 1998.

Not only have slightly more Israeli Jews visited the United States than have American Jews visited Israel, but two-thirds of the American Jews and almost a half of the Israeli Jews think that the US should have a sizeable Jewish population. They are deeply split on the idea that all Jews should live in Israel. Israelis have a higher rate of friends or relatives in the United States than the other way around.

When it comes to politics, Israelis were more willing to consider the views of the American-Jewish community than were accepted by the US Jewish sample. However, American Jews were more prepared to take public stands against Israel if they disagreed with its policies. Asked to what extent Israel should consider the views of American Jews when making policy, 60 percent of Israelis answered, "To a great extent" or "To a certain extent," compared with 37 percent of the American Jews. Respondents were also asked if US Jews should publicly support Israel even if they do not agree with Israel's policies; 65 percent of Israelis said yes compared with 40 percent of Americans. Wald and Martinez (2001) analyzed these surveys and concluded that Jewish religiosity has a common influence on most political issues but often has sharper effects in one society than the other.

The other substantial attitudinal cleavage between American Jews and Israelis is unsurprisingly related to religious identification. This reflects not only the structural differences encountered by the Israeli diaspora in America, but also one of the largest political rifts confronting the two communities today. At the heart of the political dispute are the issues of conversion, which currently exclude those of Conservative and Reform movements and restrict Israeli citizenship to the sole legitimacy and auspices of Orthodox rabbis. The attitudinal polls, while reflecting real differences between the American and Israeli communities, suggest some structural if not ideological convergence. Thus, among Israelis who describe themselves as secular (54 percent), there is considerable support for pluralism, so that even many Israelis feel that Reform rabbis should have the right to perform marriages. Interestingly, while it is important to note the similarities between the Jews of the United States and Israel regarding their synagogue attendance (28 percent report never attending), many more Israelis engage in religious or traditional practice: 88 percent of Israelis say they always or usually attend a Passover Seder; 83 percent light Hanukkah candles; 72 percent fast on Yom Kippur, the Jewish Day of Atonement; and 63 percent light Sabbath candles at least some of the time. This is considerably lower among the American-Jewish community, which evidently relegates the synagogue more to social and cultural activity than to observance (see Table 4.4).

While both groups reported that being Jewish was an important element of their self-identity (57 percent of Israelis compared to 54 percent of Americans), many more Israelis defined it as the single most important part of their identities (27 percent of Israelis compared to 13 percent of Americans). Furthermore, two-thirds of Israeli Jews objected to the suggestion of marrying a non-Jew, compared with 21 percent of the United States sample (see Table 4.5). In reality, at a time when American Jewry is experiencing such a high rate of out-marriage, the Israeli rate of intermarriage to non-Jews in the US has been estimated at 8 percent – 40 percent less than the recent average for American Jews (Gold 2000a: 416). Another sign of marked difference is that 58 percent of the Americans said that they never had a Christmas tree in their house, indicating that 42 percent had one at least once. The question was not asked in Israel, but the rate of having one would be extremely low.

As significant as the differences are, for many Israelis who observe Jewish holidays and traditions they are expressing their "Israeliness" as well as their "Jewishness." Israelis tend to perceive their designation as "Jews," a definition that implies submission to the superior status of the gentile host societies (Shokeid

Table 4.4 Religious observance: American and Israeli Jewish samples

Topic	Responses	United States	Israel
Participate in Passover Seder	Always	52%	81%
Believe in God	Without a doubt	41%	59%
Keep kosher at home	Yes	20%	46%
Synagogue attendance	Never	28%	28%
Fast on Yom Kippur	Never	43%	28%
Light Sabbath candles	Never	51%	31%

Source: Roper Center for Public Opinion Research, polls 407 and 408, sponsored by *Yediot Aharonot* and the *Los Angeles Times*, March 1998.

Table 4.5 Identity and marriage: American and Israeli Jewish samples

Topic	Responses	United States	Israel
Importance of being Jewish as part of self-identity	Very important and important	54%	80%
Would marry a non-Jew	No	21%	65%

Source: Roper Center for Public Opinion Research, polls 407 and 408, sponsored by *Yediot Aharonot* and the *Los Angeles Times*, March 1998.

1988: 5). For these reasons, Israelis in America tend not to participate in organized religious activities and depend on public institutions to socialize their children (Gold and Phillips 1996: 86–7). This is inextricably related to the differences of national identity and religion that exist in the diaspora, and underscores the struggles that those in the Israeli diaspora have to overcome in their transition from being part of a Jewish majority to part of a Jewish minority. It is important to note that, when comparing Israeli immigrants' observance of Jewish customs (i.e., lighting candles on the Sabbath and Hanukkah, attending synagogue on the High Holy Days and Sabbath, and fasting on Yom Kippur) with their patterns of practice in Israel, several studies of naturalized Israelis in New York and Los Angeles found that these practices increased in the United States (Gold and Phillips 1996: 89; Gold 2000a). This suggests that the distinctions between the two groups may widen even further as the Israeli diaspora confronts the American-Jewish community.

These attitudinal differences that center on religion and national identity substantiate the traditional dichotomy that has long separated the Israeli and American-Jewish communities, and that serve to distinguish the role of those who live inside and outside of the Israeli state. These divisions have been politically reinforced. With the globalization of the economy, and that of a diaspora community that includes increasing numbers of Israelis, the official position of Israel has continued to place importance on human capital. The Israeli state has consistently envisaged human capital as being more valuable than financial or political support from its citizens and "potential citizens" abroad. This is very significant, since it addresses the perennial assumption that Israel's policies are dependent and highly influenced by the support of Jewish fundraisers abroad, particularly in the United States. The reality resulting from the seeming division of labor, which has Jews outside Israel collecting money and leaders within Israel deciding how to spend it, has always followed the logic of Ben-Gurion's early thinking – that "one who wants to influence Israeli policy should live in Israel" (Arian 1998: 65). This has been the persistent view of both left and right political streams. Thus, in the late 1980s, the then Labor foreign minister, Shimon Peres, addressing the Conference of Presidents of Major American Jewish Organizations, stated, "We shall decide on matters of life and death in our Parliament . . . but, not to listen to you, not have a dialogue, not to express a view – who wants something so disciplined, so un-Jewish?" These comments alone generated a debate with the right-wing Likud coalition partner, Prime Minister Shamir, who renounced Peres's comments as a "regrettable attempt to circumvent Israel's democratic process by appealing to friends abroad who do not vote in Israel" (*New York Times* 1987).

Such statements are more than rhetorical, and are reinforced by institutional constraints against participation by those "citizens" who reside abroad. Israeli voting laws do not allow absentee voting, with the exception of official Israeli envoys serving in missions abroad and groups of at least ten Israeli sailors serving on Israeli flagships (0 in the 2003 elections). The estimated 300,000 to 500,000 Israelis in the US have no outlet for their political positions. Laws are occasionally proposed to allow absentee balloting, but they are always defeated, since a majority of

Israelis believe that those who live outside of the country, far from army reserve service and terrorist attacks, should not play a role in determining elections. The nationalist right-wing Likud is generally in favor; observers assess that more expatriates hold right-wing views. In contrast, the left has bitterly opposed the bill, as explained by Yossi Beilin, a candidate for the Labor Party leadership: "The cynicism of the ostensibly nationalist camp has reached new heights with a proposal which will allow former Israelis who abandoned us to send our children to the next war" (*Jerusalem Post* 1997). Many Israelis report "visions of hordes of religious Jews from the diaspora touching down at Ben-Gurion Airport, claiming instant citizenship under the Law of Return, and immediately returning to their diaspora homes, only to remerge as Israelis at election time, when they are told to vote according to the predilection of their rabbis" (ibid.). Even if the "sightings" of planeloads of voters being brought in to support one or another party are true, there is no evidence that these efforts affect the election results.

The Israeli state's approach to narrow the gap between the two groups is to target young American Jews and children of Israeli emigrants and entice them to spend time in Israel, in cooperation with Jewish organizations and federations in the United States. To this end, the Israeli government has recently agreed to co-finance, with major Jewish donors from North America and the Council of Jewish Federations, a $300 million program called "Birthright Israel" that would sponsor any Jew in the world, between the ages of fifteen and twenty-six to visit Israel (*New York Times* 1998). The assumption of "Birthright Israel" is that even a spring break spent in Israel can form a connection to Judaism and Israel for young people who have little or no affiliation. It is also seen as an effort to mend the fraying ties among the two Jewish communities. These initiatives represent renewed and heightened efforts to increase youth travel which has over the last years aimed at young people through advertisements in magazines like *Seventeen* and *Teen People*. The more recent campaign is more aggressive as it plans to use local Jewish federations to notify every Jewish couple that they will deposit in a special account a $180 check for every Jewish baby born.[8] These efforts attempt to mirror the success of government programs with second-generation Israeli youth in America. For example, *Tsabar*, the American branch of *Tzofim* (Israeli Scouts), sponsors youngsters aged ten to nineteen in eight states, and has a membership of approximately 1,500. Each summer, 200 Israeli-American youth spend a summer in Israel as part of *Hetz Vakeshet*, a program that combines elements of summer camp, outward bound, and army training (Gold and Phillips 1996: 89). These programs not only create a community bond between young Israelis with little familiarity with the country, but serve to socialize them into the "pioneering" and security spirit of Israeli life.

Globalization and the effects on community-building: one diaspora or two?

According to globalization and network theories, the ties between kin-diasporas would politically and socially empower groups as they converge over time. Our preliminary findings of Israelis and American Jews suggest that this is not necessarily the case. It is likely that these groups will in fact diverge, supporting our thesis that, while groups who live outside of the Israeli state are physically important, they will have only limited impact on Israeli domestic politics. Some of this is a result of spirited policy battles, such as the law of conversion or the status of the Reform and Conservative movements in Israel. Beyond policy issues, there are social forces at work that separate the communities. These are reinforced by the institutional constraints (e.g., voting laws) of the Israeli state. Despite and because of increasing globalization, which promotes technological innovations (e.g., jet planes, the Internet, faxes) and facilitates migration and communications, factors related to the Israeli state and national identity mitigate the relationship between the two groups. The ambivalent status of diaspora Israelis for Jews and Jewish organizations has evolved substantially since the formation of Israel more than fifty years ago, and may be interpreted more as a function of the Israeli state responding to globalization and other democratic pressures than globalization itself. The study of Israeli emigrants, as part of the newest Jewish diaspora in the context of more general demographic and attitudinal trends, exposes ideological and social tensions that differentiate the two communities, and that threaten to maintain a distance between the Israeli center and its periphery – the diaspora.

Jews developed unique forms of communal governance throughout their long diaspora history. Their organization was flexible and reflected the changing social, economic and political conditions under which they lived. These communal arrangements were designed to preserve Jewish existence and to sustain the moral imperatives shared by all Jews. Powerful tools for maintaining Jewish solidarity, identification and creativity were developed, including rabbinical writings, the daily and yearly prayer cycles, the holidays, and the Zionist movement, as well as local and even international forms of group action. These tools remain accessible to contemporary Jews, but declining proportions seem to avail themselves of them. Large numbers of the two main Jewish settlements in the world today, in Israel and the United States, are at least partly alienated from Judaism as a religious practice, and from Zionism as the destination of long years of wandering. While the relatively small but extremely cohesive sector of Jewish religious life is flourishing across great geographical distances, much of the Jewish population, not defined by their religious observance or commitment to "Zion," lack parallel tools for evolving and sustaining their corporate cultural and social lives.

In a world characterized by evolving technological means of global communication and transportation, large segments of the community appear threatened as Jews by increasing discontinuity and long-term disintegration. As Israel's role in the eyes of American Jews continues to change and to be less central, the proposition suggested by Kass and Lipset in the 1980s will be perpetuated: Israelis will remain marginal Jews, among the "proverbial marginal people" – the Jews themselves (Kass and Lipset 1982: 289). Today, the growing gap between the traditional and the modern, between globalization and national identity, between the disunity in many Jewish communities and the success and rapid growth of Israel, places these dilemmas in sharp focus.

The divisions that beset the Jewish people play out within each community and between them. With only two major concentrations of the Jewish people, the stakes for survival get higher. And yet, the tendency grows for the two communities to go their separate ways. Despite the social contact that stems from the technological and communications advances of globalization, and networks formed by increasing Israeli emigration patterns, members of the two communities increasingly become cautious spectators where the other is concerned. Since both communities prosper, albeit at different rates and in different senses, mechanisms of true mutual involvement are not readily at hand. The ambivalence between Israelis and American Jews is transformed into separatism, rather than hostility once Israelis arrive in America for an extended stay with the prospect of changing their citizenship (Shokeid 1988: 35).

The challenges facing the Jewish and Israeli diasporas are enormous. Having successfully survived through the twentieth century, with its mass murder, large-scale immigration, and struggle for the independence and security of Israel, the globalization of the twenty-first century holds hazards of its own. Manifestations of disunity abound in diaspora communal life: modernism and assimilation, separatism and political alienation pose one set of threats; arguments over religious pluralism another; how best to secure Israel's existence a third. Though part of the global village in many senses, in another sense, Israeli and American Jews seem to exist in two separate *shtetls* or villages.

Notes

1 For some theoretically insightful analyses of the political impact of diasporas, see Armstrong 1976; Sheffer 1986; Shain 1989; Cohen 1997; Esman 1994; Lipset and Raab 1995.

2 There were also other estimates and strenuous debates regarding intermarriage. See, for example, Council of Jewish Federations 1990; *Jerusalem Post* 1990. In 1990, while the total Jewish population reported in the survey amounted to 8.2 million, 2.7 million of these Jews claimed Jewish descent but did not currently consider themselves Jewish.

3 Levitt (2001) points out that "transnational communities" are not the same as diasporas, but may be included as a specific subset of the larger diaspora group.

4 Figures cited from a poll, "America's New Wave of Jewish Immigrants," by the Israel Institute of Applied Social Research, in Kass and Lipset (1982).

5 A substantial number continue to identify themselves as "Israeli" rather than American, even among second-generation groups (Uriely 1995).

6 In contrast, however, Israelis tend to rely on a substantial degree of private or informal communal activity that includes Hebrew-speaking social events, fundraising, recreational activity, Hebrew-language instruction, media, nightclubs and folk-dancing (see Gold 2000a: 413).

7 According to Shokeid's study of Israelis in New York, there was not even one voluntary association in the city during the years 1982–4, despite the fact that Israelis are not divided by anything comparable to the regional, linguistic, and caste divisions common to Indian society, for example. More recently, however, one research team identified roughly twenty-seven Israeli organizations in the Los Angeles area (Gold 2000a: 413).

8 "Chai" in Hebrew means life. The numerical value of the letters that form that word is 18: $180 = 18 \times 10$.

References

Arian, A. (1998) *The Second Republic: Politics in Israel*. Chatham, NJ: Chatham House.

Armstrong, J. (1976) "Mobilized and Proletarian Diasporas," *American Political Science Review*, vol. 70, no. 2, pp. 393–408.

Barnett, M. (ed.) (1996) "Israel in the World Economy: Israel as an East Asian State?" in *Israel in Comparative Perspective*, Albany, NY: SUNY Press.

Basch, L., Glick-Schiller, N., and Blanc, C. S. (1994) *Nations Unbound: Transnational Projects, Post-Colonial Predicaments and Deterritorialized Nation-States*. New York: Gordon & Breach.

Bauman, Z. (1998) *Globalization: The Human Consequences*. New York: Columbia University Press.

Boston Globe (1998) "Israel's Star Fades in America," May 20, pp.1 and A18.

CBS (Central Bureau of Statistics) (2003) *Statistical Abstracts of Israel*, no. 54, Jerusalem.

Cohen, R. (1997) *Global Diasporas: An Introduction*. London: University College London Press; Seattle: University of Washington Press.

Cohen, S. (1986) "Israeli Émigrés and the New York Federation: A Case Study in Ambivalent Policymaking for 'Jewish Communal Deviants,'" *Contemporary Jewry*, vol. 7, pp. 155–6.

Cohen, Y. (2002) "From Haven to Heaven: Changing Patterns of Immigration to Israel," in Levy, D., and Weiss, Y. (eds) *Challenging Ethnic Citizenship: German and Israeli Perspectives on Immigration*. New York: Berghahn Books.

Cohen, Y., and Haberfeld, Y. (1997) "The Number of Israeli Immigrants in the United States in 1990," *Demography*, vol. 34, no. 2, pp. 199–212.

Council of Jewish Federations (1990, 1998) *National Surveys*.

DellaPergola, S. (1998) "World Jewish Population," *American Jewish Year Book*, vol. 98. New York: American Jewish Committee.

Dvirei Ha'Knesset (Parliament Records) vol. 6 (1950), pp. 2035–7.

Esman, M. (1994) *Ethnic Politics*. Ithaca and London: Cornell University Press.

Evans, P. (1998) "The Eclipse of the State? Reflections on Stateness in an Era of Globalization," *World Politics*, vol. 50, pp. 62–87.

Friedberg, A. and Kfir, A. (1988) "Jewish Emigration from Israel," *Jewish Journal of Sociology*, June, pp. 5–15.

Friedlander, D., and C. Goldscheider (1979) *Population of Israel*. New York: Columbia University Press.

Glazer, N. (1957) *American Jews*. Chicago: University of Chicago Press.

Glick Schiller, N., Basch, L., and Blanc-Szanton, C. (1992) "Transnationalism: A New Analytic Framework for Understating Migration," in *Towards a Transnational Perspective on Migration: Race, Class, Ethnicity, and Nationalism Reconsidered*. New York: New York Academy of Sciences, pp. 1–24.

Golan, M. (1992) *With Friends Like You: What Israelis Really Think about American Jews*. New York: Free Press.

Gold, S. (2000a) "Israeli Americans," in Kivisto, Peter, and Runblad, Georganne (eds) *Multiculturalism in the United States: Current Issues, Contemporary Voices*. Thousand Oaks, CA: Pine Forge Press, pp. 409–20.

Gold, S. (2000b) "Transnational Communities: Examining Migration in a Globally Integrated World," in Aulakh, Preet S., and Schechter, Michael G. (eds) *Rethinking Globalization(s): From Corporate Transnationalism to Local Intervention*. London: Macmillan, pp. 73–90.

Gold, S., and Phillips, B. (1996) "Israelis in the United States," *American Jewish Year Book*, vol. 51.

Goldscheider, C. (1996) *Israel's Changing Society: Population, Ethnicity, and Development.* Boulder, CO: Westview Press.

Ha-Aretz (1994) January 21, p. 1.

Horowitz, D., and Lissak, M. (1978) *The Origins of the Israeli Polity: Palestine under the Mandate.* Chicago: University of Chicago Press.

Israel Shelanu (1995) *Going Home.* Produced in cooperation with the Office of Returning Residents, Israel Ministry of Immigrant Absorption (Supplement).

Israelis in America (1999) online: http://www.chosen-people.com/docs/curios/aboutus2/articles/MorningStar/Israelis.html (January 30).

Israelis in the US (1999) online: http://www.hamakom.com (January 30).

Jasso, G., and Rosenzweig, M. (1990) *The New Chosen People: Immigrants in the United States.* New York: Russell Sage Foundation.

Jerusalem Post (1989) "Reversing the Brain Drain," June 7.

Jerusalem Post (1990) "Intermarriage Rate of U.S. Jews Exceeds 50 Percent," June 9.

Jerusalem Post (1991) "Who Counts as a Jew?," February 19.

Jerusalem Post (1997) "Letting Them Have their Say," January 31.

Kass, D., and Lipset, S. M. (1982) "Jewish Immigration to the United States from 1967 to the Present: Israelis and Others," in M. Sklare (ed.) *Understanding American Jewry.* New Brunswick, NY: Transaction Press.

Keohane, R., and Milner, H. (eds) (1996) *Internationalization and Domestic Politics.* Cambridge: Cambridge University Press.

Kosmin, B. (1993) "New Data on Israelis in the United States Indicate that they are Not as Numerous as Believed," press release, Council of Jewish Federations, June 14.

Levitt, Peggy (2001) *The Transnational Villagers.* Berkeley: University of California Press.

Lipset, S. M., and Raab, E. (1995) *Jews and the New American Scene.* Cambridge, MA: Harvard University Press.

Machlis, A. (1998) press release, Jewish Telegraphic Agency, April 28.

Massey, Douglas, *et al.* (1993) "Theories of International Migration: A Review and Appraisal," *Population and Development Review*, vol. 19, no. 3, pp. 431–66.

Meyers, E. (1998) "Security and Immigration Policy: The Case of Israel," paper presented at the International Studies Association Convention, Minneapolis, March 17–21.

Ministry of Immigrant Absorption (1996) *The Absorption of Immigrants.* Jerusalem.

National Jewish Population Survey (2000–2001) online: http://www.ujc.org.

New York Times (1987) "Jews in U.S. to Use 'Restraint' on Matters of Israeli Security," October 12.

New York Times (1998) November 16, p. A1.

Shain, Y. (1989) *The Frontier of Loyalty: Political Exiles in the Age of the Nation-State.* Middletown, CT: Wesleyan University Press.

Sheffer, G. (ed.) (1986) *Modern Diaspora in International Politics.* New York: St. Martin's Press.

Sher, H. (1996) "Riding High-Tech," *Jerusalem Report*, July 11.

Shokeid, M. (1988) *Children of Circumstances: Israeli Emigrants in New York.* Ithaca and London: Cornell University Press.

Uriely, N. (1995) "Patterns of Identification and Integration with Jewish Americans among Israeli Immigrants in Chicago: Variations across Status and Generation," *Contemporary Jewry*, vol. 16, pp. 27–49.

Wald, K. D., and Martinez, M. D. (2001) "Jewish Religiosity and Political Attitudes in the United States and Israel," *Political Behavior*, vol. 23, no. 4, pp. 337–97.

Zolberg, A. (1981) "Patterns of International Migration Policy," in Fried, C. (ed.) *Minorities: Community and Identity*. Berlin: Springer, pp. 229–46.

Zucker, Bat Ami (1989) "Israeli Immigration Policy and Politics," in LeMay, M. C. (ed.) *The Gatekeepers: Comparative Immigration Policy*. New York: Praeger.

5 Migrant membership as an instituted process

Transnationalization, the state and the extra-territorial conduct of Mexican politics[1]

Robert C. Smith

Introduction

How should we conceptualize political community, membership and citizenship in a world where increasing numbers of immigrants and their countries of origin maintain, cultivate and deepen their formal and informal relations? Wherein concrete membership practices transcending nation-states abound?

This chapter engages these issues by analyzing the extra-territorial conduct of Mexican political life and the creation and contestation surrounding membership practices of migrants and the Mexican state. I argue that these processes have led to the creation of a transnational public sphere between the US and Mexico that manifests different degrees of membership. Theoretically, this chapter argues for the utility of rethinking the concept of membership in a political community as what Polanyi (1957) called an "instituted process," whose significance emerges within the context of the larger relations and institutions within which it is embedded (see Marshall 1950; Somers 1993). In this chapter, I analyze how migrant membership practices are embedded within four institutions and processes: 1) Mexico's domestic politics, including the regime's legitimacy crisis, secular trends toward democratization and the attempts of the PRI (Institutional Revolutionary Party) to control them through cooptation; 2) Mexico's version of dependent development, especially its policy of "*acercamiento*" (closer relations) with the US, expressed most clearly in the creation of the North American Free Trade Agreement (NAFTA); 3) the emergence over decades of migration to the US of a sometimes semi-autonomous, transnational civil society between the US and Mexico which offers migrants increasing influence; and 4) the varying contexts of reception of different Mexican groups in the US. Embedding the analysis of membership in these contexts enables one to avoid the errors of both state-centered and hard transnational approaches.

The chapter's first section proposes a theoretical framework for looking at membership as an instituted process. The second analyzes how and why the Mexican state has attempted to coopt and control the extra-territorial conduct of Mexican politics, and unintentionally helped create a transnational public sphere and new membership practices. The third section of the chapter compares different practices and degrees of membership that have emerged for migrants from the Mexican states of Zacatecas and Oaxaca. It asks why Zacatecan migrants have had a corporatist relationship with the Mexican state and based their claims on their status as Mexicans, while Oaxacans have had a more antagonistic relationship with the state and based their claims more in human rights. It further asks how engagement with the four factors noted above have strengthened or weakened their respective memberships over time and helped create a transnational public sphere. The conclusion discusses the theoretical and policy significance of the analysis.

Theoretical issues

Membership and citizenship as instituted processes

The current analysis proposes to reconceptualize membership and citizenship as instituted processes embedded within the context of transnational migration, and host and home-state national development and political strategy within the world system.[2] In this view, citizenship and membership are distinct but analytically related ways of belonging to and participating in a political community. As used here, citizenship refers to ties and relations between categories of persons and states, where these ties are in theory mutually enforceable and in general respected by other states or enforced by international treaties (see Tilly 1996). Membership describes the broader relations and practices of belonging and participation in a political community. In the context of migration, membership is usually manifest in migrants' or other diasporic members' involvement in homeland public life, and can also be institutionalized via non-legal state structures or via non-state entities or structures, including human-rights institutions or discourse.[3] Citizenship enables migrants to participate directly in democratic, formal state institutions, such as voting, to have the chance to participate directly in governing and to gain control over state resources. Membership enables participation in less formal, but still often powerful, institutions or processes, but offers no such right to a chance to govern directly.

The difference between membership and citizenship as defined here is similar to what others call formal versus substantive citizenship (Baubock 1994; Goldring 1998a, 1998b). While useful, I think that reserving the term "citizenship" to describe rights given by states and practices linked to these rights makes sense precisely because possession of state-given citizenship rights still matters so much. It is for this reason that migrants are fighting so hard – via membership practices – to expand these citizenship rights, and why so many in sending and receiving countries are resisting these changes.

Citizenship and membership can be stronger, or thicker, and weaker, or thinner, along two dimensions: a group's ability to command material, symbolic or political resources based in or controlled by the state (and hence to be able to "deliver the goods," seen on the *State institutional* axis) – or its ability to exercise its will autonomously from the state (the *Democratic autonomy* axis), including its ability to "scale up" (Fox 1996) and find outside support – for example, through relations with NGOs and international human-rights institutions which can affect how state power is used with respect to that group. Claims that strengthen membership can be made using language based in national rights and in universal human and cultural identity rights (see Soysal 1994). Figure 5.1 maps out axes of state institutional and democratic contestation for the Oaxacans and Zacatecans to be discussed in this chapter. Extra-territorial membership can be stronger than nation-state citizenship for some groups, especially within authoritarian states, such as PRI-dominated Mexico, whose cooptational politics limited effective exercise of citizenship (see Fox 1996; Smith 1997; Smith and Goldring 1994; Goldring 1997, 1998a, 1998b). Also, membership itself and claims for citizenship rights can be strengthened in particular contexts that present opportunities for mobilizing and making such claims (Tilly 1996; Tarrow 1998).

To clarify, Figure 5.1 lays out two important dimensions of political participation, showing variation in these cases along which one may evaluate the strength or weakness and evolution of both citizenship and membership. It does not distinguish between membership and citizenship, but rather provides a way to plot their strength and evolution.

The difference and limits between citizenship and membership are neither fixed nor eternal. The conditions within which states are sovereign and within which they grant citizenship and negotiate membership have changed dramatically with the current era of economic and political integration, NAFTA and the European Union (See Sassen 1996). *Hence, we should expect further redefinition of membership and citizenship.* Finally, citizenship and membership practices can be related: when migrants abroad exercise membership by lobbying for and are granted dual citizenship, or for the right to vote in presidential elections from abroad, membership practices have created new citizenship rights that can be exercised extra-territorially.

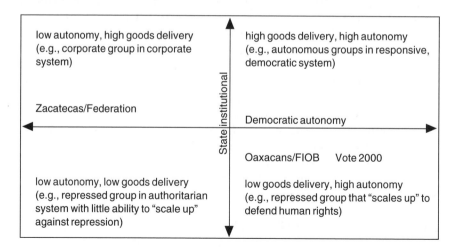

low autonomy, high goods delivery (e.g., corporate group in corporate system)	high goods delivery, high autonomy (e.g., autonomous groups in responsive, democratic system)
Zacatecas/Federation	Democratic autonomy
	Oaxacans/FIOB Vote 2000
low autonomy, low goods delivery (e.g., repressed group in authoritarian system with little ability to "scale up" against repression)	low goods delivery, high autonomy (e.g., repressed group that "scales up" to defend human rights)

Figure 5.1 State institutional versus democratic autonomous axes for plotting migrant political participation, including migrant membership and citizenship.

We begin by stating the concrete questions to guide the analysis: Why would the Mexican state make a sustained effort to cultivate and deepen relations with Mexicans in the US beginning in 1990? Why would Zacatecans in the US form a strong corporatist relationship with the Mexican state in the US and in Mexico, while Oaxacans have an antagonistic relationship with it in both places? What does the evolution of their transnational practices, including joining the Vote 2000 movement, tell us about membership as an instituted process and about the conduct of Mexican politics in this global and transnational context?

Domestic politics abroad, diasporic politics at home, and the redefinition of membership, citizenship and nation

The Program for Mexican Communities Abroad as an attempt to create the Mexican global nation

"Why now?" was the question Mexican migrants asked consular and other state officials who approached them in the early 1990s to find out how best to serve them.[4] The dramatic resurgence and expansion in the scope and intensity of the Mexican state's professed interest in Mexicans in the US follows pattern of waxing and waning interest determined by the political importance and definition of US-residing migrants (see Sherman 1999; Goldring 1997; Gonzalez Gutierrez 1997, 1998, 1993; Smith 1998a, 1998b, 1995, 1993). A defeated Mexican state attempted to protect its nationals after losing its northern territory to the US in 1848. An authoritarian Mexican state used Mexican agents to keep under surveillance Mexican expatriate politics in the US during the Porfiriato (1887–1911), with US cooperation (Gutierrez 1986; see Miller 1981 on authoritarian sending state surveillance in Europe). The revolutionary Mexican state protected US-residing Mexicans as part of a strategy of regime legitimation during the 1920s–1940s. A slightly left-leaning state created the *Comision mixta de enlace* (Hispanic Commission), providing a forum for the Mexican elite to meet with Chicano academics and students as representatives of *Mexico de afuera* (Mexico outside Mexico; see Gutierrez 1986).

The current intensification of Mexico's relationship with Mexicans in the US is part of its larger policy of *acercamiento* with the US (Smith 1996; Garcia Acevedo 1996a, 1996b). Concretely, the intent is to intensify, broaden and institutionalize the relationship with Mexicans in the US, thus significantly changing migrants' actual and potential membership practices. These steps include the Paisano program, which tries to safeguard the rights of returning migrants and reverse the perception of them as "*pochos*" (pathetic figures who do not fit in either the US or Mexico, see Monsivais, cited in Zazueta 1983; see also Smith 1993, 1995); youth exchanges and scholarship programs; and the establishment of twenty-one cultural institutes across the US, described by then secretary of foreign relations, Fernando Solana, as potential "political agents" contributing to Mexico's foreign policy goals (Garcia Acevedo 1996a, 1996b).

Creating the program and a new context for migrant membership

The flagship of the *acercamiento* policy on migration is the Program for Mexican Communities Abroad, formed in 1990 at the behest of then President Carlos Salinas de Gortari. The program's stated goals are to maintain cultural links between Mexico, its emigrants, and their children; to foster investment in the home communities in Mexico; and to protect the rights and promote the development of the Mexicans in the US. While these non-political goals do describe much program activity, analyzing its activities, rhetoric and historical context indicates that it was part of a larger strategy addressing the US, the global system, Mexico's domestic politics, and migrants' increasing importance in Mexico.

The program was on one level a response to the growing realization of the magnitude of US-bound migration and its economic contributions in Mexico. The legalization of more than 3.5 million people – more than half of whom were Mexican – through the "amnesty" provisions of the 1986 Immigration Reform and Control Act shocked the Mexican elite out of their assumption that few migrants settled in the US. Moreover, by the early 1990s, remittances from Mexico were, conservatively, more than US$2 billion, an amount roughly equal to Mexico's earnings from agricultural export, to 56 percent of its maquila (export zone) earnings and 59 percent of tourist earnings, and accounted for 10 percent of income and 3 percent of GDP nationwide (Durand and Massey 1996). My fieldnotes show program and Mexican state officials emphasizing to migrants the importance of their remittances and investments.

The program also addressed the increasing transnational political activity by opposition groups and the Mexican state government. Then opposition leader and later opposition senator, Adolfo Aguilar Zinzer, explained Mexico's sudden surge in interest in Mexican migrants in the US this way in a 1987 interview:

> There is recognition that there are many initiatives developing spontaneously in the private sector and among governors and other officials on both sides of the border that are being carried out autonomously. The Gobernacion Ministry is anxious about the possible political consequences of this, so they are trying to control it.
>
> (de la Garza and Vargas 1992: 97)

These autonomous activities included the creation in 1985 of the Program for Zacatecans Abroad by the PRI-dominated Zacatecas state government, and Zacatecan lobbying for creation of a similar federal program and better treatment by customs officials. The opposition's actions were more important. The conservative National Action Party (PAN) blocked border crossings to draw US media attention to their pro-democracy message during the 1980s. During the mid-1980s, the left-leaning Party of the Democratic Revolution (PRD) worked with Mexican pro-democracy movements already active in the US, particularly on the US–Mexico border and in California (de la Garza and Vargas 1992). Most important was the unexpected and historic break with the PRI by Cuahutemoc Cardenas to head the PRD ticket in the 1988 presidential campaign, and the alliance it made possible between migrant leaders and members of the PRD, including an insurgent elite (Martinez 1998; Perez Godoy 1998). In his 1988 campaign, Cardenas mobilized huge crowds in Los Angeles, Chicago and San Francisco, even visiting striking agricultural workers in Pennsylvania. PRD leaders in California reported being under surveillance in the US and, during later elections, being searched once they entered Mexico.

The policy of *acercamiento* with the US was the most important structure within which the creation of the Program for Mexican Communities Abroad and new membership practices were set. *Acercamiento* represented a profound rethinking of Mexico's relationship with the US and its integration into the world economy. To understand how channeling expatriate politics in the US relates to these larger strategies, we must briefly analyze Mexico's recent political and economic history.

Mexico's neo-liberal turn, beginning in 1982 with President de la Madrid and continued by his successors, broke with the historic popular pact by which the PRI had ruled since the 1930s. Stated briefly, this pact promised "peace for prosperity": labor was kept tightly controlled in return for wage increases in certain sectors; opposition parties were allowed to compete for election provided the PRI kept power; peasants and urban dwellers were subsidized in return for allegiance; and the government assumed a nationalistic stance toward the outside world and foreign intervention, especially by the United States, powerful transnational corporations, and international financial institutions such as the IMF (Cornelius *et al.* 1989, 1994; Dominguez 1982). The "pact" imposed generous terms for cooptation for many, and selective use of violence and coercion for dissenters.

Neo-liberalism opened the PRI up to the charge that it had abandoned Mexico and the poor. To defend itself and soften the effects of the neo-liberal adjustment policies, President Salinas initiated the National Solidarity Program (Programa Nacional de Solidaridad), using funds gained by selling state-owned companies to fund public works projects. While Solidarity helped many, it was also used to reward friends and punish enemies in what Dresser (1991, 1994) describes as "Neo-popular solutions to Neo-liberal problems." After Solidarity ended in 1994, the use of violence against political enemies, especially indigenous people, increased dramatically (Stahler-Sholk 1998; Kampwirth 1998).

Breaking this pact also enabled Mexico to alter profoundly its stance toward the US and toward Mexicans in the US. *Acercamiento* required that Mexico abandon the nationalistic, distrustful, sometimes hostile stance toward the United States, so that economic integration via NAFTA would not compromise Mexico's integrity and so that links with Mexicans and Mexican Americans would not be seen as Mexican intervention in United States internal affairs (de la Garza 1983, 1997; Guarnizo 1998; Smith 1996). With Mexican identity not being defined so much in opposition to the United States as before, it became possible for Mexico also to redefine its relationship with Mexicans and Mexican Americans in the United States, and to revise concepts and practices of membership and citizenship. Perhaps the clearest evidence of this change lay in the Mexican Nation initiative of the Mexican Development Plan for 1995–2000, which planned to "strengthen cultural links with Mexicans abroad and with people with Mexican roots outside Mexico, . . . to recognize that the Mexican nation extends beyond its physical borders". This position was stated succinctly to me by the program's first director, Dr. Roger Diaz de Cossio: "This is my job: to create the Mexican global nation."

Redefining the relationship with Mexicans in the US made it possible for Mexico to pursue its domestic and foreign-policy interests directly through its nationals or former nationals in the US. It did so first by deepening relations with and attempting to empower Mexicans and Mexican Americans in the US by supportive engagement with civil society organizations, such as the National Organization of La Raza and the Mexican American Legal Defense Fund, and state-level bilingual organizations. Program officials describe this as part of a strategy to "make Mexican Americans our friends" and help them become "stronger friends." Second, Mexico hired public relations consultants to lobby for NAFTA, who, according to Charles Kamasaki of the National Council of La Razza, helped broker a deal that the Chicano caucus would support NAFTA in return for creation of the North American Development Bank (NADBANK) and a retraining fund for displaced workers.[5]

Mexico also wanted to control and channel the deterritorialized conduct of Mexican politics in the US. According to Diaz de Cossio, the program served Salinas by getting NAFTA passed and by quieting opposition politics in the US (author interviews 1993, 1995). Evidence of this strategy's success comes in contrasting the massive mobilizations for Cardenas in the US in the 1988 campaign with the virtual lack of mobilization in 1994. Coopting and channeling the disaffection of US-residing Mexicans through the program helped control the image of Mexico presented to the US media, and more importantly helped legitimize the regime at home through its good works abroad. Legitimacy became increasingly important in the 1990s as Mexican elections became more competitive and transparent (Amparo Casar and de la Madrid 1998; Perez Godoy 1998). Yet, as we will see, the PRI's attempts to use the program as an extra-territorial party organization for electoral gain sometimes backfired, inadvertently helping create a transnational public sphere with greater democratic contestation.

The Mexican state's attempts to institutionalize a thin form of migrant membership in a "global nation"

The Mexican state has attempted to institutionalize migrant membership in five ways. The first four serve the PRI's interests in attempting to establish a weak, thin form of membership that program official and scholar Carlos Gonzalez Gutierrez (1997) calls "diasporic membership" (see Smith 1998a, 1998b). First, the Mexican state insinuated itself into previously largely autonomous transnational spheres of action, registering more than 500 existing or new community-of-origin clubs by mid-1998. They also organized sports leagues and supported US-based organizations (e.g., bilingual associations) aimed at empowering Mexican Americans. Second, the program helped establish state-level offices of emigrant affairs in the governors' offices in the states of highest out-migration (e.g., Guanajato, Puebla,

Michoacan, Oaxaca, Zacatecas) and parallel state-level federations of community-of-origin committees in the US. These are meant to foster direct, lasting links and effective coordination of activities between those in Mexico and the US, and to advocate for migrants vis-à-vis a Mexican bureaucracy that often regarded them as "*pochos*". Third, the program institutionalized itself by surviving two *sexenios*, or six-year presidential terms. This matters because most programs last only one *sexenio*, and because it was staffed mostly by foreign service officers who were trained or lived in the US, supported NAFTA and saw close US–Mexico ties as essential to Mexico's future. Fourth, Mexico passed a "no loss of nationality" amendment to the Mexican Constitution, which provides that one no longer loses Mexican nationality by acquiring citizenship in another country. Possessing Mexican nation-ality does not enable one to vote in Mexican elections, and has mainly helped migrant elites who are now able to become US citizens but still carry a Mexican passport and enjoy certain other advantages. The Mexican state wanted to remove an obstacle to US citizenship for Mexicans migrants, so that they would be able to defend themselves as citizens against the kind of anti-immigrant politics of the mid-1990s, such as proposition 187, and be Mexico's "friends". Toward this end, program officials routinely exhort Mexican immigrants to take out US citizenship and become politically active.

The fifth change results from democratization in Mexico, and has most affected migrant membership. In 1996, PRD Senator Porfirio Munoz Ledo included, as part of a reform of the state, legislation making it legal for Mexicans in the US to vote in Mexican presidential elections in 2000 (Martinez 1998). That the opposition could force such provisions on an unwilling PRI is evidence of the significant decentralization of power away from an omnipotent president and toward a system where Congress matters and the Chamber of Deputies, or lower house, is not controlled by the PRI (Amparo Casar and de la Madrid 1998; Perez Godoy 1998). There were two upshots. First, the failure of the Mexican Congress to pass laws implementing this constitutional change catalyzed a transnational organizing campaign among Mexican immigrants and others in Mexico and the US demanding that the state do so, an ironic "exportation" of democracy (see Martinez 1998). Second, the constitutional changes gave migrants a Mexico-based, institutionally embedded basis for their struggle, while still using their location outside the US to organize free from coercion. In terms of our theories, we can say that decentralization of power in Mexico led to the establishment of a citizenship right in the Mexican Constitution (to vote for president), and catalyzed migrant politics, leading to an intensification of migrant claims-making and other political membership practices.

Degrees and dimensions of membership in a transnational public sphere: three cases of contestation, thickening and thinning of transmigrant membership

The previous section of this chapter laid out an analysis of why the Mexican state created the Program for Mexican Communities Abroad, and how it has attempted to institutionalize a "thin" form of migrant membership. The current section analyzes how migrant membership and a transnational public sphere have actually worked and evolved for three groups: Zacatecans, Oaxacans, and the Vote 2000 movement. We identify differences in the membership practices and claims-making of Zacatecans and Oaxacans and trace them to different ways each is embedded within relevant local, national and global institutions and conditions. We analyze how the Mexican state's actions in creating a transnational public sphere have led to unintended consequences, and how democratization at home has changed membership practices abroad, particularly through mobilization around the issue of the right to vote from abroad in 2000.

Case 1 – *Zacatecans: full membership, corporatism, and political opportunity*

The Zacatecans present an ironic case of what Fox (1996) calls "semi-clientelism" and strengthening or thickening migrant membership. It is ironic that the Zacatecans exercised very thick state institutional membership (they had power and influence on politics and resource distribution) through their corporatist alliance with the Mexican state and the program, but that their membership became more autonomous from the state (thickened democratically) first, due to a mishandling of this relationship by the Mexican state and second to increasing assertions of autonomy by Zacatecans abroad. In the end, the Zacatecan Federation in California went from being the program's flagship to having its most competent members split off to form the Frente Civico Zacatecan (Zacatecan Civic Front), which supported the victorious Ricardo Monreal and the PRD in Zacatecas's gubernatorial election of 1998. Below, we analyze how this change emerged and its implications for migrant membership and a transnational public sphere.

What conditions and practices made the Zacatecan membership institutionally thick? First was the long history of Zacatecan migration to Los Angeles and their huge numbers there, as well as the more than US$300 million dollars remitted per year. Migrants inject more dollars into the state economy than the state's main industries, mining and agriculture (Alarcon 2000). More important are actual migrant membership practices, including Zacatecans' long history of autonomous state-level organizing, in contrast to most highly localized migrant organizing. Such Zacatecan organizing dates to the 1930s, with the formation of the Comite de Beneficio Mexicano and the 1966 visit of Governor Jose Rodriguez Elias.[6] While yielding few immediate results, Zacatecan leaders report that this visit made it feasible for them to think about such transnational organization and membership in the future, an important step in causing membership practices to thicken. The current era began in 1985, when then Governor Borrego visited Los Angeles and established the state-level Program for Zacatecanos Abroad and the Day of the Absent Zacatecanos (Dia de los Zacatecanos Ausentes) to honor the sacrifice of Zacatecanos abroad, a marked contrast to their normal depiction as "*pochos*" or traitors (Smith 1993). The Zacatecan state program matched with state funds whatever the local community could raise for its public works projects, almost always by migrants abroad. The federal version of this program, "Dos por Uno"

(Two for One), created in 1992, matched local with state and federal funds. These programs institutionalized membership by having migrants' economic contributions formally solicited and recognized, and migrants began to demand a public say in how the money was spent. This demand for recognition and accountability became a pivot converting the Zacatecas Federation from an arm of the PRI in California into an arena of democratic contestation allied with a nominally PRD governor.

Another way that membership was institutionalized into what some Zacatecans call a "*gobierno chico*" ("a little government") in the US was the Zacatecas governor's annual visit, in which he "holds court" at the Mexican consulate in Los Angeles. He brings key cabinet ministers, state-level program officials, and about a third of Zacatecas's municipal presidents, and announces future support, receives thanks and complaints on past projects, and inaugurates new clubs into the federation. The federation announces its donations to Zacatecas, sometimes totaling hundreds of thousands of dollars.

There is also constant traffic between Los Angeles and Zacatecas by federation leaders and state- and federal-level program officials. For example, in 1996 federation leaders were flown to Mexico to tour several sites where projects funded partly by federation dollars were under way and to quiet rumors in Los Angeles and Zacatecas that the work was not progressing well.

This strong, institutionally thick, corporatist membership benefited all included parties. The Mexican and Zacatecan states gained legitimacy by manifesting their concern for Zacatecans abroad. The Zacatecan Federation served as a model on which the program began to organize other state-level federations, and supported Mexican state positions, such as the dual-nationality provisions the government proposed and ultimately enacted. For their part, the Zacatecans received recognition and legitimacy and status from the state, and were able to multiply the impacts of their public works projects through the Two for One program. The Mexican and Zacatecan governments and the federation had a classic corporatist relationship: real benefits in exchange for real loyalty, including channeling and coopting political dissent. Frictions within the federation over the nature of this corporate relationship with the consulate played an important role in subsequent political developments.

Corporatism, clientelism and political opportunity: the federation's split and the thickening membership of the Zacatecans

The split within the Zacatecan Federation emerged within the context of two causally related processes: democratization in Mexico and the PRI's attempts to control it; and the "new federalism," particularly the decentralization of administrative practices governing the use of public funds at the local level, including those remitted by Mexicans abroad. Embedded within these two processes, migrant membership democratically thickened.

Under the federal "Two for One" program, funds remitted by US-residing migrants would be handled in the home community by a committee of trusted friends, who could refuse to release funds to municipal presidents for cause. Ramo 26 (Fund 26) replaced Two for One in 1996. Under this new federalist program, the local municipal president became responsible for having elected a municipal council that decides how to spend municipal funding, including funds remitted by migrants. In reality, the selection process is highly personalized and usually serves the municipal president's political interests. In one case in Zacatecas in 1996, an opposition (PAN) municipal president spent funds remitted by the local club for a playing field on projects in other communities, saying there was more social need there. The migrants, all still then members of the PRI, argued that the municipal president spent the money in PAN supporters' communities and pocketed the rest (Goldring 1997).

These issues of control over remitted funds and the larger relationship between the federation and the Mexican government were brought dramatically to a head during the governor's 1996 annual visit. The faction critical of Fund 26, who were being maneuvered out of power as the annual visit approached, met the governor's plane at the airport in Los Angeles before their rivals, the federation's official delegation. The critics expressed their desire to retain some control over the funds they raised, and argued that the new arrangement under Fund 26 would under-mine migrant trust. But the mechanisms for disbursing funds were not changed and the faction critical of Fund 26 was forced from power in favor of the group that came to be viewed as openly partisan and as corrupt partners of the PRI.

Perhaps the most transparent illustration of the PRI's political use of the Zacatecan Federation was its handling of the Confederation of Zacatecan Feder-ations. This umbrella organization was formed at the initiative of the consulate, the state of Zacatecas and the federal government in late 1997 to represent the interests of all Zacatecans throughout the US. Delegates of the five Zacatecas federations (in California, Illinois, Texas, Georgia and Colorado) attended. But it was commonly believed that the government intended the confederation as a way to better control the politics of Zacatecans abroad and to mobilize support for PRI candidates in the 1998 governor's race and the 2000 presidential election. The PRI hoped to use the confederation to get migrants to urge their voting relatives in Zacatecas to vote for the PRI. At the confederation convention, consular officials attempted to impose their candidate as confederation president, then subsequently tried to reconduct the election after the victory of a candidate openly critical of them, the PRI and the federation's current president. The winner publicly denounced the consular intervention as an attempt to "have under control the votes of the Zacatecanos" (author interview 1998). One federation and civic front leader described the conflict over the confederation in this way:

> The Clubs here accepted that we form the Confederation because we believed, believe, and keep believing that it can be something good for all Zacatecans, and even for other Mexicans, . . . for a common good. But our government did not have the same goals. And really we could define that the organization, was, well, was really going to be used politically at any given moment. Of course, the elections for . . . presidential elections of 2000 are

coming up. Well, I think that for the Mexican government it is important that they have some kind of control here, already, that they go controlling the organizations, so they can help themselves in that way when the elections come. The error they committed was to try to force the [five federation] leaders, that is, to accept [their choice for] President of the Confederation.

The confederation became an important institution, democratically thickening migrant membership. While the consulate intended to use the formally democratic processes of the convention to create another layer of corporatist institution, delegates instead chose a different president and then changed the consulate's version of the confederation charter so as to limit the oversight capacity of the consulate, program and Mexican and Zacatecas governments. This unintended outcome was partly the result of the Mexican state having created an arena of contestation, a transnational public sphere in which migrants did not fear state reprisals, and partly of democratization in Mexico. Ironically, this predictable error by the PRI helped convert loyal PRIistas into followers of breakaway former PRIista Ricardo Monreal.

Ricardo Monreal and Zacatecans in Los Angeles: an evolving relationship with uncertain local and national implications

Ricardo Monreal's 1998 candidacy for governor of Zacatecas represented a huge political opportunity for the faction critical of the Fund 26 and the federation's increasingly close relationship with the consulate. Monreal was an important young PRI politician in Zacatecas, and at the age of thirty-seven had already been twice a congressman from Zacatecas, once a senator, and president of both the PRI in the state and of the National Confederation of Campesinos (CNC), the most important peasant organization in the state, as well as an official in the municipal government of the largest city in the state, Fresnillo. When Monreal was not chosen to be the PRI candidate for governor, he split with the PRI and formed the Citizens Alliance, an umbrella group under which he channeled the energies of the PRD, the growing protest vote that previously went to the PAN (Arteaga Dominguez 1998), formerly unenfranchised groups and, most importantly, the huge number of the dissident PRIistas, some 20,000 of whom marched with him when he launched his independent candidacy. In the end, he defeated the PRI candidate, Pepe Olvera, by 8 percent in the state that had reported the highest percent of PRI votes (74 percent) in the 1994 presidential elections.

Monreal did not leap capriciously or burn all his bridges to the PRI when he broke with it. He became what one of his ostensible colleagues, PRD senator Cristobal Arias, calls the "PRI inconforme" ("nonconforming PRI"), that is, PRIistas by history, thought and action but operating under the label of another party, in part to protest undemocratic party candidate selection mechanisms. Monreal joined a growing group of former PRIistas, from national PRD leader Cuahutemoc Cardenas to Senate leader Porfirio Munoz Ledo, who have won some measure of power through competitive politics and decentralization of power and have provided migrants with access to an institutionalized base of support within Mexico (see Perez Godoy 1998; Martinez 1998; Smith 1998a, 1998b). The right to vote from abroad in the year 2000 elections was a crucial issue separating the PRI from the "PRI inconforme."

Monreal's candidacy and victory had important consequences for the federation in Los Angeles and for the democratic thickening of migrant membership. He actively courted Zacatecan votes in California, making three trips there during his campaign. (The PRI and PAN candidates followed, but with less enthusiastic receptions.) He ran radio ads asking Zacatecans in California to tell relatives back home to vote for him. He highlighted absent Zacatecans as agents of change and their contributions to the state's economic and social life. His campaign in California was well covered by the Zacatecas media, and Zacatecan academics believe the migrant vote mobilized by his campaign abroad was a significant factor in his victory. Monreal has continued to repeat his promises to migrants.

Most important in terms of migrant membership are two aspects of Monreal's involvement with migrants. First, he has promised to change further the relationship between Zacatecans abroad and the state government. He proposed that Zacatecans directly elect Congresspersons in the state assembly to represent those in the US, via a representational scheme. He named a prominent former Zacatecan Federation leader who broke to help form the Frente Civico Zacatecan to a cabinet-level position as secretary of migrant affairs of the state government of Zacatecas, with his main office in Los Angeles. He has also agreed to run the Zacatecas Two for One program under the old rules, not the new ones, giving migrants more control (see also Goldring 1998a, 1998b). In keeping these campaign promises, Monreal makes plausible future claims that he is making government more accountable to all Zacatecans, including the "absent ones" in the US, and positions himself well vis-à-vis wider migrant populations in future elections. His practices and promises are quite similar to those that the new Mexican president has pursued in his election. Second, Monreal also linked democratization with inclusion of absent migrants in the US in a way that has profoundly changed Mexican politics. He combined a rhetoric of including migrants in the imagined political community as a necessary step in Mexican democracy with the institutionalization of migrant membership and citizenship practices, such as campaigning in the US. Together, these moves strengthened the position of migrants and made them players in Mexican politics in ways they had not been before. This is not to say that Mexican politics has been magically reformed by transnationalization. But Monreal helped make possible the election of candidate Vicente Fox as president on a pro-migrant platform in 2000.

Case 2 – Oaxacans: attenuated, contested membership while resisting cooptation and "scaling up"

Oaxacans present a marked contrast to the Zacatecans in terms of the substance of their membership practices and claims and institutions within which they are embedded. This is especially so for indigenous Oaxacans, who are the most marginalized people in one of Mexico's poorest states, and for Mixtecs, who are the largest indigenous migrant group.[7] Zacatecans and Oaxacans have different historical relations with the Mexican and American states and the local and global economies, and have different migrant membership practices and autonomy. Hence, initial Oaxacan citizenship and membership in Mexico is less substantive than Zacatecan, which affects how transnational practices thicken and thin, strengthen or weaken, membership. Factors helping thicken Oaxacan migrant membership include their ability to "scale up" (Fox 1996) the freedom from repression and access to US media that residence in the US offers, and the political opportunity of the Zapatistas rebellion/uprising. Factors thinning their membership include their integration into extremely exploitative and globally integrated Mexican and US labor markets, their US context of incorporation, and their antagonistic relationship with the Mexican state. Oaxacans thus have a different kind or degree of migrant membership, though their interests and practices have recently coincided with the US-residing "non-conforming PRI" via the Vote 2000 coalition.

An important source of the difference in migrant membership practices stems from indigenous people's second-class citizenship and antagonistic relationship to the Mexican state compared to the mestizo Zacatecans. For example, Mexico tried in the 1940s–1950s to "modernize" indigenous people away from their languages and culture, and today still neglects many of their specific needs (Kearney 1991, 1995, 1996, 2000; Besserer 1997, 1998; Rivera 1998; Ruiz Hernandez 1993; Fox 1994a, 1994b, 1996). Because Oaxaca and Chiapas have the highest percentages of indigenous population, poverty rates and political corruption, many jokes make it seem as if "the Revolution never arrived".

This historically hostile relationship with the state manifests itself today in the formation of structures of authority, traceable back to the Conquest, parallel to the local municipal authorities in indigenous areas. While local officials are elected, real power often resides in or is shared with a council of elders (*consejo de ancianos*) in a religious "cargo" system, wherein religious and political authority are largely fused and derive from an individual's service to the town. Migrants continue to participate in these local institutions while abroad, and are summoned home to perform their "*tequio*" or "*faena*" (communal work obligation; Rivera 1998, 1999; Carrasco 1961; Wolf 1957; Kearney 1991, 1995, 2000; Smith 1995, 1998a, 1998b; Neiburg 1988). Their persistence through migration forms a foundation for larger transnational institutions addressing pan-ethnic issues, including the FIOB (Indigenous Oaxacan Binational Front). Finally, Oaxacans in the US and Mexico are closely involved in the larger movement negotiating constitutional changes to give indigenous people more local autonomy (Kearney 1996).

These different relations with the Mexican state persist in their respective diasporas. Pre-Monreal Zacatecan-state corporatist relations contrast sharply with Oaxacan wariness. Oaxacans, especially Mixtecs, view the program as an attempt to coopt them, and participate only when they can set the terms. One leader asked: "Why would the government want to be friends with us here? It is a political manipulation." The Mixtecs and FIOB strongly resisted the consulate's formation of parallel indigenous institutions in the US, such as the Oaxacan Federation, and denounced its organizing an alternative "*Guelaguetza*" (a traditional feast) in 1996 as a "commercialization of our culture." For them, it tries to coopt the *Guelaguetza* they had organized since 1994.

Zacatecan and Oaxacan stands on proposals for dual nationality also reflect their Mexican state relations. Zacatecans publicly supported dual nationality, while the Oaxacans called it "partial" and a continuation of indigenous disenfranchisement. These positions also reflect differing Zacatecan and Oaxacan contexts of incorporation in the US. Zacatecans, especially their leaders, are US citizens or permanent residents eligible for US citizenship, while Oaxacans and their leaders are mainly either undocumented immigrants or legal immigrants with a lot of family in Mexico. Dual nationality benefited Zacatecan leaders because they could now hold both US citizenship and Mexican passports, and own land in certain areas in Mexico and be majority owners in Mexican businesses. For the mostly undocumented, poor Oaxacans, only dual citizenship would do because it would restore to them the right to vote in Mexico even while their lives kept them in the US.

Zacatecans and Oaxacans also have different experiences with migration, emergent group identity, and the US and global economies. Kearney (1991, 1995, 2000) ably analyzes how indigenous migrants from Oaxaca are marginalized at four different sites: in Oaxaca, as indigenous peoples; as violently repressed labor in agriculture in northern Mexico; as exploited "*indios*" in Tijuana; and as undocumented immigrants in the US. This marginalization fostered the reactive formation of a pan-ethnic identity and organizations wherein indigenous people see their future tied not just to fellow villagers, but also to other indigenous people in Mexico and the US (Nagengast and Kearney 1990; Kearney 2000). Resulting pan-ethnic organizations facilitate transnational "scaling up" (Fox 1996; Brysk 1996).

Zacatecans are more likely to be middle class and have stable, year round employment than Oaxacans. Zacatecan migrant leaders are also largely self-employed and economically comfortable (Guarnizo 1996; Smith 1996; Zabin and Hughes 1995; Goldring 1997), and hence are more able to pursue transnational politics. Oaxacan leaders mostly work in agricultural industries for low wages, making scarce both time and money for organizing. Moreover, Besserer's work (1997, 1998) eloquently analyzes how the rhythm of indigenous Oaxacans' lives and migration is now tuned to the ripening of hybrid tomatoes in a transnational industry. Oaxacan organizations confront the formidable task of coordinating across several thousand miles of Pacific coast, from Oaxaca to Washington state.

Oaxacan geographical dispersion contrasts sharply with Zacatecan concentration, especially in Los Angeles and Orange county, California. This facilitates Zacatecans organizing and enhances their chances to convert migrant associations into local, US-oriented, political clubs in southern California. Several Zacatecans have been elected to local council seats and the state assembly, or as mayors, and many are developing relations with US politicians. Leaders estimated the federation to have 5,000 US citizen votes before the split over Monreal, a potentially strong local voting bloc. Oaxacans count few US citizens and a smaller absolute population (about 50,000 Mixtecs, the largest group; Runsten and Kearney 1994; Rivera 1998: 10), whose dispersal prevents bloc voting potential. Moreover, Latino issues such as welfare reform seem remote from indigenous Oaxacan issues of human and cultural rights and autonomy in Mexico (Besserer 1997), leading to sometimes strained relations with Latino organizations, while new Zacatecan concerns with education in the US coincide with Latino interests. These aspects of transnationalization, globalization and US incorporation have all thinned Oaxacan compared to Zacatecan migrant membership, though this could change with longer term settlement by Oaxacans.

Other aspects of transnationalization, globalization and US incorporation have strengthened Oaxacan migrant membership. First, these migrants have "scaled up" by creating pan-ethnic organizations such as the FIOB and forging links with human-rights NGOs in Mexico and the US (e.g., California Legal Rural Assistance), and other associations (United Farmworkers Union, UFW) and student groups. The FIOB has also emphasized a human-rights discourse in defining its members as indigenous people whose rights are recognized by international bodies, has sent delegates to the first Indigenous National Congress (INC) organized by the Zapatistas in Chiapas in 1996–7, and has served as the official link conduit between the INC in Mexico and indigenous people in the US (Rivera 1998: 5; Kearney 1996; Brysk 1996). The ability of FIOB leaders to scale up is also strengthened by their repeatedly intertwining histories of struggle in Oaxaca as students and then as strikers in northern Mexico, thus conserving the social energy of these actions (Hirschman 1970, 1984; Fox 1996).

The FIOB has been able to create a far-reaching organization that thickens membership. It has set up offices in Oaxaca and California, established a base of twenty-two communities in Oaxaca and signed work agreements with that state, and organized binational mobilizations linking their local issues with larger indigenous issues and human-rights discourse, including ecological human rights (Kearney 2000; Brysk 1996; Rivera 1999, 2001; Velasco Ortiz 1999). In February 1997 the FIOB protested in front of the consulates in Fresno and Los Angeles, in Tijuana, and at tourist archeological sites in Oaxaca. Using human, indigenous and national-rights discourse, they demanded the government honor agreements with the Zapatistas and the FIOB, and attend to such local demands as resolving local communal land disputes. The FIOB elected a municipal president and a representative in the Oaxaca state assembly, angering local political bosses in 1998 (Rivera 1998).

Freedom from state repression and access to US media within the charged context of *acercamiento* and the Zapatistas has thickened Oaxacan migrant membership. FIOB leaders say they can protest human-rights abuses in Mexico more effectively because that state cannot repress them in the US. One told me: "If something happens in Oaxaca, we can put protesters in front of the Consulates in Fresno, Los Angeles, Madera . . . " Consular officials told me that migrants clearly got attention because they were in the US and could sully Mexico's image, a power that increased with the Zapatistas. Consular officials confided that Mexico wanted to portray itself as a good place to do business, and avoid images of indigenous people fighting the government at home and protesting it abroad. This charged context thickened Oaxacan migrant membership. FIOB leaders also appealed to the Mexican state's own rhetoric of its "nation extending beyond its borders."

FIOB mobilizations point out the importance of the factors discussed above in strengthening migrant membership: transnational scaling up, the conservation of social energy, access to US media, the US context of incorporation, the context of *acercamiento*, and operating in a public sphere wherein the home state cannot repress dissent. Despite conditions that would tend to weaken their membership, such as extreme marginalization and dispersion in Mexico and the US, Oaxacans have been able to strengthen their political claims-making and migrant membership.

Case 3 – The "Vote 2000" movement: migrant membership claims based in the Mexican constitution and practiced abroad

A final case of claims-making and migrant membership is what I call the Vote 2000 movement, composed of migrants in the US and Mexico, opposition leaders from the PRD and PAN, "non-conforming" PRIistas, Mexican and US academics, NGOs and others. This became a key issue in the 2000 presidential elections, in which the eventual winner, the PANista Vicente Fox, strongly supported migrant voting rights, in contradistinction to the PRI's refusal, during summer of 1999, to enact the legislation needed to make this constitutional right into law. The campaign to get the vote from abroad began with PRDistas abroad in the 1980s (Martinez 1998), and gained impetus by being institutionalized in 1996 Mexican constitutional changes (Perez Godoy 1998) and by the work of US-residing Mexican and Mexican-American activists who visited Mexico in 1998. The 1998 report of the impressively autonomous Federal Electoral Institute (IFE) stating the feasibility of implementing migrants' right to vote from abroad in 2000 also spurred action, despite the PRI's protestations. These events catalyzed migrants' transnational politics by giving stronger legal and political basis to their membership claims.

Whether migrants can vote from abroad matters for practical and symbolic reasons. First, nearly 8 million Mexican nationals live in the US, about half of all Mexicans have a relative in the US, and about one-third will make a trip in their lifetime (Massey and Espinosa 1997). Hence, migrants could theoretically determine a Mexican presidential election, though the requirements of current electoral laws make that unlikely.[8] Second, public sentiment, especially among migrants, increasingly views awarding "*los ausentes*" ("absent ones" or migrants) the right to vote as a condition for making Mexico truly democratic. To oppose this right is to oppose democracy and side with an authoritarian past. "Never Again a Mexico Without US!" proclaims one Vote 2000 coalition organization. Finally, Vincente Fox's advisors believe that the migrant vote was key to their victory (author interviews, 2000).

The Vote 2000 movement significantly changed the nature of migrant membership claims-making during the campaign. First, it helped propel the issue to national prominence and to move control over debate on such issues out of Mexico City into migrant-sending states, including the relatively unimportant Zacatecas, whose small Autonomous University has championed the issue. It even published the Declaration of Zacatecas in 1998, proclaiming (in the name of Governor Monreal) that migrants should be given the right to vote from abroad and to participate in Mexican public life, in part because of their ongoing contributions. Second, it has fostered a broad US-residing migrant-Mexican domestic opposition coalition with strong roots, both in Mexican opposition parties and groups and in US civil society, including Latino neighborhood and political organizations. This created horizontal links between immigrant groups in the US and Mexico and between different migrant organizations in Mexico, and vertical links with political parties. It also creates improbable bedfellows such as the Frente Civico Zacatecan and the FIOB – respectively, "non-conforming PRIistas" and indigenous supporters of the Zapatistas in Chiapas. Finally, the Vote 2000 movement has helped strengthen defense of human rights and civil society. When the FIOB director was threatened with death by masked gunmen in January 1999 (presumably hired by local caciques angered by FIOB's growing electoral success), a national and international campaign demanded protection. Contrary to past responses, Oaxaca's governor assigned the director armed guards. This protection campaign was more effective because it drew on horizontal links of migrant groups in the US and in Mexico, and on vertical links to the opposition and non-conforming PRIistas in Mexico and to the US media. Such links are perhaps the movement's most important political outgrowth because they strengthen civil society, democratic processes and migrant membership.

Conclusion

This analysis shows that there are different ways of belonging to a national political community. Mexican migrants have become an increasingly important part of Mexican politics, and have strengthened both their membership (e.g., through de facto participation in politics) and citizenship (e.g., through changes in the constitution) practices and claims. Yet they have not done so uniformly. Indeed, Oaxacans' and Zacatecans' different relationship to the state and labor markets in Mexico and the US, and to Mexico's larger strategic integration with the US, have yielded stronger membership for Zacatecans than for Oaxacans, and greater ability to exercise their Mexican citizenship rights and participate in politics both in Mexico and in the US. While the FIOB has, for example, been able to use the freedom it has by virtue of being in the US to organize and even to win local municipal elections in Oaxaca, Zacatecans – even divided into two organizations – still have access to the governor of the state and his staff in ways unimaginable to their Oaxacan counterparts. Oaxacans still must appeal to international human-rights regimes and defenders in the US to help protect them in Mexico. Zacatecans instead focus their energies more on influencing politics in and getting resources from their home state, getting more recognition from the Mexican state for their organizations in the US, and, increasingly, on local electoral politics in the US.

However, despite these differences, Zacatecans and Oaxacans have both benefited in making their claims by being in the US, by Mexico's strategy of integration with the US and of *acercamiento* with Mexicans there, and by the Mexican state's own extension of itself into the US. The Program for Mexican Communities Abroad and the strategy of *acercamiento* helped create the political space that changed Zacatecans and Oaxacans in the US from "*pochos*" into valued members of the "Mexican global nation." The secular processes of democratization and decentralization of power in Mexico also facilitated this change and the demand for greater inclusion by migrants. Finally, this analysis illustrates the importance of differentiating between citizenship and membership. Migrants have used membership practices such as public protests in the US for Oaxacans and the collaboration between Zacatecans in the US and the Zacatecas government to press for expanded citizenship rights, including the right to vote for the president from abroad and the right to elect representatives for those living abroad. That migrants see a difference between these broader membership practices and the concrete, enforceable ties that citizenship rights offer is important, and needs to be taken seriously by theorists too.

This analysis documents how politics in one large, important migrant sending country has changed because of migration and globalization, integration with the US, and Mexican democratization. Migrants were much more a part of the Mexican political community in the year 2000 than they were just ten years previously. Moreover these changes, increased democratic contestation among them, resulted not simply from blunt pressure of global norms, but also from the political actors, including migrants, in the US and Mexico. It shows a state elite in the PRI whose development strategy of integration with the US and global economies had the contradictory effect of enhancing the ability of the regime's opponents to use its position in the US to press for gains.

Coda – November, 2003

As an author, it is interesting to look now at this paper, written in 1999–2000 and published in longer form in 2003 in *International Migration Review*. More than three years into Vincente Fox's six-year term as president, migrants living abroad still do not have the right to vote, and, if things continue as they are, they will not get it during his term. In this context, I wish to take two quick glances backwards at migrant membership in Mexican politics. In 1999, I told officials of the PRI, PRD and PAN that they were mistaken in their firm conviction prior to the 2000 elections that most migrants would vote for the PRD or PAN, and that the PRI would be helping amalgamate the opposition by voting down the right-to-vote legislation in 1999. While it is true that by the time of the 2000 elections most migrants did support *el cambio* (change) – 65 percent of those voting in a symbolic election in Chicago, long a PRD stronghold, voted for Fox, and he won two of three symbolic votes in New York as well – this result was in significant part induced by the PRI's actions, which were perceived by many as anti-migrant and anti-democracy. Those who actually voted in the 2000 election (by returning to

Mexico to vote at the border, where special voting centers had been set up) actually supported Labastida by a slim margin, 46 percent to Fox's 41 percent, with Cardenas getting 12 percent, as reported by Enrico Marcelli and Wayne Cornelius (2003).[9] The reasons for this support are various, but my sense is that PRI supporters were more likely to have the IFE electoral credential and to be registered in the National Registry of Voters. This is so because, of the three parties, the PRI had organized migrants abroad most intensively, using the government, for the ten years preceding the election. Hence, I had argued before the election that the PRI would be likely to win at least as many actual votes as the opposition, even if its popular support was less. Cornelius and Marcelli's findings suggest that this argument was correct.

But what has happened to migrant membership since the 2000 election? There have been several notable movements. One is that migrants living in the US have not simply waited for the implementation of the right to vote, but have, rather, actively pursued positions through the political parties in Mexico. With strong support from their migrant base, five or six migrants ran as serious candidates for the 2003 congressional elections in Mexico for *plurinominal*, or regional representation. Moreover, they publicly ran *as migrants* who said they would live in the US and represent their constituents there. One, Manuel de la Cruz, from Zacatecas, seemed as if he had enough support to get a spot through the PRD, but was not picked by his party after a strong showing. A second development was the passage during summer 2003 of a state-level law in Zacatecas giving migrants abroad the right to vote in state elections there. Since it is not prohibited by the state constitution, nor expressly prohibited by the national constitution, it will be interesting to see how the issue is negotiated in the coming years. Unless challenged, it suggests that migrants could carve out some kind of transnational federalism, creating subnational political institutions to help govern their subnational, transnational, communities.

Notes

1 The author gratefully acknowledges the support of Barnard College and a Special Assistant Professor Pilot Grant; the Hewlett Foundation and Institute for Latin American and Iberian Studies at Columbia University, especially Douglas Chalmers; the International Center for Migration, Ethnicity and Citizenship at the New School for Social Research, especially Aristide Zolberg; the Social Science Research Council's Program on International Migration and the Andrew Mellon Foundation; the Oral History Project at Columbia University and the Rockefeller Foundation; and John Gledhill, Chuck Tilly, Paul Silverstein, Michael Kearney and anonymous reviewers for *International Migration Review* who read earlier versions of the paper. This chapter is a shortened version of an article that appeared under the same name in *International Migration Review*, vol. 37, no. 2, pp. 297–343. Address correspondence to Robert Smith, Associate Professor of Sociology, Immigration Studies and Public Affairs, Baruch College, City University of New York, 135 E. 22nd St., NY, NY 10010; robert_smith@baruch.cuny.edu.

2 My debt to Margaret Somers (1993) is clear here, though I have redefined public sphere more broadly than she and set the concept within a different set of institutions and forces. My analysis is consistent with Polanyi's 1957 essay.

3 This is why it makes sense to talk about European Union citizenship: it is in an organization that is sovereign in some way, answers to no higher authority, has the authority to regulate movement, and mediates the relationship between individuals and the community. Some observers have conceptualized European Union citizenship as "fragmented citizenship" because it simultaneously provides more than one set of rights as an individual, more than one means of access to these rights, and more than one sense of belonging in a national community. See Weiner's (1997) interesting discussion of the evolution of EU citizenship (see also Hanagan 1998).

4 Beginning with this question helps advance the chapter's larger task of analyzing the current historical context within which the processes of membership, citizenship and nation are being redefined. This section analyzes why and how the Mexican state attempted to create the "Mexican global nation," setting up the analysis of migrant membership practices that follows.

5 Author interview with Kamasaki 1996. The theory was that Latino business persons, especially Mexican Americans, would be ideally placed as cultural intermediaries to facilitate the new business ventures. This has not happened for a variety of reasons, including the lack of knowledge of large-scale business among most Latino entrepreneurs and the preference of Mexican companies for dealing with large American firms (Spener 1996).

6 Governor Rodriguez Elias visited Zacatecan leaders in California to strengthen links with their homeland, to tell them to "behave and not to forget us," according to a municipal president who went on that mission. He also met with local California authorities, including Governor Brown (Sr.), to see if agreements could be worked out with them on issues of mutual interest, particularly those providing for the protection of the rights of Zacatecans residing in California.

7 I focus here mainly on Mixtecs and their organizations, such as the FIOB, which have had a more antagonistic relationship with the PRI-dominated government than have the more PRI-oriented Zapotecs, who nonetheless still experience most of the same contexts of incorporation in the US and of origin in Mexico. On this, see Rivera 1999; Velasco Ortiz 1999.

8 These requirements include that one hold the new electoral credential, and that one be registered in the still to be created National Registry of Voters. I think that the PRI's anti-vote stance is ill-conceived even from a purely self-interested point of view. I predict that the PRI and PRD would each gain a plurality of the vote, while the loser would be the conservative PAN, which is seen as the party of the rich. The PRI would do well because, through the program, it has organized in the US for ten years, and because many of the most active members of the program have the goal of keeping the PRI in power. The PRD would do well partly because of its long history of organizing, but mainly as a protest vote.

9 They note that this finding is based on a small sample size, and hence is not definitive.

References

Alarcon, R. (2000) "Remesas de migrantes Zacatecanos," in *Migracion internacional y desarollo regional*, ed. H. Rodriguez and M. Moctezuma. Senate of Mexico and the Autonomous University of Zacatecas.

Amparo Casar, M., and de la Madrid, R. R. (1998) "Las elecciones y el reparto del poder," *Nexos*, no. 247.

Arteaga Dominguez, E. (1998) "Las elecciones recientes en Zacatecas," paper presented at the Conference on Migration and Regional Development, Autonomous University of Zacatecas, Mexico.

Baubock, R. (1994) *Transnational Citizenship: Membership and Rights in International Migration.* Aldershot: Edward Elgar.

Besserer, F. (1997) "La transnacionalizacion de los oaxacalifornianos: la comunidad transnacional y multicentrica de San Juan Mixtepec, Oaxaca," paper presented at El Colegio Michoacan, XIX Coloquio de Antropologia e Historia Regionales, Zamora, Michoacan, October.

——(1998) Notes on the Case of Felipe Sanchez. Personal communication.

Brysk, A. (1996) "Turning Weakness into Strength," *Latin American Perspectives*, vol. 23, no. 2, pp. 38–57.

Carrasco, P. (1961) "The Civil–Religious Hierarchy in Meso-American Communities: Pre-Spanish Background and Colonial Development," *American Anthropology*, vol. 63, pp. 483–97.

Cornelius, W. A., Craig, A., and Fox, J. (eds) (1994) *Transforming State–Society Relations in Mexico: The National Solidarity Strategy*. La Jolla, CA: Center for US–Mexico Studies.

Cornelius, W. A., Gentleman, J., and Smith P. (1989) *Mexico's Alternative Political Futures*. La Jolla, CA: Center for US–Mexico Studies.

de la Garza, R. (1983) "Chicano–Mexican Relations: A Framework for Research," *Social Science Quarterly*, vol. 63, no. 2.

——(1997) "Foreign Policy Comes Home: The Domestic Consequences of the Program for Mexican Communities Abroad," in de la Garza and J. Velasco (eds) *Bridging the Border: Transforming Mexico–US Relations*. Lanham, MD: Rowman & Littlefield.

de la Garza, R., and Vargas, C. (1992) "The Mexican Origin Population of the United States as a Political Force in the Borderlands," in L. A. Herzog (ed.) *Changing Boundaries in the Americas*. San Diego: University of California Press.

Dominguez, J. (1982) *Mexico's Political Economy: Challenges at Home and Abroad*, Beverly Hills, CA: Sage.

Dresser, D. (1991) *Neopopulist Solutions to Neoliberal Problems: Mexico's National Solidarity Program*, San Diego: Center for US–Mexico Studies, University of California.

——(1994) "Bringing the Poor Back In: National Solidarity as a Strategy of Regime Legitimation," in W. Cornelius, A. Craig, and J. Fox (eds) *Transforming State–Society Relations in Mexico: The National Solidarity Strategy*. La Jolla, CA; Center for US–Mexico Studies.

Durand, J. and Massey, D. (1996) "Migradollars and Development: A Reconsideration of the Mexican Case," *International Migration Review*, vol. 30.

Fox, J. (1996) "How Does Civil Society Thicken?," *World Development*, vol. 24, no. 6, pp. 1089–103.

Garcia Acevedo, R. M. (1996a) "Aztlan and the Program for Mexican Communities Abroad," paper presented at American Political Science Association meeting, San Francisco.

——(1996b) "Aztlan and Mexico," in David Maciel and Isidro Ortiz (eds) *Chicanas/Chicanos at the Crossroads*. Tucson: University of Arizona Press.

Goldring, L. (1997) "El estado mexicano y las organizaciones transmigrantes: reconfigurando a nacion, ciudadania, y relaciones entre estado y sociedad civil?," paper presented at XIX Coloquio at El Colegio de Michoacan, Zamora, Michoacan, Mexico, October 22–4.

——(1998a) "The Power of Status in Transnational Communities," in M. P. Smith and L. E. Guarnizo (eds) *Transnationalism from Below*. New Brunswick, NJ: Transaction Publishers.

——(1998b) "From Market Membership to Transnational Citizenship?," *L'Ordinaire Latino-Americano*, vol. 173–4 (July–Dec), pp. 167–72.

Gonzalez Gutierrez, C. (1993) "The Mexican Diaspora in California: The Limits and Possibilities of the Mexican Government," in K. Burgess and A. Lowenthal (eds) *The California–Mexico Connection*. Berkeley: University of California Press.

——(1997) "Decentralized Diplomacy: The Role of Consular Offices in Mexico's Relations with its Diaspora," in R. de la Garza and J. Velasco (eds) *Bridging the Border: Transforming Mexico–US Relations*. Lanham, MD: Rowman & Littlefield.

——(1998) "The Mexican Diaspora: Current Challenges for the Mexican State" paper presented at a conference "States and Diasporas" organized by the Latin American Institute, held at Casa Italiana, Columbia University, May 8–9, 1998.

Guarnizo, L. (1998) "The Rise of Transnational Social Formations: Mexican and Dominican State Responses to Transnational Migration," *Political Power and Social Theory*, vol. 12, pp. 45–94.

Gutierrez, J. A. (1986) "The Chicano in Mexicano-North American Foreign Relations," in T. Mindiola, Jr., and M. Martinez (eds) *Chicano-Mexican Relations*. Houston: Mexican American Studies Program, University of Houston.

Hanagan, M. (1998) "Irish Transnational Social Movements, Deterritorialized Migrants, and the State System: The Last One Hundred and Forty Years," *Mobilization: An International Journal*, vol. 3, no. 1, pp. 107–26.

Hirschman, A. O. (1970) *Exit, Voice and Loyalty*. Cambridge, MA: Harvard University Press.

——(1984) *Getting Ahead Collectively: Grassroots Experiences in Latin America*. Elmsford, NY: Pergamon Press.

Kampwirth, K. (1998) "Peace Talks, But No Peace," *New York: North American Congress on Latin America*, vol. 31, no. 5.

Kearney, M. (1991) "Borders and Boundaries of State and Self at the End of Empire," *Journal of Historical Sociology*, vol. 4, pp. 52–74.

——(1995) "The Local and the Global: The Anthropology of Globalization and Transnationalism," *Annual Review of Anthropology*, vol. 24, pp. 547–66.

——(1996) *Reconceptualizing the Peasantry: Anthropology in Global Perspective*, Boulder CO: Westview Press.

——(2000) "Transnational Oaxacan Indigenous Identity: The Case of Mixtecs and Zapotecs," *Identities*, vol. 7, no. 2, pp. 173–95.

Marcelli, Enrico, and Cornelius, Wayne (2003) "Immigrant Voting in Home Country Elections: Potential Consequences of Extending the Franchise to Expatriate Mexicans," Department of Society, Human Development and Health, Harvard University.

Marshall, T. H. (1950) *Citizenship and Social Class*. Cambridge: Cambridge University Press.

Martinez, J. (1998) "In Search of our Lost Citizenship: Mexican Immigrants, the Right to Vote, and the Transition to Democracy in Mexico," paper presented at the conference on "States and Diasporas" held at Casa Italiana, Columbia University, New York, May 8–9.

Massey, D., and Espinosa, K. (1997) "What's Driving Mexico–US Migration? A Theoretical, Empirical and Policy Analysis," *American Journal of Sociology*, vol. 102, no. 4, pp. 939–99.

Miller, M. J. (1981) *Immigrants in Europe: An Emerging Political Force*. New York: Praeger.

Nagengast, C., and Kearney, M. (1990) "Mixtec Ethnicity: Social Identity, Political Consciousness and Political Activism," *Latin American Research Review*, vol. 25, no. 2, pp. 61–91.

Neiburg, F. G. (1988) *Identidad y conflicto en la sierra mazateca: el caso del Consejo de Ancianos de San Jose Tenango*. Mexico: Instituto Nacional de Antropologia e Historia, Escuela Nacional de Antropologia e Historia.

Perez Godoy, M. (1998) "Social Movements and International Migration: The Mexican Diaspora Seeks Inclusion in Mexico's Political Affairs, 1968–1998," PhD diss., University of Chicago.

Polanyi, K. (1957) "The Economy as an Instituted Process," in K. Polanyi, C. Arensberg and H. Pearson (eds) *Trade and Market in the Early Empires.* Chicago: Henry Regnery.

Rivera, G. (1998) "Political Activism among Mexican Transnational Indigenous Communities and the Mexican State," paper presented at the conference on "States and Diasporas," held at Casa Italiana, Columbia University, New York, May 8–9.

——(1999) "Migration and Political Activism: Mexican Transnational Indigenous Communities in a Comparative Perspective," PhD diss., University of California, Santa Cruz.

——(2001) "Transnational Political Strategies: The Case of Mexican Indigenous Migrants," in N. Foner, R. Rumbaut and S. Gold (eds) *Immigration Research for a New Century: Multidisciplinary Perspectives.* New York: Russell Sage Foundation.

Ruiz Hernandez, M. X. (1993) "Todo indigenismo es lo mismo," Ojarasca [Mexico].

Runston, D., and Kearney, M. (1994) *A Survey of Oaxacan Village Networks in California Agriculture.* Davis, CA: California Institute for Rural Studies.

Sassen, S. (1996) *Losing Control? Sovereignty in an Age of Globalization: The 1995 Columbia University Leonard Hastings Schoff Memorial Lectures.* New York: Columbia University Press.

Sherman, R. (1999) "From State Introversion to State Extension: Modes of Emigrant Incorporation in Mexico, 1900–1996," *Theory and Society*, vol. 28, pp. 835–78.

Smith, R. C. (1993) "De-Territorialized Nation Building: Transnational Migrants and the Re-Imagination of Political Community by Sending States," *Occasional Papers Series*, New York University, Center for Latin American and Caribbean Studies.

——(1995) "Los ausentes siempre presentes: The Imagining, Making and Politics of a Transnational Community," PhD diss., Columbia University.

——(1996) "Domestic Politics Abroad, Diasporic Politics at Home: The Mexican Global Nation, Neoliberalism, and the Program for Mexican Communities Abroad," paper presented at the American Sociological Association.

——(1997) "Transnational Migration, Assimilation and Political Community," in M. Crahan and A. Vourvoulias-Bush (eds) *The City and the World.* New York: Council on Foreign Relations.

——(1998a) "The Changing Nature of Citizenship, Membership and Nation: Comparative Insights from Mexico and Italy," paper given at the Transnational Communities Programme, Manchester, England.

——(1998b) "Reflections on the State, Migration, and the Durability and Newness of Transnational Life: Comparative Insights from the Mexican and Italian Cases," *Soziale Welt*, 12, pp. 197–220.

Smith, R. C., and Goldring, L. (1994) "Transnational Migration and Social Citizenship," proposal to the National Science Foundation, January.

Somers, M. (1993) "Citizenship and the Place of the Public Sphere: Law, Community, and Political Culture in the Transition to Democracy," *American Sociological Review*, vol. 58, no. 5, pp. 587–620.

Soysal, Y. N. (1994) *Limits to Citizenship: Migrants and Postnational Membership in Europe.* Chicago: University of Chicago Press

Spener, D. (1996) "Small Firms, Small Capital and the Global Commodity Chain: Some Lessons from the Tex-Mex Border in the Era of Free Trade," in R. P. Korzeniewicz and W. C. Smith (eds) *Latin America in the World Economy.* Westport, CT: Greenwood Press.

Stahler-Sholk, R. (1998) "The Lessons of Acteal," *New York: North American Congress on Latin America*, vol. 31, no. 5.

Tarrow, S. (1998) *Power in Movement: Social Movements and Contentious Politics.* Cambridge: Cambridge University Press.

Tilly, C. (ed.) (1996) *Citizenship, Identity and Social History.* Cambridge: Cambridge University Press.

Velasco Ortiz, L. (1999) "Comunidades transnacionales y conciencia etnica: indigenas migrantes en la frontera Mexico–Estados Unidos," PhD diss., El Colegio de Mexico.

Weiner, A. (1997) "Making Sense of the New Geography of Ccitizenship: Fragmented Citizenship in the European Union," *Theory and Society*, vol. 26, pp. 531–59.

Wolf, Eric (1957) "Closed Corporate Peasant Communities in MesoAmerica and Central Java," *Southwestern Journal of Anthropology*, vol. 13, no. 1.

Zabin, C., and Hughes, A. (1995) "Economic Integration and Labor Flows: Stage Migration in Farm Labor Markets in Mexico and the United States," *International Migration Review*, vol. 29, no. 2.

Zazueta, C. (1983) "Mexican Political Actors in the United States and Mexico: Historical and Political Contexts of Dialogue Revisited," in M. Garcia y Griego and C. Vasquez (eds) *US–Mexico Relations: Conflict and Convergence.* Los Angeles: UCLA Center for Chicano Studies and Latin American Center.

6 Politics from outside

Chinese overseas and political and economic change in China

Amy L. Freedman

Introduction

This chapter looks at ethnic Chinese living outside of China. There is a lively debate over terminology used to refer to this group. Most commonly they are referred to as "overseas Chinese," or *huaqiao*. The problem with this term is that it was originally used to describe Chinese sojourners, Chinese nationals who happen to be living temporarily outside of China's borders. This group is now much smaller than the number of ethnic Chinese who are citizens of the county where they reside. Therefore, I will refer to "Chinese overseas" to indicate that this chapter is concerned with ethnic Chinese outside of China, most of whom are foreign nationals, but a crucially important group of Chinese nationals overseas are also important. While the number of Chinese citizens abroad is relatively small, this chapter will show that some of them have been very active in mobilizing people and support for political and economic change at home. There is no accurate count of Chinese overseas, but most estimates put the figure between 25 and 30 million, 80 percent of whom live in South-East Asia (Wang 1995; Pan 2000).

In addition to clarifying who is the subject of study here, I must stipulate the area of focus in this chapter. When one discusses Chinese overseas, what constitutes "overseas"? Are all Chinese outside of mainland China part of the area of study, in which case how should one think about the populations of Taiwan, Hong Kong and Macao? Generally the term Chinese overseas refers to ethnic Chinese *not* currently living in the People's Republic of China, Taiwan, and Hong Kong. While most of this chapter follows this convention, I will discuss the special role that Chinese in Hong Kong, Taiwan and, to a lesser extent, Macao have had on domestic changes on mainland (People's Republic of) China.

Substantively, this chapter examines the relationship between ethnic Chinese overseas and the internal politics of the People's Republic of China. While it is difficult if not impossible to attribute political and economic change to any one or two specific factors,[1] one can explain the links between different groups and the effects that might result from such relations. I will come back to this point shortly. Since 1978 there have been enormous changes in China. The most pronounced transition has been economic. In the space of twenty-three years China has essentially gone from a socialist, centrally planned economy, with virtually no private ownership, to a mixed economy where the private sector is surpassing the public in productivity and importance. While eschewing the term "capitalism,"[2] China is for most intents and purposes a (state-led) capitalist economy. Private ownership of businesses and property is allowed and it is no longer politically dangerous to aim at getting rich and making a profit. Additionally, people are given far more room for private expression, thought, and activity than was ever the case under Mao. As long as practices and ideas are not viewed as threatening to the current regime, people are allowed a considerable degree of personal freedom. For example, people are relatively free to choose their own job, marry whom they like, consume information from a variety of sources, and generally go about daily life with far less intrusion from the state than was true from 1949 to 1978.[3]

This chapter will look at if, and how, Chinese overseas have impacted these economic, social, and political changes. In addition, this chapter looks at how the relationship between Chinese overseas and the government of China has changed over time. While the link between the two was once encouraged by the Chinese regime, the tie has been reversed. Now, one could argue that it is the Chinese diaspora that fosters continued contact between its members and their ancestral homeland.

The organization of the chapter is as follows: First there is a discussion about the history and current status of Chinese immigration. The chapter then turns to a discussion of political and economic changes in China and the links between the diaspora and domestic transitions. The demonstrations in Tiananmen Square in the spring of 1989 and the continuing crackdown against the Falun Gong are discussed, with particular emphasis on the links between activists abroad and events within China. The chapter then moves to address economic shifts and the impact of investment in China by Chinese overseas. One of the things that the economic changes highlight is the significant extent of decentralization of power that has occurred in China; this section of the chapter makes the argument that decentralization of power has opened the door to greater influence from Chinese overseas in economic decision-making, but that this has not necessarily led to greater political liberalization. Finally, the chapter looks at the implications of economic change for theoretical debates about the nature of civil society and its possible role in democratization, and second about international relations literature and the links between domestic and international behavior.

Chinese immigration

Immigration was once seen as a discrete process. A person or a family would leave their homeland and move to a new country. Ties between the immigrant and the "old country" would fade and over time the newcomer would become more interested in the social, political, and economic life of their new country. The assumption of much of the 1950s literature on migration was that immigrants would acclimate and by the second or third generation assimilate with the larger culture around them.[4] Implied in this analysis was the idea that ties with the homeland would weaken over time. This vision of migration and acculturation has been radically altered in the last ten years. Not only do new immigrants maintain close ties to family in their homeland, but they also remain interested and involved in the social and political life of their birthplace. New scholarship on the continued links between immigrants and the life they left behind has called into question the previous assumption that earlier immigrants became estranged from homeland affairs. It is now understood that immigrants in past generations also had more extensive links to the home country than scholars once believed. While Chinese immigrants were no exception to this, they did face certain additional difficulties in maintaining ties to China.

In the mid-fifteenth century, under the Ming dynasty, China forbade maritime expeditions. The basic reasons for this included an image of China as a land-oriented country with little need for things and ideas from outside the Middle Kingdom, and a social hierarchy that positioned traders and merchants at the bottom of the heap. Those who ignored this imperial edict were forbidden from returning to China. This, of course, made it significantly more difficult to maintain close ties with social, economic and political life back home. The ban on leaving China was relaxed in the mid-nineteenth century, and it was finally lifted only in 1893 (Wang 2000: 43). Despite the prohibition on overseas travel, many thousands of Chinese left the Middle Kingdom for South-East Asia and the Americas. Many of these migrants were traders and unskilled laborers, but there were also a significant number of students, intellectuals and businessmen who journeyed overseas. Over time some Chinese intermarried with the local population[5] and put down roots that would become permanent. Other Chinese immigrants lived apart from the indigenous population of the host countries and maintained distinct "Chinese" cultural practices and characteristics. During this early period the links that existed between the immigrant communities and the homeland were mostly informal. Some communication occurred, but it was slow and unreliable. Chinese overseas could not look to the Chinese imperial court for any type of protection or advocacy, and those who had succeeded in leaving China seemed to effect little impact on domestic politics at home.

As revolutionary movements in China began to gather steam in the late nineteenth and early twentieth centuries, the ties between Chinese overseas and events back home seem to become more significant. At the same time there was a dramatic increase in the number of Chinese students who traveled to Japan, Europe, and the United States to study. These students would become the basis for much of the philosophical and financial development of the Kuomintang (KMT), the Nationalist Party soon to threaten imperial rule. The connection between the diaspora and events in China was forged and encouraged by the KMT. The party looked to Chinese overseas to raise funds and to generate support for dramatic political change in China.

Ties between the KMT and the Chinese diaspora

The best example of the connection between Nationalist forces and Chinese over-seas can be seen by looking at the period just before the overthrow of the Qing dynasty. Most famously, Sun Yat-sen, father of modern China, spent a great deal of time in Japan and the United States raising money for his cause. Perhaps more important than this financial link, Chinese nationals abroad were able to organize and form political opposition groups, plan strategy, and begin the struggle to overthrow the imperial system in China. In the early 1900s Japan was the basis for Sun's leadership of a new generation of student youth. In Tokyo, Sun developed his "Three Principles of the People": Nationalism, Democracy, and the People's Livelihood (a sort of vague socialism). At the first meeting of the revolutionary group in Japan in 1905, Sun gathered more than 400 Chinese students; they took an oath to work for the overthrow of the Manchus and to form a new Chinese Republic (Fairbank 1983: 216). Sun derived his support from the new merchant class among Chinese overseas and from students, intellectuals and army officers within China.

Sun fostered links between his supporters outside of China and groups within China through various means. Using Japan as their base Sun's group of students began publishing a monthly newspaper, *The People* (*Min bao*), smuggling 2,000 copies into China to distribute to students and intellectuals there. Likewise, when Chinese students studying abroad went home they were encouraged to continue promoting Sun's Three Principles. By all accounts their efforts were greatly successful. From 1905 through 1911 anti-Manchu sentiment swept through China. The last emperor ceded the throne in 1911 and the Nationalist Party, the KMT, consolidated power over key areas of China by the mid-1920s. Chiang Kai-shek was the head of this new republic. Chiang married Soong Meiling, daughter of financier T. V. Soong. Madam Chiang had graduated from Wellesley College and had strong family ties to the United States. She and some of her family members served as effective lobbyists for American support of the KMT.

Once in power the Nationalists continued to look overseas for financial support. And, fearing internal threats, the KMT also sought to prevent any opposition from groups within and outside of China. To do this, it maintained a whole international network of security forces to make sure that overseas Chinese stayed loyal to the Nationalist cause. This watchfulness became particularly apparent during the Second World War and the civil war that followed it. During the Second World War Chinese in American cities were urged to contribute to China's war effort. The National Salvation Fund, a community agency run by patriotic businessmen with strong ties to the KMT, solicited contributions.

> Those who refuse to contribute to the war fund ought to be punished. I have just paid my bi-monthly dues last week. I paid eighteen-fifty. According to my business, I would not have to pay so much. What of it? If we should lose to the Japs, what good is the money? So I decided to do my best. Some are beaten for refusal to pay the war fund. I think they deserve it.
>
> (Siu 1987: 225)

Even after the Japanese were defeated, the KMT kept an eye on Chinese communities throughout North and South America, as well as in South-East Asia.

They did this to ensure continued support for the regime and to prevent the Communist Party from soliciting assistance from Chinese overseas. Despite massive fundraising and continued political support from overseas, the KMT lost the civil war and the Chinese Communist Party (CCP) took control of China officially on October 1, 1949.

With the Communist Party in power many Chinese overseas shifted their focus to Taiwan. The KMT maintained its security apparatus overseas and kept a close watch on Chinese communities to prevent any sympathy or support for the CCP from developing. For example, in Latin America from the 1950s through the 1980s the KMT created the "Free Overseas Chinese" federations. In both Latin America and South-East Asia and the United States the Nationalist Party sponsored a variety of cultural, educational and political activities. In part this was to help the Chinese communities maintain ties to the Republic of China on Taiwan, and in part this involvement served a political function. KMT involvement in the diaspora was a way of maintaining a political presence within communities overseas so that there was little chance that expatriates would develop any sympathies to the Communist Party on the mainland (Freedman and Brooks 2001: 24). The lineage associations that characterize Chinatown social, political, and economic organization were often closely tied to the KMT (Kwong 1996).

The CCP comes to power

After the Communist Party came to power in China in 1949 the new government set up a bureaucratic agency to coordinate policy toward Chinese overseas. It was proclaimed that the new rulers of China would take the responsibility of protecting the legal interests and the rights of Chinese overseas. The real goal of this agency was to safeguard the remittances from overseas.

Most of the mainland Chinese dependants of overseas Chinese relied upon remittances sent back by their relatives as their primary means of subsistence. The overseas Chinese remittances constituted an important source of hard currency for the mainland, as expressed by Nan Hanzen, the director of the People's Bank of China, in 1950:

> Our country's new economic construction is going under way, we need as much foreign currency as possible to import the necessities of our economic construction. Both the individual and government can benefit from the remittance. I calculated that the overseas Chinese remittance in one year is equivalent to the gross economic income of Shanxi Province (with a population of about ten million), it means our state has a province overseas in addition.

> (Quoted in Zhuang 1998: 16)

From about 1960 until the early 1980s immigration from the People's Republic of China to the Americas, South-East Asia and Europe was reduced to a small trickle.[6] It was difficult for Chinese to get out of China without assistance from relatives overseas, and in both South-East Asia and the US immigration restrictions prevented large numbers of Chinese from leaving.

Despite all the rapid changes taking place in China under the CCP from 1949 to 1978, most Chinese overseas identified the KMT as the locus of their interest. This was true for several reasons. First, the KMT, as already mentioned, worked at maintaining links between itself and Chinese overseas. Second, many Chinese overseas hoped to see the KMT retake control of the mainland. Two significant changes occurred to alter the connection between the Chinese diaspora and the KMT. First, the US changed their immigration laws in 1965, allowing increasing numbers of Chinese from the People's Republic to enter the United States. Later, Deng Xiaoping embarked on a program of economic reforms, which included the opening of China to travel and investment by foreigners.

Before 1965, immigrants were admitted to the United States based on a quota system, which favored European immigrants and virtually excluded immigrants from Asia, Latin America, and Africa. Quotas were instituted in 1924 with the express intention of maintaining America's racial and ethnic balance at the time. The 1965 Immigration Act replaced these preferential set-asides for a flat number: 20,000 immigrants would be allowed from countries outside of the Western hemisphere. Two different groups of Chinese benefited from these legislative changes. Under the new provisions, preference was to be given to uniting families of American citizens and to those with professional skills. Since the first Chinese immigrants to the US had come from the economically disadvantaged, mainly rural and southern mainland, the family unification stipulation allowed thousands of Chinese to reinvigorate urban Chinatowns. The other group of ethnic Chinese who took advantage of the change was a significant pool of professionals from Hong Kong and Taiwan (Freedman 2000: 122). The significant influx of Chinese to the United States added an element of diversity to the communities' political attentions. As Peter Kwong (1996) demonstrates, by the 1980s the KMT's hold on Chinese Americans' political loyalty had shifted. Many professionals had left Taiwan in part because of political repression and a lack of good job opportunities, these immigrants were less likely to idealize the KMT and want to support it from afar. Likewise, immigrants from the People's Republic may not have been diehard communist backers, but, after growing up with ceaseless vilification of the KMT, they were not prone to identifying with the enemy.

Post-1978 reforms

In 1978 Deng Xiaoping initiated the Four Modernizations as a way of improving China's ailing economy. The four areas targeted for reform were industry, agriculture, defense, and science and technology. For the purposes of this chapter, Deng's reforms had four significant effects. First, one of the four pillars of economic reform was the opening of China to the outside world. Chinese overseas began investing in the mainland, and China became increasingly integrated with Hong Kong and Taiwan. Second, China began to allow greater economic and then social freedom at home, allowing Chinese citizens access to new information, ideas and trends from around the world. Third, China began to send large numbers of students overseas for higher education. Some of these students returned to China, bringing with them ideas about life in the US, Europe, Japan, Australia, etc. Some students remained in countries where they went to study and were ripe for mobilization should the right catalyst come along. Lastly, in order to implement economic reforms, Deng and his supporters in China began a dramatic program of decentralizing economic decision-making. This has resulted in greater opportunities for local areas to encourage foreign investment and for overseas investors (both ethnic Chinese and others) to forge partnerships with local government officials and state enterprises, thus providing both local elites and investors with the opportunity to influence the pace and nature of economic reforms.

The cumulative effect of the economic changes was that by the 1980s life for many people in China had gotten dramatically better. By 1989 many Chinese, especially those in big cities, had access to a huge variety of consumer goods, new sources of information, and the ability to choose their own profession and workplace. Opportunities to make money, and ways to spend that money, increased exponentially. However, with the dramatic changes an old problem returned to China: corruption. Officials and their families were perceived to have disproportionate access to privatizing companies, permits to study abroad, and access to prestigious jobs. Resentment about this privilege grew steadily in the 1980s.

Tiananmen Square protests and suspicion of outside interference

In the spring of 1989 Hu Yaobang died. Hu had been Deng's chosen successor in the mid-1980s but had been pushed aside when he was perceived to be too liberal in favoring greater openness in China. When Hu died students from around Beijing converged on Tiananmen Square to honor him and commemorate his passing. The government tried to dissuade the students from such public outpourings of grief but they would not be deterred. Students visited Tiananmen Square daily and laid flowers at the center of the public plaza. Back on their campuses they began efforts to organize independent student unions and "democracy clubs." More and more students began converging on the square. What began as an expression of grief for Hu's death became a demonstration against inequities resulting from reforms. The students called for an end to corruption, greater accountability of leaders to the people, and a faster pace for reforms. Suddenly the world began to pay attention to what was going on in Beijing. Tens of thousands of students and ordinary people from Beijing and beyond were demonstrating in the capital of China about the need for faster reforms and even greater change from above.

Ethnic Chinese in Taiwan and Hong Kong, as well as those in the US and Europe, began looking into what they could do to show their support for the protestors in Beijing. Before long food, money, tents, fax machines and messages of support were streaming into Beijing from around the globe. Much of the support was from Chinese overseas. At Baxter and Canal streets in Manhattan's

Chinatown a banner was hung reading "Patriotic Overseas Chinese – Donate for your sons and daughters who are fighting for human rights and freedom in China" (Pace 1989). As the demonstrations continued through the spring the students began to take a tougher line. They demanded a meeting with Chinese leaders and they drafted a formal letter of conditions to be met in order for them to clear the square. Many students went on a hunger strike to get the government to take them seriously. Students from a Beijing art college created a papier mâché statue modeled after the Statue of Liberty which they called the Goddess of Democracy. In addition, the students became savvy at playing to the Western media. Banners and signs in the square appeared in English as well as Chinese. Students told American reporters that they were fighting for democracy.

The Chinese government interpreted these actions as a direct threat to order and stability in China. One of the things that worried hardliners like Li Peng the most was what they interpreted as foreign influence on the students. It seemed to these conservative leaders that ideas and rhetoric about democracy and accountability had come directly from the West. While the students never said that they favored overthrowing the regime, they simply were suggesting ways to improve it, the government feared that they were influenced by too many students studying overseas[7] and by the corrupting ideas entering China from the United States and elsewhere. The Chinese government directly criticized groups such as the New York-based Chinese Alliance for Democracy, formed in 1983.

The alliance publishes a magazine called *China Spring*, which has been a forum for Chinese intellectuals to express their views on how to improve life and politics in China. In 1989 the organization supported the Beijing demonstrators and drew tremendous criticism from the Chinese government for being behind the protests. Another group of Chinese overseas was also mobilized by the Tiananmen demonstrations. The United Association of Scholars and Students from the People's Republic of China in the United States of America held demonstrations in the US to show their support of those in Beijing. In Hong Kong a million people, or a sixth of the territory's population, jammed the colony's streets to show their enthusiasm for what the students in Beijing were doing.

> As the marchers set off for the Hong Kong offices of the New China News Agency, Beijing's de-facto embassy in the colony, they chanted "Down with Li Peng," the Chinese Prime Minister, "Down with Deng Xiaoping," the paramount leader. At the news agency, a staff member gave a speech and employees of a pro-Beijing newspaper waved banners of support from their office windows.
>
> (Vines 1989)

All of these actions alarmed leaders in Beijing. Within the politburo (the apex of power within the party) officials were divided as to how they should handle the protesters in the square. Some leaders, notably Zhao Ziyang, Deng's chosen successor at the time of the protests, wanted to listen to the students' demands and take seriously their requests for greater accountability and an end to corruption.

Hardliners, like Prime Minister Li Peng, advocated clearing the square by any means necessary. We now know with some confidence that the decision was left up to Deng Xiaoping.[8] On June 4, 1989, the tanks that had retreated to the outskirts of Beijing moved into the center of the city and proceeded to shoot all citizens in their way. An argument can be made that the links drawn between the Chinese overseas and the demonstrators in Beijing gave the hardliners additional justification for ending the protests, regardless of the cost. Being able to paint the students as agents or forces from the West enabled conservative leaders to convince their moderate counterparts that the demonstrations were a threat to Chinese stability and even Chinese sovereignty.

How accurate were these fears? We know that these organizations and others were supporting the demonstrators in Beijing; however, it would be difficult if not impossible to argue that they instigated or prompted the protests to begin in the first place.[9] The role of the Chinese Alliance for Democracy (CAD) can serve to illustrate this point. Chen Jun, a member of the CAD, returned to China in 1987 and initiated a petition to demand the release of political prisoners such as Wei Jingsheng. During the Tiananmen protests CAD provided the students with donations and information. It also urged its members around the world to send "a million letters to China and to make a million calls to tell the truth" (He 1997: 99). While it is impossible to say that overseas groups changed fundamentally the nature or extent of the protests, transnational groups such as the CAD did have an impact in two significant ways:[10] first in that the Chinese government *perceived* them to be important behind-the-scenes actors; and, second, these groups were able to lobby foreign governments to put pressure on China during and particularly after the demonstrations. One additional opposition group is the Front for Democratic China (FDC). Student leaders from the Tiananmen Square demonstrations founded the FDC. Once safely in the US and elsewhere, these young activists quickly began reaching out to foreign governments and NGOs for assistance in criticizing the Chinese government from abroad. The FDC publishes a Chinese magazine, *Democratic China* (He 1997: 86). The US, France, Germany and Australia all made it easy for Chinese students and exiles to apply for permanent residency. The US went even further in assisting those fleeing from China after June 4, 1989. "Also, a free office and free telephone in the Congress building were offered by one of President Bush's supporters to Chinese students. This facilitated lobbying activities for Chinese students and exiles" (He 1997: 93).

While these groups are pushing for a democratic China, what they mostly do is expose human-rights violations in the country, and they pressure foreign governments to exercise influence on Beijing to release political prisoners. Opposition groups in exile have also tried to build support within Chinese overseas communities. Their success in doing this has been mixed. After the massacres at Tiananmen Square many Chinese were outraged and willingly gave time and money to opposition groups. Yet, over the last decade much of this support has waned. Why might this be the case? Chinese overseas are a diverse community. Many of the Chinese business elites overseas want to maintain good relations with the People's Republic of China for business purposes, so they are less likely to be outspoken against the regime. Others in the Chinese diaspora are more in tune with the domestic politics of their adopted country and spend less time worrying about and being engaged by issues in China. One last reason that support for opposition groups may have faded recently has to do with American rather than Chinese politics. Since Bill Clinton's re-election campaign in 1996 and the accusations against Chinese Americans of illegal campaign contributions, and since the justice department charged Wen Ho Lee, a scientist at Los Alamos, with stealing nuclear secrets for China, many Chinese Americans have become resentful of the United States, and some have become more protective of the current Chinese regime (perhaps as a defensive reaction to the US polity, which seems increasingly hostile).

In addition to the overtly political links between the Chinese diaspora and mainland China, there is a growing spiritual or religious connection. Since the 1980s people in China have been given a measured degree of freedom to practice religious beliefs. While some have returned to traditional Buddhist or Confucian practices, or have adopted Christianity, many others have turned to spiritual movements. One such sect, the Falun Gong, has received a great deal of attention.

Falun Gong

Over the last four years the Chinese government has confronted what it sees as a serious threat to stability, "morality" and, ultimately, its ability to maintain control. What has triggered this confrontation is a spiritual group known as the Falun Gong. Falun Gong combines the breathing exercises of *qigong* with additional prescriptions about living a balanced, moral life. In the spring of 1999 the movement managed to coordinate thousands of supporters to stage a large, peaceful sit-in surrounding Zhongnanhai, the leadership compound in Beijing. These people were able to amass thousands of adherents around the complex without causing alarm in the security forces. Once assembled, members commenced breathing exercises and meditation. Their publicly stated goal was to convince the government not to ban the organization as a cult. In practice, they also wanted to illustrate their huge following and their ability to organize right under the noses of China's leaders. Their demonstration outside Zhongnanhai, and the countless number of members who continue to come to Tiananmen Square to sit down and meditate in a single act of defiance against the regime, has brought the fury of the party upon members.

> The Falun Dafa Information Center has verified details of 665 deaths since the persecution of Falun Gong in China began in 1999. Government officials inside China, however, report that the actual death toll is well over 1,600, while expert sources estimate that figure to be much higher. Hundreds of thousands have been detained, with more than 100,000 being sentenced to forced labor camps, typically without trial.
>
> (Falun Dafa Information Center 2003)

The government has responded against the spiritual group with a massive program of re-education for adherents and a propaganda war to discredit the movement. A front-page essay in the *Liberation Army Daily*, the official mouthpiece of the military, stated: "Western anti-Chinese forces have spared no effort to engage in ideological infiltration to achieve their goal of overturning our socialist system and subverting our state" (Eckholm 2001). It has been easy for the CCP to portray this group's activities as foreign-led, since the founder of the movement, Li Hongzhi, lives in exile in New York. Other articles of propaganda have called the group's members "running dogs of foreign anti-Chinese forces" (ibid.). While it is unknown how many members of the group there are in China, estimates in 1999 put the figure in the millions. While numbers of those who publicly affiliate with Falun Gong have shrunk significantly, it is presumed that many of the group's believers have simply become more quiet and private in their practice and adherence to the sect's principles.

The real reason for the government's hostility against the sect has little to do with its spiritual practices or its supposed foreign element. The Communist Party is threatened by the group's ability to organize and attract members both through the Internet and via word of mouth. The fact that they could do this without a clear leadership hierarchy and virtually without detection by the security apparatus has the regime tremendously worried.

In addition to the very political attempts by Chinese overseas and Chinese nationals to push for greater political freedoms in China and for groups seeking religious or spiritual freedom, there is another group of Chinese in the diaspora who have perhaps made the biggest impact on China's social and economic transformations: the business community.

Investment in China from Chinese overseas and "greater China"

As part of Deng Xiaoping's four modernizations, foreign investment began entering China in the early 1980s. Since Deng began the process of opening China up to trade, travel and investment, southern China has become increasingly integrated with Hong Kong, Macao and Taiwan. The term "greater China" has been used to refer both to potential political and strategic implications of the integration of southern China, Hong Kong, Macao, Taiwan, and overseas Chinese, and to economic interdependence among the territories and communities already listed. I use the term in the latter sense; economic coordination.[11]

During the 1980s, China's gross national product grew at an average 9.2 percent a year. China became the target of large amounts of direct investment. Many Chinese overseas originally came from southern China, and once China opened to foreign investment many Chinese businessmen began investing in their home provinces. By the early 1990s Chinese overseas business accounted for about 80 percent of the total investment and about 40 percent of Chinese exports (Story 1999) (see Table 6.1).

Table 6.1 Foreign direct investment in China (in millions of US dollars)

Source	1998	1999	2000	2001
Hong Kong	$6,985 (41.1%)	$7,758 (52.4%)	$7,791 (78.1%)	n/a
Japan	$1,306 (5.4%)	$363 (1.6%)	$937 (3.0%)	$2,161 (5.6%)
Taiwan	$2,035 (38.2%)	$1,253 (27.7%)	$2,607 (33.9%)	$2,784 (38.8%)
United States	$1,497 (1.1%)	$1,641 (0.9%)	$1,602 (1.0%)	$1,236 (1.1%)

Source: JETRO 2002, p. 20.

Note
Numbers in parentheses represent the percent of each countries' total FDI outflow.

Chinese business networks cut across Asia Pacific.

> From Guangzhou to Singapore, from Kuala Lumpur to Manila, this influential network – often based on extensions of the traditional clans – has been described as the backbone of the East Asian economy. A substantial amount of cross-investment and trade takes place, often on a family basis. Frequently, these business ties involve "overseas" Chinese who are dealing with people in the province of China from which they or their ancestors migrated (*tongbao* or compatriots).

> (Weidenbaum 1993: 4)

Investment from Hong Kong and Taiwan dwarfs investment from the rest of the globe. While it is impossible to know how much of this investment is from ethnic Chinese versus other business interests, we do know that ethnic Chinese businesses from South-East Asia, North America and Australia invested heavily in Hong Kong and Taiwan before China's opening to the West, and that many of these firms were among the first to wade into the China market once it opened in the late 1970s. Chinese overseas investment comes primarily through Hong Kong and Taiwan for several reasons. First, the post-Second World War developments in South-East Asia and in China itself had a profound effect on the Chinese diaspora. The communist takeover in China severed the links between Chinese businessmen in South-East Asia and their homeland. Because of the CCP's victory, Hong Kong became the focus of much economic restructuring and attention in Asia (Yen 1998: 97). Once the People's Republic of China opened its doors to investment many ethnic Chinese businesses already had links to Hong Kong (and to a lesser extent to Taiwan). It was generally the Hong Kong arm of the business that would undertake new projects in China. Until recently, direct investment from Taiwan to the mainland was forbidden. However, many Taiwanese were already doing business in Hong Kong, so again Hong Kong became the conduit to investment in China.

What impact has this investment had? As part of the reform process initiated in 1978, local areas (provinces and municipalities) were given greater control of their budgets and more discretion in determining what type of foreign investment, and how much, they wanted in their area. Port cities such as Guangzhou and Shenzen were given even greater freedom to attract foreign investment. This gave local bureaucrats and local party leaders new sources of power. From the other end, businesses interested in forming partnerships with companies in China (the route that most investment takes to get a foot in the door of China's potentially huge market) now had to work through this group of local officials. Many of these local elites stood to gain from their new connections to outside businessmen. The political change or impact from these relationships is decidedly mixed.

On the positive side, the legal system in China has slowly been reformed to protect business interests: concepts such as contract law and essentially private property rights have begun to evolve in China (Lubman 1999). Much of this reform came about because of the need to encourage and facilitate economic growth from foreign investment. More negatively, there are not many incentives for foreign investors or their Chinese partners to advocate democratization. Despite a great deal of social science literature on the connection between capitalism and democracy, the market imperative[12] does not require democracy to thrive, and in some cases democracy may harm vested economic elites. Chinese overseas business interests that have learned to "work the system" may be content with the status quo. Thus, it becomes difficult to argue that Chinese overseas investors have done much to further political reform in China.

Additionally, with its opening to the West, China *has* prospered economically. Economic growth increases incomes and standards of living for hundreds of thousands of Chinese (mostly those in urban and coastal areas). More and more Western products, movies, ideas, fashions, and amenities permeate Chinese life. With these things comes an understanding about how people live outside of China. This knowledge fosters both a sense of relative deprivation and high expectations; reforms must be carried on so that people can continue see their lives change for the better. The CCP's legitimacy is based on this. People seem willing to accept a lack of democracy as long as there is economic growth to satisfy more material aims. This is particularly true for the expanding middle class in the cities.

Political implications of Chinese overseas activity

Implications for civil society

Political science literature is filled with articles about civil society and the role that it plays in domestic politics and political change. At its most basic, civil society is taken to encompass organized groups within the population that operate "autonomously" from the government. In theory these groups articulate the interests of their constituents to the government in the hopes of influencing policy decisions. Philippe Schmitter's work on civil society argues that it should ideally be independent of the state, be able to take collective action, not seek to overthrow the government, and act within pre-established rules and norms (Schmitter 1995). Civil society groups can exist in the economic arena, the cultural and artistic realm, and the political arena. In much of the literature on transitions to democracy (beginning with Weber and continuing in one form or another to Huntington, Schmitter and O'Donnell, Diamond and others) civil society plays a role in demanding greater openness from an authoritarian regime. These demands, along with internal divisions, could bring about political change. Because the economic reforms in China were so successful, and since a middle class now exists and is allowed a significant degree of privacy in economic, social, and cultural life, scholars in the 1980s began to examine to what extent civil society was developing in China.

Problems with the civil society approach

While there is little consensus about the nature and extent of civil society in China,[13] it is clear that in China today individuals do have the ability to form organizations to reflect their common interests. It is, however, difficult to determine how independent these groups are from state intervention. For example, there are a myriad of professional organizations in China, such as a bar association for lawyers and a professional association for doctors. Yet, these groups are organized by the party and, while the party may not directly interfere with the associations' discussions and agendas, there is clearly a constraint placed on such "official" organizations. It would therefore be a mistake to see them as truly "autonomous." Outside of such recognized groups, there are now also associations that are more independent from the party. Yet it is impossible to tell if these groups attempt to express their policy preferences to the state and, if so, if there is any impact that comes out of such interest articulation. A further problem with using the idea of civil society to understand efforts at influencing change in China is that virtually none of the literature on civil society takes into account transnational organizations such as diaspora groups.

As the material presented earlier shows, there are links between Chinese overseas and people and groups within China that have been very active in mobilizing support for further economic, political, and social (religious) liberalization. Civil society literature neglects this international aspect. Whether one wants to portray Chinese overseas actors themselves as examples of civil society (as He 1997 seems to want to do), or whether one views the Chinese diaspora as playing a secondary role to domestic actors within China (supplying information, financial and moral support) who might then play a part in bringing about greater change, the diaspora is hard to fit into existing models of civil society. If anything, this international element to civil society has given the Communist Party greater justification in refusing to institute any political reforms. When there is civil unrest in China, like the Tiananmen Square protests and the Falun Gong's challenge to the party, hardliners in the party point to the foreign connection as a justification for taking a more harsh approach to opposition events.

The one area where I think there has been significant change has been the decentralization of power that has taken place since 1978. This power shift means that, when Chinese overseas investors establish close working relationships with local leaders and bureaucrats, they are in a position to influence local rules and regulations to work in their favor. While this is clearly an example of the impact of the Chinese diaspora on domestic changes in China, it has not necessarily led to greater liberalization overall, nor has it led to institutionalized changes at either the local or the national level.

Challenges to political science

Conventional literature on civil society does not take into account an international or transnational element. And international relations literature tends to look at the behavior of nation-states either as a product of balance of power variables or as a result of domestic politics. It does not often look at how transnational groups and international events impact domestic politics. In this case, activists in the Chinese diaspora have organized internationally and have forged links with other non-government groups such as Amnesty International to further their cause of democracy in China. Likewise, domestic events such as the Tiananmen Square protests become internationalized, perhaps changing how national leaders choose to address the problem. None of these dynamics are captured in mainstream international relations scholarship.

Conclusion

As stated earlier, because of the closed nature of Chinese politics it is impossible to say with any certainty what elements influence political and economic changes in China. However, I want to offer three tentative conclusions about the role of the Chinese diaspora and political and economic reforms in China. First, we know that there has been a considerable degree of decentralization in China and that new local elites have been empowered to develop close links with investors, many of whom are Chinese from overseas. I have speculated that this puts ethnic Chinese businessmen from outside of China in a position to influence certain regulations that may affect their interests in China.

Second, greater openness in China has resulted in the creation of a middle class and has made many, many Chinese aware of what life is like outside of China. Information and ideas have been brought to China from members of the diaspora who return to visit family, from students who go abroad and return, and from a new set of global Chinese media outlets that supply information via satellite TV, the Internet, and newsletters. Many of these suppliers of information originate outside of China and were originally meant to cater to Chinese overseas. It is unclear at this point if Chinese (middle class or otherwise), armed with greater knowledge about other political systems, will form more autonomous organizations (the basis for civil society) and demand political change. Since the Tiananmen Square protests in 1989 the most outspoken groups to challenge the regime have been farmers burdened by heavy taxes and workers fighting for the right to form independent labor unions and for better working conditions, unemployment benefits, secure pensions and job protection. Both students and the middle class have been largely quiescent.

Third, one might almost argue that links between the Chinese diaspora and domestic voices for change have had a *negative* impact on political liberalization. The Chinese government has been able to point to outside interference from the West as an excuse to crack down on both the students in Tiananmen Square and members of the Falun Gong. It would be easy to dismiss this as convenient propaganda, but in both instances hardliners within the party have been able to consolidate power over more moderate leaders and thus prevent any real political change from occurring. Additionally, when Chinese overseas form organizations critical of the CCP and lobby foreign governments to condemn China or implement policies detrimental to China, the regime becomes defensive and more convinced that greater openness and freedom will jeopardize their power. Ultimately, it seems that there are important links between the Chinese diaspora and changes taking place in China currently. However, it is too soon to say what impact Chinese overseas activity will have on political and economic reforms in China.

Notes

1 This is particularly true for Chinese politics. While much is known about Chinese political institutions – we know that the standing committee of the Communist Party Politburo is the nexus of power, and that the general secretary of the party traditionally holds a preponderance of power – it is virtually impossible to know with any certainty why or how policy decisions get made. Likewise, it is problematic to talk about interest articulation in China. At the time this chapter is being written, China's political system is still closed to formal means of civic input on the policy-making process.

2 Deng Xiaoping described China's new economic system as "socialism with Chinese characteristics."

3 This is not to say that China is a free country. There are significant constraints on people's choices about education, employment, and information gathering. The Communist Party still exercises its ability to decide what constitutes subversive activities, ideas, or actions. It is generally believed that one is freer to criticize the government in private, but that any public display of criticism still risks reprisals and possible jail.

4 The classic work that many scholars continued to draw on in the 1950s which exemplified this idea was Zangwill, I. (1909) *The Melting Pot: A Drama in Four Acts*, New York: Macmillan Press.

5 The *babas* and the *nonyas* in Malaysia are a good example of this phenomenon. Chinese men who traveled or migrated to ports such as Malacca married local Malay women. In such families a blend of Chinese and Malay customs developed. The men generally insisted on retaining Chinese traditions like language and filial piety, but culinary practices became more mixed.

6 The exception to this was immigration to Taiwan and Hong Kong. There were three significant waves of migration from China to Taiwan and Hong Kong. The first occurred after the CCP came to power, and the second was during and immediately after the Great Leap Forward (Mao's attempt at massive collectivization of agriculture and industry) from 1957 to 1960, when many thousands of Chinese left China for Hong Kong and Taiwan. The third wave of migration was set off by the Cultural Revolution from 1965 to 1975. Outside of these periods there certainly were many Chinese who

became disenchanted with the communist regime and left to try life elsewhere, but the three periods above saw much larger numbers of people leaving.

7　At the time of the demonstrations there were approximately 40,000 students from China studying in the US (Pace 1989).

8　See Nathan and Link (2001), which contains official documents from the highest organs of power about the decision to crack down on the protesters in the spring of 1989.

9　To say that the Tiananmen protests were the work of outside agitators would rob the courageous students and citizens of Beijing of their initiative and goals in the movement.

10　It is also reported that the CAD and the FDC have secret branches in major cities in China (He 1997: 96).

11　As Harry Harding notes, there is wide variation in how the term "greater China" is used. As mentioned above, it can refer to commercial links between Chinese territories (some include Singapore in the list already mentioned), and some use it in assessing prospects for political unification. The problem, of course, of discussing political unification is that it implies expansionism toward neighboring areas. For a more thorough discussion of this discourse, see Harding, H. (1995) "The Concept of 'Greater China': Themes, Variations, and Reservations," in Shambaugh, D. (ed.) (1995) *Greater China: The Next Superpower?* New York: Oxford University Press.

12　For a good article on the rise of "illiberal democracies" (those countries with a vibrant capitalist economy and some features of democratic institutions but where real accountability and the protection of civil rights and civil liberties may be lacking), see Zakaria (1997).

13　For interesting work on civil society in China, see the work of Dorothy Solinger and Chan *et al.* (1998).

References

Chan, A., Kerkvliet, B., and Unger, J. (1998) *Transforming Asian Socialism.* St. Leonards, NSW: Allen & Unwin.

Eckholm, E. (2001) "China Steps up War on Sect, but Some Denounce Attacks," *New York Times,* February 7, p. A3.

Fairbank, J. (1983) *The United States and China.* Cambridge, MA: Harvard University Press.

Falun Dafa Information Center (2003) "'China Lies, People Die': Practitioners of Falun Gong Rally in New York City's Times Square," www.faluninfo.net, April 23.

Freedman, A. (2000) *Political Participation and Ethnic Minorities: Chinese Overseas in Malaysia, Indonesia, and the United States.* New York: Routledge.

Freedman, A., and Brooks, E. (2001) "Globalized Chinese Capital in Central America," *Asia Pacific: Perspectives,* vol. 1, no. 1.

He, B. (1997) *The Democratic Implications of Civil Society in China.* New York: St. Martin's Press.

JETRO (2002) *White Paper on International Trade and Investment.* Japan External Trade Organization.

Kwong, P. (1996) *The New Chinatown.* New York: Hill & Wang.

Lubman, S. B. (1999) *Bird in a Cage: Legal Reform in China after Mao.* Stanford, CA: Stanford University Press.

Nathan, A. J., and Link, P. (eds) (2001) *The Tiananmen Papers: The Chinese Leadership's Decision to Use Force Against their own People – in their Own Words.* New York: Public Affairs.

Pace, E. (1989) "Chinese in the United States Voice their Disappointment," *New York Times,* May 20.

Pan, L. (ed.) (2000) *The Encyclopedia of Chinese Overseas.* Cambridge, MA: Harvard University Press.

Schmitter, P. C. (1995) "On Civil Society and the Consolidation of Democracy: Ten General Propositions and Nine Speculations about their Relation in Asian Societies," paper presented at the International Conference on Consolidating the Third Wave Democracies: Trends and Challenges, Taipei, August.

Siu, P. C. P. (1987) *The Chinese Laundryman: A Study in Social Isolation*, ed. J. K. W. Tchen. New York: New York University Press.

Solinger, D. J. (1999) *Contesting Citizenship in Urban China: Peasant Migrants, the State and the Logic of the Market.* Berkeley: University of California Press.

Story, J. (1999) "Time is Running Out for the Solution to a Chinese Puzzle," *The Times*, July 1.

Vines, S. (1989) "Million March in Hong Kong to Support Beijing Students," *The Guardian*, May 22.

Wang, G. (1995) "Greater China and the Chinese Overseas," in Shambaugh, D. (ed.) *Greater China: The Next Superpower?* New York: Oxford University Press.

Wang, G. (2000) *The Chinese Overseas: From Earthbound China to the Quest for Autonomy*, Cambridge, MA: Harvard University Press.

Weidenbaum, M. (1993) "Greater China: The Next Economic Superpower?," *Contemporary Issues*, vol. 57.

Yen, C. (1998) "Modern Overseas Chinese Business Enterprise: A Preliminary Study," in Wang, L., and Wang, G. (eds) *The Chinese Diaspora: Selected Essays, vol. 1.* Singapore: Times Academic Press.

Zakaria, F. (1997) "The Rise of Illiberal Democracy," *Foreign Affairs*, vol. 76, Nov/Dec.

Zhuang, G. (1998) "The Policies of the Chinese Government towards Overseas Chinese (1949–1966)," in Wang, L., and Wang, G. (eds) *The Chinese Diaspora: Selected Essays, vol. 1.* Singapore: Times Academic Press.

7 Opposing constructions and agendas

The politics of Hindu and Muslim Indian-American organizations

Prema Kurien

Introduction

According to the high level committee on the Indian diaspora of the Indian government, as of January 2001, there were approximately 20 million diasporic Indians in countries around the world. The number includes both non-resident Indians (NRIs), or Indian citizens living outside India, and persons of Indian origin (PIOs), people of Indian background or ancestry (up to the fourth generation) who are citizens of other countries.[2] The largest concentrations were in South-East Asia, the Caribbean, North America, the Middle East, South Africa and the UK. The committee also estimated that the $300 billion income of this group was close to the GDP of India as a whole (Singhvi 2000).

There were almost 1.7 million individuals of Asian-Indian origin in the United States according to the 2000 census, and the community was also one of the fastest growing in the country, with a growth rate of 105.87 percent between 1990 and 2000. Although only a small proportion of the global Indian diaspora, Indians in the United States wield a disproportionate influence because of their location in a country which is at the center of the global system, and because they are also one of the wealthiest and most educated groups, both within the diaspora and within the United States as a whole. Thus, Indian Americans have contributed a great deal to the "globalization" of Indian politics. This chapter focuses on the political mobilization of Hindu and Muslim Indian immigrant groups in the United States based on their very different constructions of Indian identity. While many differences between Indian immigrants, such as region, language and caste, are in the process of weakening, religious differences and tensions seem to have been exacerbated in the immigrant context. I examine the reasons for this development and its implications for religion and politics in India.

The dominant Hindu and Muslim Indian-American organizations have developed opposing constructions of "Indianness." Hindu Indian-American organizations view India as a Hindu society whose true nature has been sullied by the invasions of Muslims, the British, and the post-colonial domination of "pseudo-secular" Indians. They are working for the establishment of a Hindu *rashtra* (nation) in India and are strong supporters of the *Hindutva* (Hinduness) movement, currently a dominant force in Indian politics. Muslim Indian-American organizations have an opposing and more inclusive definition of Indianness, viewing India's multi-religious history and society as evidence that India is a multi-religious and multicultural society. They are striving to safeguard India's secularism and, toward this end, some of them have entered into coalition-type relationships with lower-caste groups. Both types of organizations are working to influence Indian politics in line with their respective interests. This has led to an exacerbation of the conflict between the two immigrant groups.

In 2000, Indians were the third largest Asian group in the United States (after the Chinese and Filipinos) but were the largest Asian group in nineteen states around the country. Indians were most concentrated in New Jersey and New York, but the state with the largest number of Indian Americans was California, with 18.75 percent (about 315,000) of the national total. My study is based on an examination of the activities of two umbrella organizations in southern California – the Federation of Hindu Associations (FHA) and the American Federation of Muslims from India (AFMI) which represent the two different positions very clearly. The FHA is based in southern California. Although the AFMI is a national organization to unite Indian Muslim organizations around the country, its president in the late 1990s, Aslam Abdullah, was a southern California resident, and the local chapter has been particularly active in attempting to construct an alternative to the Hindu nationalist perspective of the FHA. I have focused on the FHA and the AFMI because they are fairly representative of the dominant Hindu and Muslim Indian-American organizations. It is, however, important to emphasize that the composition, platform and goals of neither organization are representative of the average Hindu and Muslim immigrant in the United States. This seeming contradiction will be discussed further a little later in the chapter.

Data on these organizations were collected over a period of two years (1996–8) through in-depth interviews with leaders and members of the organizations and participation in some of the meetings and activities of each (including the 1997 annual AFMI meeting in San Jose). This research was supplemented by fieldwork in India over the summer of 1997 to examine the impact of these organizations on Indian society and politics. In addition, I monitored their activities between 1995 and 1999 through an examination of their own publications in newspapers, magazines and newsletters, and the accounts of their activities given in Indian-American newspapers.

After presenting some background on Indian immigrants in the United States and the two organizations, I examine the opposing constructions of the FHA and the AFMI. To explain the differences in the constructions of "Indianness" of the two and the reason for the exacerbation of tensions between Hindu and Muslim Indians in the United States, I draw on three approaches dealing with immigrant religion and politics. The first approach views diasporic politics as being an outcome of the marginalization experienced by immigrants. While marginalization is certainly an important contributing factor to the politicization of Indian immigrants, this perspective cannot explain why such politicization is largely on religious lines and why Hindu Indian organizations tend to promote reactionary causes and Muslim Indian organizations support liberal politics.

The second approach, which deals with the reasons that religion and religious identity become more important for immigrants, explains some of the reasons for mobilization along religious lines. According to this perspective, religion and religious organizations increase in salience for immigrants because of the disruption and disorientation caused by the immigration experience and because religious organizations become the means to form ethnic communities and identities in the immigrant context. A third approach argues that immigrants mobilize on ethnic lines since ethnicity is a resource that can bring material benefits to groups in host societies and provides further information on why immigrant groups become politicized around constructions of ethnicity. My theoretical perspective combines these three approaches and extends them to explain why tensions between religious groups from the same country can be exacerbated in the immigrant context and why this leads to separate and competing constructions of national identity. I also distinguish between factors motivating the leadership of such groups and those motivating the mass of supporters. Finally, I examine the consequences of the political struggles between Hindu and Muslim Indian immigrant groups on religion and politics in India.

Indian immigrants in the United States

Immigration is a selective process, and therefore immigrant populations are rarely representative of the population of the home country. It is important to keep this in mind as we discuss constructions of "Indianness" by Indian Americans. Immigration from India to the United States occurred during two different historical periods. The first phase was between 1899 and 1914, when around 6,800 Indians arrived in California. Most of the Indians were peasants from Punjab province, and they took up farming in rural California.

The second phase of immigration began after the passage of the 1965 Immigration and Naturalization Act. This immigration was largely family based and brought Indians from all over India and from a variety of religious backgrounds. It is now common to talk about "two waves" of post-1965 Indian immigration to the United States. The "first wave" Indians came under the "special skills" provision of the act and were thus mostly highly educated, fluent English speakers from urban backgrounds, who entered into professional and managerial careers. This explains why Indians are among the wealthiest and most educated foreign-born groups in the United States. According to the 1990 census, the median family income of Indians in the United States was $49,309, well above that for non-Hispanic whites, which was $37,630 (Waters and Eschbach 1999: 315); 43.6 percent were employed either as professionals (mostly doctors and engineers) or managers, and 58.4 percent had at least a bachelor's degree (Shinagawa 1996: 113, 119). The highly selective nature of the immigration can be seen by the fact that, in the same year, the per capita income in India was $350, and only 48 percent of Indians were even literate (i.e., could read and write their own names).[3]

There are indications that the "second-wave" immigrants might bring down some of the high socio-economic measures reported above. Many of this group are relatives of the first-wave immigrants sponsored under the "family reunification" provision of the 1965 act, and do not have the same educational or professional status as those in the first wave. In 1996, for instance, of the total 44,859 Indian immigrants admitted, 34,291 were admitted under family sponsorship and only 9,919 in employment-based preferences (Springer 1997).

Supporters of the *Hindutva* movement characterize India as a Hindu country. Although Hindus constitute the overwhelming majority, over 80 percent of the population,[4] religious minorities are a significant presence in India, particularly given their location (most religious minorities are concentrated in urban areas and in a few regions of the country) and absolute numbers. Muslims comprise over 12 percent of the population, and there are more Muslims in India than in neighboring Pakistan, an Islamic state. Christians (both Protestants and Catholics) and Sikhs each constitute around 2 percent of the population.[5] Indian religious minorities also have a very long history in India, going back over sixteen centuries in the case of Christians and eleven centuries in the case of Muslims.

There are no national or regional figures on the proportions of Indians in the United States belonging to various religions. However, indirect evidence indicates that Hindus are underrepresented in the United States in relation to their proportion in India,[6] showing the presence of significant numbers of Indian religious minorities. Among religious minorities, Sikhs and Christians seem to be particularly overrepresented. While upper castes form only around 25 percent of the Indian population, given the elite nature of the immigration to the United States, all the available indirect evidence indicates that most Indian Americans are of this background.

Indian immigrants in southern California

Estimates put the number of Indian Americans in the southern California region at over 170,000.[7] The area in and around Los Angeles has the third highest number of Indian immigrants of any region in the country (Portes and Rumbaut 1990: 38). While support for the *Hindutva* project can now be found among sections of the Hindu Indian community all over the United States, there is a particularly strong and aggressive movement in southern California. A significant section of the southern California Hindu Indian population seem to support the movement either passively or actively.

In other areas of the country where there are large numbers of Indians, such as New York, Chicago, Boston and San Francisco, many Hindus have mobilized against the movement (although, for the most part, such counter-movements tend to be overshadowed by the *Hindutva* forces). In many of these areas, the counter-movements are often initiated by Indian-American groups (both students and faculty) on college and university campuses (Misir 1996). The Indian-American discourse in these areas has therefore emerged as a contested terrain between such groups and the more conservative established Indian immigrant community. However, this is not the case in southern California. While there are groups such as the Coalition for a Secular and Egalitarian India (now renamed Coalition for an

Egalitarian and Pluralistic India), founded by some members of the AFMI and a few other Indians of various religious backgrounds, and the Indian Progressive Study Group at the University of California, Los Angeles, who have been attempting to project an alternative voice, by and large they have not succeeded in making any appreciable dent in the support for *Hindutva* in the region.

The establishment of the two organizations

The *Hindutva* movement calling for a Hindu state has gained strength in India since the late 1980s, and in 1998 the BJP (Bharatiya Janata Party), the party supporting Hindu nationalism, came to power after winning the national elections. Since the BJP was not able to obtain an absolute majority in parliament, it formed a coalition government with its allies. New elections were called in 1999 and the BJP and its allies were returned to power. A watershed event in the movement that first propelled the BJP into the limelight was the demolition of a sixteenth-century mosque in north India, on December 6, 1992, by *Hindutva* supporters, despite attempts by the government to prevent it. According to members of the *Hindutva* movement, the Babri mosque had been built by a Muslim emperor over a temple which commemorated the spot where the Hindu god Ram was born. Communal riots followed the demolition and several thousands, mostly Muslims, were killed.

The seeds of the *Hindutva* movement in America were first sown by the international Hindu organization the Vishwa Hindu Parishad (World Hindu Council), VHP for short, founded in India in 1964. The VHP's American branch (VHPA) was established in the 1970s on the East Coast. However, as a tax-exempt religio-cultural organization, the VHPA cannot pursue a political agenda and thus, at least officially, it has remained devoted to promoting Hinduism and pursuing cultural and social activities.

As the term *Hindutva* or Hinduness implies, the movement has several facets. Besides the explicitly political aspects, it stresses the greatness of Hinduism and Hindu culture, the importance of Hindu unity, and the need to defend Hinduism and Hindus against discrimination, defamation and the pressure to convert to other religions. This is the source of its power and appeal, enabling the movement to recruit even apolitical supporters.

The Federation of Hindu Associations (FHA)

Southern California has been the center of the explicitly political Hindu nationalist movement for several years, even before the formation of the FHA (Jha 1993). It was formed in Artesia, Orange county, in early 1993 in the wake of the demolition of the mosque (which the activists claim inspired and energized them). The FHA was one of the first Hindu umbrella organizations to be based in the United States (earlier Hindu American groups were branches of organizations based in India), and it launched its major activities in 1995. In the short period of a few years FHA activists have emerged as a powerful force within the Indian community – locally and nationally as well as in India – and the organization has been very successful in recruiting supporters and influencing community affairs. Although it is based in southern California, its leadership has close ties with like-minded individuals and organizations around the country. Since the VHP cannot support an overt political platform, the founding goal of the FHA was to unify Hindu Americans to "specifically pursue Hindu political interests."[8] In its first few years of operation, the FHA refused to get itself registered as a religious organization and thus obtain tax-exempt status, since this would have meant that, like the VHP, it would not be able to promote an overt political agenda. But, under pressure from donors, it registered in 1997. However, its platform did not really change. The activists are mostly wealthy, middle-aged, upper-caste north Indian businessmen with established businesses, often in the care of wives or relatives. Their economic security gives them the leisure and the resources to pursue their Hindu nationalist activities.

The FHA sponsors visits of *Hindutva* leaders from India to southern California and now has a lot of influence over such leaders and the Indian politicians who support Hindu nationalism. In the first few years of its existence, one or two of the most extremist of such individuals were given the "Hindu of the Year" award by the organization. They have also been trying to influence American foreign policy by assiduously wooing politicians in an attempt to communicate their ideas regarding Indian society and politics.

The FHA leadership propagates their ideas by organizing and speaking at religious celebrations at which the message of *Hindutva* is given and through copious writings and frequent full-page advertisements in Indian-American newspapers. Since 1996 they have been organizing an annual open-air celebration in southern California for Diwali, a major Hindu festival, which reportedly draws several thousands of attendees every year.[9]

The American Federation of Muslims from India (AFMI)

The American Federation of Muslims from India, a national organization, was formed in Washington in 1989 as a social service organization dedicated to the uplifting of Muslims in India (who, for a variety of reasons, remain well behind the Hindu community in terms of education, income and employment). The activists are mainly established professional men, several of whom are medical doctors. Their programs focus particularly on improving the educational status of Indian Muslims. However, subsequent to the demolition of the Babri mosque, the opposition to *Hindutva* and the promotion of secularism and communal harmony in India has become an important goal. Since 1994, the AFMI has formed a coalition with *Dalit* (lower castes formerly considered "untouchable") groups to support the advance of all the underprivileged groups in India.

According to Dr. Aslam Abdullah, president of the AFMI, there are around 300 Muslim Indian families in southern California with whom the southern California branch of the AFMI has direct or indirect contact. This branch of the AFMI has been very active, particularly in the wake of the Babri mosque demolition. In 1993 they organized a big function and fundraiser to help victims of the riots, which was attended by 600 people. Dr. Aslam Abdullah told me that the AFMI had collected $25,000 for the cause (from all over the United States) and sent the money to India. The annual convention in the following year with the theme of "Pluralism and Secularism – Issues and Challenges for India" was organized in Los Angeles.

The AFMI has become very successful at fundraising in the United States and sponsors a range of social activities in India targeted at Muslims and *Dalits*. Like the Hindu organizations, the AFMI also sponsors the visits of prominent Indian politicians and public personalities who support their platform. Besides their yearly conference in the United States, they hold an annual conference in India. The AFMI works with other organizations such as the Indian Muslim Relief Council (IMRC), and national Muslim organizations such as the Muslim Public Affairs Council (MPAC), to stay in regular contact with legislators and has become a significant political lobby group in Washington. In 1995, several AFMI members were invited to the White House to meet with State Department officials and attend a reception hosted by Mrs. Clinton (AFMI 1995: 3).

Despite their names, neither the FHA nor the AFMI represent all Hindu or all Muslim Indian Americans. Although the FHA is a dominant force in this region, many Hindus in southern California are not interested in or are opposed to their political agenda. I am aware that this is the case even with some organizations which are officially members of the FHA. FHA activists themselves have mentioned that they have faced opposition from some temples and individuals. In a letter to *India West*, an Indian-American weekly, several faculty and graduate students, mostly of southern California universities, protested FHA's conferring of the "Hindu of the Year" awards on two individuals in India whose statements are believed to have incited violence against Muslims. They had this to say: "Most of us are Hindus; nor are all of us 'secularists' and we most emphatically repudiate the attempt of the FHA to speak for us and to speak for 'Hindus'. It is curious that self-styled Hindus here appear to know better the meaning of 'Hinduism' than do most Hindus in India" (Lal *et al.* 1995).

Similarly AFMI does not represent all Muslim Indian Americans. The AFMI is described as an organization of "professionals and activists who are dedicated to the cause of peace and justice for all" (AFMI 1996). As such, the organization is both progressive and social service oriented, and thus does not represent conservative Indian Muslims or those groups such as the Tablighi Jamaat (which have a significant presence in southern California) who eschew politics completely and whose focus is exclusively on the moral and religious character of the individual (Ahmad 1991: 517).

The opposing constructions of the FHA and the AFMI

In this section, I present the constructions of Indian history of the FHA and the AFMI, as well as their very different visions of the ideal Indian state and their political strategies. I will also demonstrate the ways in which Hinduism and Islam are reformulated by both groups to fit their respective political agendas.

The FHA's constructions of Indian history and the ideal Indian state

For *Hindutva* proponents, the Vedic age (around 1500–1000 BC) represents the essence of Indian culture. According to the FHA, the true Vedic Hindu "essence" was besmirched by successive foreign invasions and can only be restored by a Hindu state. Thus, the FHA sees Indian culture and civilization as Hindu, and true Indians as Hindus (which includes groups like the Sikhs, Buddhists and Jains whose religions originated in India out of the Hindu civilization). Groups such as Muslims and Christians are viewed as resident aliens whose loyalties are suspect, since they owe allegiance to religions that originated outside India.

The interpretation of the Muslim period is central to the different historical constructions of Hindu and Muslim organizations. In an advertisement for a Hindu center that it wants to build in southern California, the FHA declares that it views the Muslim period as "a prolonged national struggle [by Hindu kings] against foreign Islamic imperialism and not the conquest of India" (FHA 1997c). Thus the FHA makes it clear that, in its perspective, Islamic control over India was attempted but never really accomplished and that therefore the Islamic rulers played no role in creating modern Indian society or culture. A memorandum the FHA presented to the Indian ambassador states its position on the nature of the Islamic period even more explicitly:

> The FHA feels that the government of India fails in her duties to teach the factual history of the past invaders, by not telling our generations that invaders from Islamic blocs destroyed our culture, people and their temples. Instead, these ruthless barbarians are depicted and praised as kings of cultural achievements.
>
> (FHA 1997b)

A big grievance of the FHA is that, while India was partitioned on the basis of religion to create Pakistan, an Islamic state, no Hindu state was given to the Hindus. What further aggrieves the FHA is that, after demanding an Islamic state, most of the Muslims stayed in India and are now demanding a secular state and special concessions from the government (FHA 1995a: 117). The FHA views the post-independent period as being one dominated by "pseudo-seculars" who have been "pampering" minorities and engaging in "Hindu bashing."

The demolition of the Babri mosque on December 6, 1992, is seen as a watershed event by both groups. However, what the demolition of the mosque represents is perceived in opposite ways. For the FHA, it symbolized the fact that the Hindus who had suffered injustices for so long had finally decided to assert themselves. Thus it marked the beginning of a new era, one where Hindus were going to be in power. An FHA publication summarizes their feelings: "[O]n December 6th of 1992 when the Babri structure was demolished in Ayodhya to restore the history and rebuild the Ram *mandir* [temple], an awakening of [the] Hindu soul took place to turn the direction of glorious Hinduism and make all of us so proud" (FHA 1995a: 76).

The FHA's vision of what a Hindu *rashtra* will look like was presented in an article written by Prithvi Raj Singh (1996b), president of the FHA, in the *India Post*, entitled, "Can '*Hindutva*' Be Indian Nationalism." While Hindu groups are to be given full "freedom of thought and action" in a *Hindutva* state, Singh maintains that "*Hindutva* culture will enforce restriction[s] on some portions of other religions like Islam or Christianity," such as the right to preach that their deity is the only God. Nor will the *Hindutva* state "allow anyone to convert any child to any faith, until the child becomes a[n] . . . adult." Another restriction is that "outside resources of money and power cannot be used to erect . . . Mosques or Missionary churches" (1996b: A29). (Note that he does not say anything about outside resources for Hindu temples.)

Although Singh states that "local people and [the] local population of Muslims will be exempt from any mistreatment for atrocities committed by their invading forefathers in the past," his caveat that "injustices committed by those invaders, like destruction of Hindu temples or forceful conversions shall be corrected," is ominous. Singh adds that marriage and divorce procedures will be standardized (currently these are governed by the "Personal Laws" of each religion) and that the Islamic call to prayer from minarets of mosques will not be allowed, "as it disturbs the basic rights of non-believers of Islam." (Here again, he does not say anything about prayers and music broadcast from temple loudspeakers.) Singh concludes, "[t]hus *Hindutva* culture will be a blessing to the soul-less society of Western style governments. Without imposing religious teachings and directions, the culture will bring religious values into public life" (Singh 1996b: A29).

The AFMI's constructions of Indian history and the ideal Indian state

The AFMI contests the FHA's claim that the Vedic age represents the essence of Indian culture, arguing instead that Indian culture is an amalgamation of several influences, with Islamic culture being a very important component (since the Islamic period of around nine centuries constitutes the longest single era in Indian history). The AFMI also disagrees with the FHA's claims of Islamic brutality and forced conversions by stating that, but for one or two exceptions, most of the Muslim rulers practiced a policy of religious tolerance, with many even sponsoring Hindu temples and celebrations. In an advertisement published in Indian-American newspapers, the AFMI argues, "if force had been used [in conversions] . . . Muslims would not be a minority given the length of Muslim rule," and concludes that "[p]resent India is the result of a long interaction between Hinduism and Islam" (AFMI 1993: 18).

In short, while the FHA sees Indian culture as Hindu, for the AFMI India is "a multi-racial, multi-cultural, multi-lingual and multi-religious country which in the past has never been a single political entity and never a nation politically." Thus the AFMI argues that, in such a country, "any attempt to impose lingual, religious, or cultural uniformity and homogeneity or superiority of any race will lead to division, destruction and segmentation. To keep such a variegated people and country together, . . . India must of necessity . . . remain secular and culturally plural" (Qureshi 1994: 14).

What is of interest is that, while most historians of India now argue that it was under British rule that Hindu–Muslim cleavages were created, neither Hindu nor Muslim projects discuss the role of the British or the British period except very cursorily at best. While the FHA blames partition on the Muslims, the AFMI and other progressive Muslims argue that partition was the handiwork of the British and a few Islamic leaders who by no means represented the viewpoints of the majority of Muslims in India. The AFMI also points out that, in the period when Muslims were supposedly being pampered, their position deteriorated so much that now "their plight is worse" than that of the *Dalits* (AFMI 1993).

For the AFMI, December 6, 1992, the day the Babri mosque was demolished, was "a day of national shame" (Abdullah 1993: 23) and a day "which showed . . . that, [w]hat is gazing into their [Indian Muslim] faces is either annihilation and extinction, or a dark tunnel with no light at the other end" (Afzal 1993: 57).

The AFMI's viewpoint and vision of the future is, not surprisingly, very different from that of the FHA. It strongly opposes the creation of a Hindu state in India and instead would like to see a pluralistic, secular society committed to social justice and democracy with special social and economic provisions to help minorities and disadvantaged groups. It also wants to safeguard the current religious protections for minorities such as the "Personal Law" and the right to establish educational institutions to preserve and promote their religious ideas.

It is not surprising that the different constructions of "Indianness" and the different visions of an ideal Indian state of Hindu and Muslim organizations are grounded in a very different interpretation of Indian history. Ethnic groups try to construct themselves as natural, ancient and unchanging socio-cultural units that individual members have an obligation to uphold. The invoking of an idealized and generally sacralized past has thus been central in the attempts to create a new or redefined ethnic identity (see, for instance, Marty and Appleby 1991: 835). History is the anchor grounding conceptions of a primordial peoplehood and an authentic culture. The resuscitation of ancient grievances also justifies current negative treatment of other groups. History therefore becomes central in defining the "essence" of Indian culture, in legitimizing current policies, and in providing a blueprint for the future.

Affirmative action or the reservation system

Besides these fundamental differences in the interpretation of Indian history and in their vision of an ideal Indian state, the two groups differ in their viewpoints on many other issues. One contentious point is their position on reservations (affirmative action) for lower castes. The FHA is strongly opposed to the Indian reservation system, which it views as being discriminatory toward "Hindus" since upper castes bear the brunt of the system. The AFMI on the other hand supports the reservation system and has been demanding its extension to Muslims and to the lower castes of other religious groups (currently it is only for lower-caste Hindus in most north Indian states).

Critics of *Hindutva* such as the AFMI argue that the movement, while claiming to represent all Hindus, is actually an upper-caste project, since it is supported primarily by the upper castes and since proponents of *Hindutva* are opposed to reservations for the lower castes. *Hindutva* groups have become acutely conscious of the need to gain the support of the lower castes (who constitute the majority of the population) and, while not yielding on the reservation issue, they now speak out against caste discrimination and have been wooing lower castes through special programs.

In the battle between *Hindutva* and anti-*Hindutva* forces, the lower castes have become the pivotal swing factor. Anti-*Hindutva* parties, realizing that they can gain political power only by uniting the lower castes and minorities together, have also been targeting these groups. It is not accidental that the AFMI decided to form an alliance with the *Dalits* in the wake of the Babri mosque demolition and the gains made by the BJP. Besides emphasizing that *Hindutva* is really an upper-caste movement, against the interests of lower castes, groups such as the AFMI also challenge the upper-caste assertion that *Dalits* are really "Hindu," since, in traditional Hinduism, "untouchables" were regarded as falling outside caste Hindu society. Recently, several prominent *Dalit* leaders in India have endorsed this position by coming out publicly to state that they did not see themselves as Hindus (see, for instance, Iliah 1996). This is a very significant challenge to *Hindutva* because the idea of India being a Hindu majority country (the basis of the Hindu nationalist movement) can only be sustained if the lower castes are counted as Hindu. Lower castes in India have become increasingly mobilized and militant, and there have been caste clashes between lower and upper castes throughout the country over the past few years. What implications this will have for the *Hindutva* movement remain to be seen.

The position of women

In the struggle between *Hindutva* and Islamic groups, the respective position of women in Hinduism and Islam has become a politicized issue. *Hindutva* supporters argue that it is only in Hinduism that women are respected and revered and men and women are given equal rights. According to the FHA:

> From religious, cultural, social and individual aspects, a woman has the same rights as a man in Hindu society. "Where women are honored, gods are pleased", declare Hindu scriptures. Hindus have elevated women to the level of Divinity. Only Hindus worship God in the form of Divine Mother.
>
> (*India Post* 1995)

Thus it claims that a Hindu *rashtra* is necessary to rescue Indian Muslim women from the oppression they now have to experience under the Muslim Personal Law (see also Kurien 1999: 666).

Not surprisingly, the AFMI and other modernist Muslim organizations disagree that Islam is oppressive toward women. Najma Sultana, a former president of the AFMI, argues that "Islam the religion got hijacked by men whereas true Islam has the most equitable system for genders of any world religion" (Sultana 1996, citing a statement by Karen Armstrong).

Reinterpretation and politicization of religion

Both the FHA and the AFMI offer interpretations of their respective religions consonant with their political goals (Kurien 2002). Thus, the FHA argues that, "being a compassionate and tolerant religion, Hinduism has been discriminated [against] and invaded" (FHA 1995a: 80), and that therefore it is time to construct a more assertive Hinduism. To counter the threat of lower-caste members being drawn to secularist, anti-*Hindutva* parties, the FHA and other Hindu nationalist groups also emphasize that the caste system "was never integrally connected with the inner spirit of Hindu religion" and that "[t]here is no religious sanction to the practice of [a] caste system of any kind in the primary Hindu scriptures" (*India Post* 1995).

The AFMI, proclaiming that "Islam demands full participation of its followers in activities that help humanity achieve peace and justice," asserts that its fight against injustice and inequality (and its common platform with *Dalits*) is a response to this Islamic obligation (AFMI 1996). This is a significantly different interpretation of Islamic political obligation than that conventionally offered by Muslims.

The importance of pluralism

Prithvi Raj Singh, the president of the FHA, argues that a pluralistic religion is essential in the contemporary world. He writes, "Modernism . . . requires all religions to affirm [the] truth of other traditions to ensure tranquility" (Singh 1997). According to the FHA, Islam is anti-modernist by this criteria. It argues that it is only Hinduism which is truly tolerant and pluralistic and therefore that it is the most suitable religion for the twenty-first-century world. Again, it contends that only a Hindu *rashtra* will be genuinely secular (here secularism means that the state will treat all religions equally).

Interestingly, the AFMI seems to agree about the importance of pluralism. Thus, it disputes the characterization of Islam as fundamentalist and anti-modern and quotes verses from the Quran emphasizing tolerance and respect to all religions to make the case that Islam is indeed a pluralistic religion (Siddiqui 1994: 3; Akhtar 1994: 16–17).

What they say about each other

In 1995 the president of the FHA and some other Hindu activists released a statement condemning the AFMI's activities in the wake of the latter group's announcement of a coalition with *Dalits* and Buddhists. In the statement, the FHA said that AFMI's actions "speak of their agenda of pseudo-secularism and deplorable partnership for political gains, by creating unnatural and artificial alliances of *Dalits* and Buddhists with Muslims, thereby nurturing wedges between them and the Hindus". They go on to exhort them to "shun such divisive and anti-national policies" and to "mingle and melt with the mainstream of Indian culture and civilization" (FHA 1995b). AFMI members have refrained from making any public statements about the FHA since they want to steer clear of getting involved in inter-group politics among Indian Americans. However, privately, they strongly condemn the activities of the FHA, describing its members as upper-caste ideologues and religious fundamentalists.

Explaining the opposing constructions and positions

Since the constructions of both the FHA and the AFMI are typical of conservative Hindu and liberal Muslim Indian positions in the United States, it would be a mistake to focus on the specifics of the two organizations or their leadership to explain the opposing stands. Also, a lot of the rhetoric is quite similar to the positions of like-minded groups in India, so the constructions are not completely "made in the U.S.A."[10] However, there are differences in the terminology and some of the particular issues highlighted. Thus, the emphasis on pluralism and gender equality and the exhortation by the FHA to the AFMI to "mingle and melt with the mainstream Indian culture" are more in tune with the American context than the Indian. The question, then, is why such positions have become dominant in the United States and how such constructions are being used by Indian Americans.

Why is it that the support for *Hindutva* is so strong among Hindus in the United States – by many indications, stronger than the support for the movement among Hindus in India? Why is it that this highly educated, well-placed professional group is pursuing reactionary politics? Even more importantly, why are Hindu Indian Americans demanding a religious state in India which would deny minority religions the very rights, such as religious freedom, state secularity and affirmative action, that they enjoy in the United States? By the same token, why is the Muslim Indian-American voice more liberal than the Muslim voice in India? The answer to these questions is complex. In an attempt to provide an explanation, I will turn first to a brief review of three approaches dealing with immigrants and immigrant politics.

Response to immigrant marginalization

Scholars consider diasporic politics to be a response to the social, cultural and economic marginalization experienced by immigrants. According to this perspective, participation in ethnic nationalism brings recognition and status from compatriots (both fellow immigrants and those at home) and compensates for the marginality and loss of social status experienced by immigrants in the host society (Helweg 1989; Juergensmeyer 1988; Rajagopal 1995).

Undoubtedly, immigrant marginality and the attempts to compensate for it are important reasons for the involvement of immigrants in ethnic communities and, possibly by extension, in diasporic politics. However, this perspective cannot explain why political mobilization is largely on religious lines and why marginalization affects immigrant groups differently – in other words, why there is variation in the type of politics supported by different immigrant groups.

The increasing salience of religion for immigrants

Although not dealing specifically with immigrant politics, scholars such as Will Herberg (1960), reflecting on the patterns of European immigration to the United States at the turn of the century, and Stephen Warner (1993) and Raymond Williams (1988), discussing contemporary immigration, argue that religion and religious identity take on a significance in the American context that is not the case in the home country. As Raymond Williams puts it, "Immigrants are religious – by all counts more religious than they were before they left home" (1988: 29). There are two main reasons for this development. First, the disruptions and disorientation caused by settlement in a new environment means that migration frequently becomes a "theologizing experience" (Smith 1978: 1175, cited in Warner 1993: 1062), resulting in intensified religious commitment. Many of the Indian immigrants I have spoken to mentioned that they had become more religious after coming to the United States, where for the first time they had to think about the meaning of their religion and religious identity, something they could take for granted in India.

However, even more importantly, religion becomes more salient because, in the immigrant context, it creates and sustains ethnicity. Warner argues that this is particularly the case in the United States because Americans view religion as the most acceptable and non-threatening basis for community formation and ethnic expression (1993: 1058). Religious organizations become the means of maintaining and expressing ethnic identity not just for non-Christian groups such as the Hindus but also for groups such as the Chinese Christians (Yang 1999), Korean Christians (Min 1992; Hurh and Kim 1990) and Maya Catholics (Wellmeier 1998).

There is another factor, specific to the case of Indian immigrants. The idea that the essence and superiority of Indian culture (over Western) lies in the spiritual or inner realm was first propagated as part of the anti-colonial movement (Chatterjee 1993). Indian immigrants who are acutely conscious of the negative stereotypes of India prevalent in the United States have taken over this characterization. Thus, in the Indian case, the preconditions for religion being the carrier of ethnic identity and the basis of political mobilization were already in place. Immigration only served to strengthen these tendencies.

Ethnicity as a resource in multi-ethnic societies

A third body of literature argues that immigrants mobilize on ethnic lines because ethnicity is a resource that can bring material benefits to groups in their host societies. In most multicultural states, national origin is officially recognized as the basis for ethnicity. Such recognition can secure the group social, political and economic resources since such resources are generally distributed on the basis of ethnicity. Thus ethnic groups work to make their homelands visible to the public (Dusenbery 1995). Dusenbery, discussing the case of Canadian Sikhs, argues that they supported the *Khalistan* movement calling for a separate homeland in the Indian state of Punjab, not because of a nostalgic desire to return to the homeland but because they realized that they would not be recognized as a distinct ethnic group in Canada (their "real" homeland) unless they had their own country. This approach provides more information regarding why immigrant groups become politicized and also explains why groups might adopt different strategies depending on their size and location in the homeland.

* * * * *

To explain the opposing constructions and strategies of groups like the FHA and the AFMI we need to synthesize these three perspectives, each of which provides one piece of the answer. It is also important to make a distinction between factors motivating the leadership of such groups and those motivating the mass of supporters.

Immigrant marginality heightens the need to interact with co-ethnics, to maintain close emotional and social ties with the homeland, and to obtain status and recognition within the community. In immigrant contexts, religion becomes the means to create ethnic communities and identities, and thus the attachment to religion and religious institutions is intensified. Again, the bonds between co-religionists is strengthened and that between immigrants from different religious backgrounds is weakened. Since national origin is officially recognized as the criterion for ethnicity in the United States (and other multicultural states), the different religious groups also develop definitions of nationality from their own perspective, resulting in differences in the construction of homeland culture and identity along religious lines. Official policies are based on the assumption that people who share national origins also share cultural values and political concerns. Since this is often not the case, control over the definition of national identity becomes a valuable resource for immigrants, giving rise to competition between the religious groups to define homeland cultural and political concerns in their own interest.

Dominant and minority religious groups generally have very different political interests and definitions of the relationship between religion and nationality. Dominant groups generally view their religion as the basis of national culture and cohesion. This strategy of the dominant group is threatening to religious minorities and can lead to different responses, depending on the size and distribution of the particular religious minority in the homeland and the history of its relationship with the majority group. Religious minorities like the Sikhs of India, who are largely concentrated in one region of the home country, may try to initiate a movement for a separate state.[11] However minorities, such as the Muslims of India, who are dispersed through the homeland have little choice but to contest the claim of the dominant group by asserting that the home country is multi-religious and multicultural. While these constructions also take place in the home country, they are often informal and not clearly articulated or publicized. Again, in the home country, members of both majority and minority groups manifest a diversity of responses.

Religio-politics takes on a new intensity in the immigrant context for the reasons already mentioned. Since constructions of ethnicity become the means to unify the immigrant group and to gain visibility and resources, ethnic constructions forged in the diaspora are generally much more clearly formulated and articulated. The diversity characteristic of the home communities is not manifested for two inter-related reasons. First, the immigrant community tends to be much smaller and more homogenous. Second, as a minority community in a new and often hostile environment, there is more pressure to present a unified public face and therefore dissent is more strongly suppressed.[12] As third-world immigrants, and as prac-tioners of religions that are negatively perceived in the United States, members of both Hindu and Muslim Indian-American organizations stress that they are professional and that their religions are sophisticated, pluralist and gender equal. I will now turn to an explanation of the differences between the two types of organizations.

Hindu Indian-American organizations

Hindu Indian Americans tend to be more supportive of the *Hindutva* ideology and politics for several reasons. Firstly, since Hindus are the dominant (and majority) group, both in India and among Indian Americans, the conflation of a Hindu and Indian identity, already taking place in India, is only reinforced in the diaspora since religion becomes the basis of ethnicity. As Dusenbery (1995) argues for the case of Sikhs in Canada, the need for a spiritual homeland as the legitimizer and anchor of ethnic identity becomes particularly pronounced in such contexts. Thus, the cry of the FHA, "Where is the country for the Hindus?" (1995a: 117) becomes the central plank of their platform.

Hindu Indian Americans who were in the majority in India, become a racial, religious and cultural minority in the United States and have to deal with the largely negative perceptions of Hinduism of the wider society. It is therefore not surprising that the "Hinduism under siege" *Hindutva* message, particularly its emphasis on the greatness of Hinduism and the need for Hindu pride, resonates so much more in this embattled context. The large majority of Hindu Indian Americans are supporters of Hindu organizations for these reasons and tend to be largely unaware or uninterested in the political agenda of such organizations (Kurien 1998).

Third, the anti-Muslim platform of the *Hindutva* movement also fits in well with the anti-Muslim sentiment in the United States, and groups such as the FHA have been using this to strengthen their case in their discussions with American politicians and to build alliances with other groups in this society (see Kurien 2001). In its interaction with American politicians and public officials, the FHA does not mention Hindu nationalism but instead emphasizes the tolerance and pluralism of Hinduism.

Muslim Indian-American organizations

I have argued that, for groups such as the Muslims, the only way to counter directly the constructions of the *Hindutva*-oriented organizations is by emphasizing that India is not Hindu but multi-religious and therefore should have a secular government. Another important reason for the liberal Muslim Indian-American political voice is the fact that the more conservative Muslim Indian-American groups are either apolitical like the Tablighi Jamaat or are against involvement in secular politics. By default, then, it is the more liberal Muslim Indian Americans who become involved in socio-economic and political activities *as Indians*. This probably explains why it is that, although the dominant Muslim voice in India has been conservative and fundamentalist (largely as a reaction to the *Hindutva* movement), Muslim Indian Americans have adopted a liberal, secularist position. It is also likely to be an attempt to counter the American perception of Muslims as fundamentalist.

* * * * *

In both the Hindu and the Muslim case, it appears that there is a fundamental difference in the reasons for the participation of the leadership and the members. The leadership seem to be involved largely because of the resources (e.g., political power, status and recognition) they hope to obtain from ethno-politics. Many were involved in politics in the homeland or come from families who were politically active (although not always in the type of politics they are currently advocating).[13] Many of the supporters of such groups, however, participate in the activities of religious organizations because they experience marginality and intensified religious and nationalistic commitment as a consequence of immigration.

While it is difficult to say for sure, the reason that there are no major counter initiatives to the *Hindutva* movement in southern California, unlike in other large American cities, may have to do with the absence of strong South Asian programs in the university campuses in the region. In other major American cities, the campus-based Indian-American groups have located themselves within larger Asian-American structures and have been very active in liberal politics. In discussions and interviews that I conducted, Indian-American students at both the major campuses in the region – the University of California, Los Angeles, and the University of Southern California – complained about being excluded from or marginalized within Asian-American programs and of racism by East-Asian American students and faculty. The hegemonic East-Asian presence in southern California has therefore hampered Indian involvement in liberal Asian-American politics both on college campuses and outside, and has also had the effect of rendering Indians invisible as an ethnic group in this region.

The impact of the two types of organizations

Impact on India

As I go on to demonstrate, the two types of organizations have had important consequences for politics in India. The strong moral and financial support of Hindu Indian Americans has been crucial, both in bringing the BJP to power in India (and keeping them there) and to many of its central (and controversial) policies. While there is clear evidence of close ties between groups such as the FHA and the AFMI and their Indian counterparts, it is harder to assess the actual nature of the relationship and exactly what concrete impact such Indian-American organizations have on Indian politics and policies. I present below some of the scattered evidence that is available.

The FHA was not only one of the first Hindu umbrella organizations to be based in the United States, but it also took the lead in being the first expatriate Hindu organization to reach out publicly to the Indian citizenry. In January 1993, describing themselves as "Concerned NRIs [non-resident Indians] of Southern California," its leaders issued a full-page advertisement in all the editions of the *Indian Express*, a widely read English-language paper in India, urging their "brothers and sisters in India" to work toward making India a Hindu country (personal interview; Mckean 1996: 319). FHA leaders claim that they received hundreds of enthusiastic and supportive letters from Hindus in different regions and of differing socio-economic backgrounds.

It is now well understood that much of the financial support for the *Hindutva* movement in India comes from the United States (see Rajagopal 2000: 474; Anderson 1998: 73). Ajit Jha, a journalist, has described the southern California region as being "a goldmine of funds for the BJP" (Jha 1993). However, it is difficult to estimate even approximate amounts because most of the money is sent through undocumented channels. Through a careful analysis of the funding received by the VHPA (Vishwa Hindu Parishad of America) over the past decade, Biju Mathew (2000: 123) notes that, by the organization's own documentation, $2.6 million of the money that was legally transferred to India did not go to the charitable causes for which it had been raised – a sizeable amount of money, particularly by Indian standards. Mathew (2000: 123–5) also points out that the money that was transferred illegally and through "matching gift" corporate dollars probably far exceeded the $2.6 million that was legally transferred. With the proliferation of Hindu organizations in the United States, there are many other sources of funding in addition to the VHPA, further increasing the financial clout of Indian Americans within the *Hindutva* movement and the Indian political system.

While there are no figures of the amounts involved, Muslim organizations such as the AFMI are also funneling large sums of money into India. According to Aslam Abdullah, the Indian Muslim Relief Council raises around $2 million a year to help projects in India. The AFMI and its progressive allies (such as the Coalition for an Egalitarian and Pluralistic India) have also placed advertisements in Indian newspapers, but have targeted Indian-language papers. It is likely that the efforts of both American *Hindutva* groups such as the FHA and the anti-*Hindutva* groups such as the AFMI influenced the election results of spring 1998 – with the support of the *Hindutva* forces helping the BJP and that of the anti-*Hindutva* organizations undermining the party's hegemony (making it necessary for it to seek the backing of other parties to form a government).

In a public acknowledgment of the support the BJP received from NRIs, particularly in the United States, the party presented a budget in June 1998 which had several special provisions for members of the Indian diaspora willing to invest dollars in the country. Among these was a person of Indian origin (PIO) card, costing $1,000 and valid for twenty years, entitling the holder to several benefits, such as a visa-free visit to India, and economic, financial and educational benefits equivalent to those offered to NRIs, such as the right to own and dispose of property in India, the ability to open bank accounts in India on a par with rupee accounts maintained by resident Indians, and the inclusion of PIO children under NRI quotas in educational institutions, including medical and engineering colleges.[14] The government also raised the limit on shareholding for NRIs in Indian companies, and launched new funds to obtain NRI dollars with competitive rates of interest.

Shortly after taking over the reins of leadership in the country, the BJP also embarked on a nuclearization program that culminated in the now historic explosions of May 1998. American *Hindutva* groups such as the FHA had long been advocating nuclearization for India (Singh 1996a, 1997). Although the initial support for the nuclearization program in India quickly evaporated in the wake of the explosions in Pakistan and the increasing prices consequent on the sanctions (both of which led to protests around the country), the BJP government's actions dramatically increased its popularity among Indian Americans. Not surprisingly, groups such as the FHA and its Hindu nationalist allies were jubilant at the nuclear explosions. A statement signed by the Overseas Friends of the BJP and other Hindu organizations asserted, "The vast majority of Indian Americans who comprise one of the most educated groups in the US, and the 900 million people of India, have given their overwhelming support to India's testing" (Rajagopal 2000: 486). My survey of Indian-American newspapers and websites indicated that they were not too far off the mark regarding the response of Indian Americans, since large sections of even those (largely) Hindu Indian Americans who had been relatively apolitical seemed to come out strongly in support of the Indian government's actions with jingoistic assertions of nationalistic pride and fervor. At the same time, another group in the southern California region, spearheaded by the AFMI and its partners, condemned the action in no uncertain terms and has been trying to mobilize people to take a stand against nuclearizing the tensions between India and Pakistan.

The BJP wasted no time in harnessing the enthusiastic response to its nuclearization program by Indian Americans. (In fact, the party's confidence in going ahead with its program despite the certainty of sanctions was based on its confidence that it could count on the support of the overseas Indian community to offset the effects of the sanctions.) Calling on the NRIs to "stand up for India at this critical hour" (*India West* 1998), the Indian government launched a Resurgent India Bond to enable NRIs to help the Indian government tide over international sanctions. The response to the scheme was so positive that the government far exceeded its target of $2 billion, mopping up $4.6 billion by the time of its close at the end of August 1998 (Nanda 1999, p. 1). With its large pro-liberalization Hindu Indian-American business constituency in the United States and India, the BJP hastily abandoned its nativist "*swadeshi*" platform and came out strongly in support of liberalization. The AFMI, however, has been more cautious, urging the government to take efforts to ameliorate the effects of liberalization on lower classes and castes.[15]

Hindu Indian-American organizations have also been pressing the BJP government for representation in the Indian parliament. Under such pressure, the prime minister announced that a separate department would be created within the External Affairs Ministry to act as a link with NRIs (*India Journal* 1999a) and to deal with their concerns. This department, the Non-Resident Indians' Division, set up a high level committee in September 2000 to travel to countries around the world and study the Indian diaspora. Their goal was to develop a comprehensive database of "achievers, entrepreneurs, experts and eminent people in every field from amongst the NRIs and PIOs." The database would also list the top fifty companies run by the NRIs and PIOs in each country. In addition, the committee was forming sub-groups to study topics of particular relevance to NRIs and PIOs (Singhvi 2000). The committee submitted its report and recommendations to the Indian government in January 2002. On its recommendation, the granting of dual citizenship to people of Indian origin living in "certain countries" (the US, the UK, Canada, Australia, New Zealand and Singapore) was announced with great fanfare at the first government-organized convention of the Indian diaspora held in New Delhi in January of 2003.

American foreign policy

The politicization of Indian Americans (largely through the *Hindutva* movement) has brought about significant shifts in American foreign policy toward India and Pakistan. Both Hindu and Muslim groups are also trying to influence American foreign policy toward India and Pakistan by contributing heavily to the campaigns of politicians they believe to be sympathetic to their interests. The outcome of the Kargil conflict between India and Pakistan demonstrated the influence of Indian Americans. In 1999, India and Pakistan got into a conflict over the incursion of Pakistani troops into Kargil on the Indo-Pakistani border. The conflict was resolved only when Clinton intervened and urged the Pakistani president to withdraw his forces. According to a front-page article in the *Washington Post* on October 9, 1999, it was the pressure that Indian immigrants put on congress members that forced Clinton to intervene on behalf of India. The *Post* article went on to conclude that it was the generosity of Indian Americans in political campaigns that had been responsible for the growing support for India in the earlier pro-Pakistan American administration and that "Indo-Americans [have become] a powerful and effective domestic lobby" (cited in *India Journal* 1999b). An Indian-American newspaper pointed out that, with around 130 members in 2000, the Indian caucus on Capitol Hill is one of the largest caucuses of any country (*India Post* 2000).

In an article in the *Indian Post*, the chairman of the high level committee, Dr. L. M. Singhvi, called the NRIs the "National Reserve of India" for their role in helping the Indian government after the nuclear tests and during the Kargil conflict, by "explaining our viewpoint and creating a favorable public opinion" in the United States (Singhvi 2000). Similarly, on his trips to the United States, the Indian prime minister, Atal Behari Vajpayee, repeatedly encourages Indian Americans to get involved in American politics and "build and maintain contacts at different levels with US Congressmen and Senators" in order to influence American foreign policy (*India Journal* 1999b).

Indian-American Muslims have also played a critical role in protecting the interests of India on the Kashmir issue. In an email of January 9, 2001, to the Islamic Supreme Council of America (ISCA), Dr. Mohammed Ayoob, a respected Indian-American Muslim leader, protested the organization's advice to Muslims in the United States to support the Pakistan–Kashmir caucus, claiming that this was "highly objectionable from the perspective of Indian Muslims residing in the country who consider anti-India propaganda as much directed against them as against other segments of the Indian community and the Government of India." In his email Dr. Ayoob pointed out to the council that more Muslims lived in India than in Pakistan or even the entire Arab world, that Muslims in Kashmir constituted only 2 percent of Indian Muslims, and that the organization should therefore not engage in partisan politics that supported one group of Muslims at the expense of another. The next day, Dr. Ayoob received an apology from the general secretary of the ISCA and a promise to look into the matter.

Conclusion

I have argued that, since religion becomes the basis of group formation in the United States, Hindu and Muslim Indian Americans have separate organizations from the local to the national level. Such organizations also become proxy "ethnic" associations. As Hindu and Muslim Indians have very different histories, political interests and social concerns (as majority and minority religious groups), they have systematic differences in the way they construct the meaning and content of an "Indian" identity. Due to the importance of ethnic recognition and visibility in obtaining state resources, Hindus and Muslims compete to obtain such state recognition for their definition of national identity, leading to the exacerbation and politicization of religious cleavages.

Although the existence of subgroups within ethnic categories has not been adequately recognized, this article shows how significant such cleavages can be. It also shows that, under conditions of insecurity and marginality of the kind that are being experienced today by many immigrants, the conflicts are likely to be made worse and possibly even exported back to the home countries. Since the FHA and the AFMI and other similar organizations have been in existence only for a few years, it is hard to predict how the tension between them will develop and to what extent either side will be successful in imposing their agenda on Indian or United States foreign policy. However, undoubtedly, both types of organizations will have profound consequences for the globalization of Indian politics and for inter-religious relations in India.

Notes

1 This research was supported by a grant from the Southern California Research Center (SC2) at the University of Southern California. Earlier versions of the chapter were published in *Ethnic and Racial Studies* (http:www.tandf.co.uk), 2001, ("Religion, Ethnicity and Politics: Hindu and Muslim Immigrants in the United States," vol. 25, no. 2, pp. 263–93), and in Marta Lopez-Garza and David R. Diaz (eds) *Asian and Latino Immigrants in a Restructuring Economy: The Metamorphosis of Southern California*, Stanford University Press, 2001 ("Constructing 'Indianness' in Southern California: The Role of Hindu and Muslim Indian Immigrants," pp. 289–312). I am grateful to Rey Koslowski for his suggestions.

2 The official website of the committee is at www.indiandiaspora.nic.in. The Indian government coined the terms NRI and PIO in the early 1970s, setting up schemes to permit both groups to deposit money in special accounts with competitive rates of interest (Rajagopal 2001: 242).

3 World Bank figures, 1990.

4 This is only if the *Dalits* (lower castes, formerly considered "untouchable"), who constitute around a fifth of the population, are considered Hindu. The controversy over who is considered Hindu is discussed later in the article.

5 1990 census figures.

6 Fenton (1988: 28) estimates that, in 1985, around 65 percent of the Indian immigrants in America came from a Hindu family background.

7 Rough estimate based on projections from the 1990 and 2000 censuses.

8 Statement made by Mr. Prithvi Raj Singh, president of the FHA, at a banquet organized to raise money for the construction of a local temple (Saberwal 1995). Despite its professed goal, the FHA could not maintain internal unity, and in late 1998 a section of the organization broke away to form a parallel organization, the American Hindu Federation (AHF).

9 They claim that around 20,000 people attended their Diwali-Dussera function in 1999 (FHA 1999).

10 This is Williams's (1992: 230) term regarding the development of what he characterizes as an "American Hinduism" (1992: 239).

11 Thus the *Khalistan* movement was initiated by Sikh immigrants outside India (Mahmood 1996: 257).

12 Bhattacharjee (1992) and Dasgupta and Dasgupta (1996) have made the same argument with respect to gender models among Indian Americans.

13 Some of the leaders of Hindu organizations come from families who were involved in the Indian freedom struggle as Gandhian followers.

14 http//iic.nic.in/vsiic/piocard.htm.

15 Presentations at the 1997 annual AFMI meeting and discussions with some of its leaders.

References

Abdullah, A. (1993) "A Day of National Shame," *The Minaret*, Jan/Feb, pp. 23–6.

AFMI (1993) "United We Stand, Divided We Fall," *Newsbrief*, vol. 3, no. 1, p. 18.

——(1995) *Newsbrief*, vol. 5, no. 2.

——(1996) "Editorial," *Indo-US Relations in the 21st Century: A Global Perspective*. Newark, NJ: AFMI [brochure, 6th Annual Convention].

Afzal, O. (1993) "The Way Ahead," *The Minaret* (Jan/Feb), pp. 57–8.

Ahmad, M. (1991) "Islamic Fundamentalism in South Asia: The Jamaat-i-Islami and the Tablighi Jamaat," in Marty, M., and Appleby, R. S. (eds) *Fundamentalisms Observed*. Chicago: University of Chicago Press, pp. 457–530.

Akhtar, H. (1994) "Secularism and Pluralism in India," *AFMI Newsbrief*, vol. 4, no. 4, pp. 15–18.

Anderson, B. (1998) "Long Distance Nationalism," in Anderson, *The Spectre of Comparisons: Nationalism, Southeast Asia and the World*. London: Verso, pp. 58–76.

Bhattacharjee, A. (1992) "The Habit of Ex-nomination: Nation, Woman and the Indian Immigrant Bourgeoisie," *Public Culture*, vol. 5, no. 1, pp. 19–44.

Chatterjee, P. (1993) *The Nation and its Fragments: Colonial and Postcolonial Histories*. Princeton, NJ: Princeton University Press.

Dasgupta, S., and Dasgupta, S. D. (1996) "Women in Exile: Gender Relations in the Asian Indian Community in the U.S.," in Maira, S., and Srikanth, R. (eds) *Contours of the Heart: South Asians Map North America*. New York: Asian American Writers Workshop, pp. 381–400.

Dusenbery, V. (1995) "A Sikh Diaspora? Contested Identities and Constructed Realities," in van der Veer, P. (ed.) *Nation and Migration: The Politics of Space in the South Asian Diaspora*. Philadelphia: University of Pennsylvania Press, pp. 17–42.

Fenton, J. (1988) *Transplanting Religious Traditions: Asian Indians in America*. New York: Praeger.

FHA (Federation of Hindu Associations) (1995a) *Directory of Temples and Associations of Southern California and Everything You Wanted to Know about Hinduism*. Artesia, CA: FHA.

——(1995b) "Support to Separatism 'Pseudo-Secularism' Condemned," *India Post*, Nov 24, p. A4.

——(1997a) "Ideal Hindu Temple," *India Post*, August 29, p. A27 [advertisement].

——(1997b) "FHA Memorandum," *India West*, Feb 21, p. C20.

——(1997c) "A Hindu Center," *India Post*, Jan 24, p. BIII [advertisement].

——(1999) "FHA is Overwhelmed," *India Journal*, Nov 26, p. A7 [advertisement].

Helweg, A. (1989) "Sikh Politics in India: The Emigrant Factor," in Barrier, G., and Dusenbery, V. (eds) *The Sikh Diaspora: Migration and Experiences Beyond the Punjab*. Delhi: Chanakya Publications.

Herberg, W. (1960) *Protestant, Catholic, Jew: An Essay in American Religious Sociology*. 2nd edn, Garden City, NY: Doubleday.

Hurh, W. M., and Kim, K. C. (1990) "Religious Participation of Korean Immigrants in the United States," *Journal for the Scientific Study of Religion*, vol. 29, no.1, pp. 19–34.

Iliah, K. (1996) *Why I am Not a Hindu: A Sudra Critique of Hindutva Philosophy, Culture and Political Economy*. Calcutta: Samya Publications.

India Journal (1999a) "Separate Department to be Created for NRIs: Vajpayee," October 22, p. A3.

——(1999b) "Indo-Americans Now Wield Great Influence in U.S. Politics," August 15, p. A3.

India Post (1995) "Hindu Philosophy has No Place for Caste System Says FHA," March 17, p. 6.

India Post (2000) "NRIs Behind Surge in Indo-US Ties," *India Post*, October 6, p. 4.

India West (1998) "Singh Asks NRIs to Stand by India in Critical Hour," June 19, p. A30.

Jha, A. K. (1993) "Saffron Sees Red: Secular Groups Pose a Challenge to the Hindutva Brigade," *India Today*, August 15, p. 56g.

Juergensmeyer, M. (1988) "The Logic of Religious Violence: The Case of the Punjab," *Contributions to Indian Sociology* (n.s.), vol. 22, no. 1, pp. 65–88.

Kurien, P. (1998) "Becoming American by Becoming Hindu: Indian Americans Take their Place at the Multi-Cultural Table," in Warner, R. Stephen, and Wittner, Judith G. (eds) *Gatherings in Diaspora: Religious Communities and the New Immigration*, Philadelphia: Temple University Press.

——(1999) "Gendered Ethnicity: Creating a Hindu Indian Identity in the U.S.," *American Behavioral Scientist*, vol. 23, no. 3, pp. 648–70.

——(2001) "Religion, Ethnicity and Politics: Hindu and Muslim India Immigrants in the United States," *Ethnic and Racial Studies*, vol. 24, no. 2, pp. 263–93.

——(2002) "'We are Better Hindus Here': Religion and Ethnicity among Indian Americans," in Kim, J. H., and Pyong, G. M. (eds) *Building Faith Communities: Asian Immigrants and Religions.* Walnut Creek, CA: Altamira Press.

Lal, V. *et al.* (1995) "Shame of Award to Thackerey," *India West*, June 23, p. A5.

Mahmood, C. K. (1996) *Fighting for Faith and Nation: Dialogues with Sikh Militants.* Philadelphia: University of Pennsylvania Press.

Marty, M. E., and Appleby, S. (eds) (1991) *Fundamentalisms Observed.* Chicago: University of Chicago Press.

Mathew, B. (2000) "Byte-Sized Nationalism: Mapping the Hindu Right in the United States," *Rethinking Marxism*, vol. 12, no. 3, pp. 108–28.

McKean, L. (1996) *Divine Enterprise: Gurus and the Hindu Nationalist Movement.* Chicago: University of Chicago Press.

Min, P. G. (1992) "The Structure and Social Functions of Korean Immigrant Churches in the United States," *International Migration Review*, vol. 26, winter, pp. 370–94.

Misir, D. N. (1996) "The Murder of Navroze Mody: Race, Violence and the Search for Order," *Amerasia Journal*, vol. 22, no. 2, pp. 55–76.

Nanda, A. (1999) "1998: A Year of NRI Confidence in India," *India Post*, Jan 1, pp. 1, 36.

Portes, A., and Rumbaut, R. G. (1990) *Immigrant America: A Portrait.* Berkeley: University of California Press.

Qureshi, A. R. (1994) "Secularism and Pluralism in India," *AFMI Newsbrief*, vol. 4, no. 4, pp. 13–15.

Rajagopal, A. (1995) "Better Hindu than Black? Narratives of Asian Indian Identity," paper presented at the annual meetings of the SSSR and RRA, St. Louis, Missouri.

——(2000) "Hindu Nationalism in the U.S.: Changing Configurations of Political Practice," *Ethnic and Racial Studies*, vol. 23, no. 3, pp. 467–96.

——(2001) *Politics after Television: Hindu Nationalism and the Reshaping of the Public in India.* Cambridge: Cambridge University Press.

Saberwal, S. (1995) "FHA Unity Banquet Raises $20,000 for Norwalk Temple, Support Emphasized at Sangeet Sandhya," *India Post*, July 28, p. DSW6.

Shinagawa, L. H. (1996) "The Impact of Immigration on the Demography of Asian Pacific Americans" in Hing, B. H., and Lee, R. (eds) *The State of Asian Pacific America: Reframing the Immigration Debate: A Public Policy Report.* Los Angeles: LEAP Asian Pacific American Public Policy Institute and UCLA Asian American Studies Center, pp. 59–126.

Siddiqui, M. (1994) "Islam and Pluralism," *AFMI Newsbrief,* vol. 4, no. 4, pp. 3–4.

Singh, P. R. (1996a) "The 'Fighting Machine' and Hindus," letter to the editor, *India Post,* October 11, p. A26.

——(1996b) "Can 'Hindutva' Be Indian Nationalism," *India Post,* August 16, pp. A28–9.

——(1997) "Discussing Religious Role Models," letter to the editor, *India Post,* March 14, p. A26.

Singhvi, L. M. (2000) "NRIs Should Mean National Reserve of India," *India Post,* September 29, p. A64.

Smith, T. (1978) "Religion and Ethnicity in America," *American Historical Review,* vol. 83, December, pp. 1155–85.

Springer, R. (1997) "Indians Jump to Third Place in Immigration to U.S.," *India West,* May 2, p. A22.

Sultana, N. (1996) "Empowerment of Muslim Women through 100% Literacy by Year 2005," in AFMI, *Indo-US Relations in the 21st Century: A Global Perspective.* Newark, NJ: AFMI.

Warner, S. (1993) "Work in Progress Toward a New Paradigm for the Sociological Study of Religion in the United States," *American Journal of Sociology,* vol. 98, March, pp. 1044–193.

Waters, M. C., and Eschbach, K. (1999) "Immigration and Ethnic and Racial Inequality in the United States," in Yetman, N. R. (ed.) *Majority and Minority: The Dynamics of Race and Ethnicity in American Life,* 6th edn, Needham Heights, MA: Allyn & Bacon, pp. 312–27.

Wellmeier, N. J. (1998) "Santa Eulalia's People in Exile: Maya Religion, Culture, and Identity in Los Angeles," in Warner, S., and Wittner, J. (eds) *Gatherings in Diaspora: Religious Communities and the New Immigration.* Philadelphia: Temple University Press, pp. 97–122.

Williams, R. B. (1988) *Religions of Immigrants from India and Pakistan: New Threads in the American Tapestry.* Cambridge: Cambridge University Press.

——(1992) "Sacred Threads of Several Textures: Strategies of Adaptation in the United States," in Williams, R. B. (ed.) *A Sacred Thread: Modern Transmission of Hindu Traditions in India and Abroad.* Chambersberg, PA: Anima Publications, pp. 228–57.

Yang, F. (1999) *Chinese Christians in America: Conversion, Assimilation and Adhesive Identities.* University Park, PA: Pennsylvania State University Press.

8   A marooned diaspora

Ethnic Russians in the near abroad and their impact on Russia's foreign policy and domestic politics

Robert A. Saunders

Introduction

In 1991, the Soviet Union came to an abrupt end, leaving approximately 25 million ethnic Russians outside the borders of the Russian Federation.[1] By all measures, this community represented a rather ill-prepared diaspora. Nearly three-quarters of all Russians living in the non-Russian republics considered the USSR to be their homeland as late as December 1990 (Payin 1994). Within a year, this "homeland" no longer existed, and Russians outside of the newly created Russian Federation were faced with a sudden identity crisis.[2] When making the decision to immigrate to what would become the independent states of Central Asia, Transcaucasia and the Baltics, Russians had little or no idea that they would one day be part of a diasporic community facing the daily challenges of immigrants around the world. These Russians, who had previously occupied a role as *primi inter pares* in the imperial periphery, were instantly reduced to second-class citizens and in some cases faced the possibility of expulsion from increasingly hostile states (Tuminez 2000: 184). In the years since the demise of the Soviet Union, ethnic Russians in the Newly Independent States (NIS) have proved an interesting study due to their impact on the politics of their states of residence and on the Russian Federation's foreign policy and domestic politics.

Due to the long history of Russian immigration to far-flung parts of the Russian and later Soviet state, the idea of a Russian diaspora in the borderlands is a relatively new one. Previously, the Russian colonizers were thought of in terms of tsarist subjects or Soviet citizens with every right to settle where they did, since the territories formed an integral part of the empire. Since the collapse of the Soviet Union, the term "diaspora" has gained significant use in the discourse of ethnic Russians living in the Newly Independent States; however, national minority (*natsional'noe men'shinstvo*) is still the preferred term of some to discuss Russians and other minorities in the post-Soviet space.[3] The term diaspora is even controversial in some quarters, since Russians in certain areas (particularly in northern Kazakhstan and eastern Ukraine) consider the term ill-fitting if not outright offensive, as there has been a continuous Russian presence in the area for centuries (see BBC 2002b).

Millions of Russians immigrated to the Russian Federation during the 1990s, exercising their right under the new country's freshly minted nationality law, which entitled those with a strong emotional attachment to the Russian or Soviet state to "return" to their ancestral homeland and assume Russian citizenship. In 2001, the number of "near abroad" Russians had dropped to 19 million, signifying a migration of approximately 6 million to the Russian Federation or third countries, including the US. Those who chose to stay quickly adapted to their new surroundings and increasingly assumed the mantle of diaspora as best they could under such challenging circumstances. Barred from political activity based on ethnic affiliation in many NIS countries (Kazakhstan, Georgia, etc.) and stripped of citizenship in other states (the Baltics), ethnic Russians have increasingly utilized alternative measures to effect political change in their states of residence, including lobbying elites within the Russian Federation to act on their behalf. Although many Russians have employed the standard tools of diasporas, i.e., *exit* and *voice*, the use of proxy politics – that is, the representation through outside parties – conducted through Russian foreign policy stands as a key mark of distinction for this immigrant group.

Far from rejecting calls to action, federation politicians from every point on the political spectrum have rallied in support of "offshore" Russians. The national obsession with ethnic countrymen (*sootechestvenniki*) colors Russia's foreign policy directives and has been sewn into the fabric of nearly every political platform within the country (Tuminez 2000: 199–201). This trend has had serious consequences for the Russian Federation's internal and external political situation. Russia's nascent democracy has seen this issue become a political battleground in regional elections, with candidates attempting to outmaneuver each other to appear more "protective" of the countrymen in neighboring states. And at the federal level, Russian foreign policy is increasingly tied to the condition (or perceived condition) of ethnic Russians and Russian-speakers in the Newly Independent States.

This trend has had implications not only for bilateral relations with the newly formed states of Eurasia, but also for Russia's relationship with the European Union and even its budding friendship with the United States. In the Baltics, Russia is relentless in applying pressure through international organizations, trade, and security relationships to ensure better treatment of its countrymen in Estonia, Latvia and (to a lesser extent) Lithuania. Most Russians have left Transcaucasia as a result of untenable social, political and economic conditions, including ethnic conflict and chronic unemployment, but those who remain receive substantial financial support for cultural institutions and education from Russia's Duma. Lastly, the Russian Federation has demonstrated strong support for two breakaway republics, Abkhazia in Georgia and the (Slavic) republic of Transdniestria in eastern (Latinate) Moldova, prompting difficulties with a host of states concerned about the stability of South-Eastern Europe and the Caucasus. In Central Asia, questions regarding the Russian population increasingly provide fodder for resuming Russian hegemony over, if not outright political domination of, its southern neighbors.

Russia's seemingly overzealous interest in the Russian populations of Kazakh-stan, Uzbekistan and Kyrgyzstan serves as an integral part of what is referred to as the Russian Monroe Doctrine. Viktor Ilyin, philosophy professor at Moscow Technical University, recently defined the concept: "The exclusive right of control over the former fragments of the [Russian] empire and support of the friendly regional regimes there is the prerogative of Russia, which strives to reintegrate the [former Soviet] Union space under its leadership" (quoted in Torbakov 2003). Use of the term by the Russian intelligentsia is not a recent phenomenon. In January of 1994, Adranik Migranian, a political scientist based in Moscow, published "Russia and the Near Abroad" in *Nezavisimaia Gazeta*, outlining his ideas for a Russian Monroe Doctrine which he had formulated somewhat earlier. Despite the involvement of Moscow in the internal affairs of the Newly Independent States and the diaspora's use of proxy politics, it is now abundantly clear that the dire predictions (violent ethnic conflict, separatist struggles, etc.) of many Western political scientists and politicians are not coming true. Rogers Brubaker's study of the Russians in the Near Abroad, *Nationalism Reframed*, drew countless parallels between the Russians and the Germans of Eastern Europe in the interwar period (1918–39). This analogy now seems quite a bit off the mark.

This chapter is organized into five main parts, beginning with a discussion of the novel idea of a Russian "diaspora" in the states which comprised the former Soviet Union. This will be followed by a brief narrative detailing the historic conditions that led to the existence of a substantial Russian diaspora in the non-Russian republics of the former Soviet Union before its collapse in 1991. The chapter will then discuss the nationalizing projects of several of the Newly Independent States formed out of the ruins of the USSR, focusing specifically on those states with a higher percentage of ethnic Russians within their borders.[4] The discussion will next provide a synopsis of the Russian Federation's actions to "protect" its countrymen in the near abroad through its foreign policy. This will be followed by an analysis of the diaspora's role in Russia's domestic politics. Finally, the essay will conclude with some observations on the future of the Russian diaspora and the possibility of the development of a transnational, rather than nationalistic, identity among the Russian and Russian-speaking populace of the NIS.

As I will argue, Russia has effectively employed its diaspora as a mechanism to reassert hegemony in its borderlands, often putting the people there in direct confrontation with their states of residence over issues of national security. Diasporic Russians, however, have seen few discrete benefits from this flurry of activity, and recent polls show they are growing resentful of Moscow's meddling in their relations with their states of residence (Barrington *et al.* 2002). Yet as ties between the federation and the other former Soviet republics grow, they are well placed to take advantage of the situation as an increasingly transnational group, belonging neither wholly in Russia nor outside of it. That being said, any appearance of symbiosis at this point is largely illusory – the relationship as it stands favors only the Russian Federation.

Russians in the near abroad: diaspora or imperial minority?

For most of the twentieth century, the term Russian diaspora conjured up images of exiled aristocrats pining away for the days when infallible tsars and long-bearded patriarchs lorded over Mother Russia. But in 1991 the composition and the very idea of the Russian diaspora was radically altered as New York, Paris and London were eclipsed by Riga, Almaty and Tiraspol. Russians who did not have the "good fortune" of living within the borders of the new Russian Federation found themselves turned from pampered colonists into unwanted immigrants almost overnight. Unlike more traditional diasporic communities, such as Chinese of South-East Asia or Germany's Kurdish population (covered in this volume by Amy L. Freedman and Alynna J. Lyon, Emek M. Uçarer respectively), Russians in the near abroad were psychically ill-prepared for the challenges facing them in the post-Soviet world.

For centuries, tsarist and Soviet imperial policies encouraged relocation of Russians to the imperial periphery. In the seventeenth and eighteenth centuries, Russian Cossacks moved into Siberia as fur-trappers, traders and professional adventurers. In the first half of the nineteenth century, imperial Russia's steady advance in the deserts and steppes of Central Asia attracted settlers in search of commercial opportunities in the newly subjugated cities of the old Silk Road. In the second half of that century, incipient industrialization beckoned Russians to the oil fields of Transcaucasia and the fast-developing cities in the Western Provinces. After the Bolshevik Revolution, immigration flows of Russians to historically non-Russian areas continued.

The Soviet republics with the highest percentages of Russians – Estonia, Latvia and Kazakhstan (see Table 8.1 below) – coincidentally suffered significant population losses of the titular majority during the mid-twentieth century, a fact that tended to breed particular resentment against resident and arriving Russians. During the Great Patriotic War, Lavrentii P. Beria, head of the Soviet state security apparatus, the NKVD, oversaw the deportation of 140,000 Lithuanian, Latvian and Estonian landowners, entrepreneurs and members of the educated elite to the interior of the Soviet Union (Knight 1993). This created a vacuum which was quickly and systematically filled by immigrants from other parts of the Soviet Union, principally Russians. Agricultural migration figured prominently in Kazakhstan due to Nikita S. Khrushchev's "virgin lands" program, which attracted millions to the Kazakh SSR only a few short decades after the cata-strophic policies of forced collectivization and sedentarization resulted in the deaths of over a third of the Kazakh population.[5]

By the early 1990s, Russians, together with considerable communities of Ukrainians and Belorussians, constituted a majority of the industrial labor force in the Baltics (Baev and Kolstø 2003). As of the 1989 census, Russians in Kazakhstan were clearly the majority in the cities and represented about 37 percent of the total population. According to Baurzhan Zhanguttin, ethnic Russians represented a plurality in most skilled professions, including healthcare, physical culture, and social security (40 percent); science and scientific services (53 percent); and

Table 8.1 Indigenes versus Russians in the NIS (2002)

State	Population	Indigene	Russian	Other	No. of Russians
Armenia	3,330,099	93%	2%	5%	67,000
Azerbaijan	7,798,497	90%	2.5%	7.5%	195,000
Belarus	10,335,382	81%	11%	7%	1,137,000
Estonia	1,415,681	62%	30%	8%	425,000
Georgia	4,960,951	70%	6%	24%	298,000
Kazakhstan[1]	16,741,519	53%	30%	17%	5,022,000
Kyrgyzstan	4,822,166	54%	12%	34%	579,000
Latvia	2,366,515	56%	30%	14%	710,000
Lithuania	3,601,138	80%	9%	11%	324,000
Moldova	4,434,547	65%	13%	22%	576,000
Tajikistan	6,719,567	69%	3%	28%	202,000
Turkmenistan	4,688,963	77%	7%	16%	328,000
Ukraine	48,396,470	78%	17%	5%	8,227,000
Uzbekistan	25,563,441	74%	5.5%	20.5%	1,411,000

Source: Country profiles from *Asia and Pacific Review World of Information Comment and Analysis* (2002), *Europe Review World of Information* (2002) and the *CIA World Factbook* (2002).

Note

1 There are some disagreements about the statistics in Kazakhstan. Official government sources state that Kazakhs do have a majority in the country, while other sources suggest a mere plurality (45–7 percent).

management (48 percent). Education was one of the few areas where Kazakhs (42 percent) maintained a small lead over Russians (36 percent) (2002).

Russians in the near abroad represent a unique diaspora with only limited commonalities to other dispersed immigrant communities. As a marooned imperial minority, Russians outside of Russia are most frequently compared to Germans who found themselves beached outside the rump successor states of the Hohenzollern and Habsburg empires.[6] Strong similarities also exist between offshore Russians and Englishmen in British India, Afrikaaners and other European settlers in South Africa and *pieds noirs* in Algeria. For Russians in the states where they represent a substantial percentage of the population (Kazakhstan, Latvia and Estonia), the communities are relatively contiguous with the Russian nation residing in the federation, causing them to resemble German minorities in interwar Eastern Europe. In other states (Georgia, Tajikistan, Uzbekistan, etc.), Russians are generally located in metropolitan areas and lack contiguity with the rest of the Russian nation. Therefore, the Russian diaspora after 1991 shares spatial distribution patterns with both the contiguous imperial (German and Austrian) and far-flung colonial (British and French) examples discussed above. I personally draw a parallel with Mexican settlers who ended up on the "wrong" side of the border at the conclusion of the Mexican–American War (1846–8). Mexicans in America's South-west saw the border cross over them rather than the other way around. Curiously, both the Mexicans and the Russians are consigned to a particular role in their "new" societies, i.e., immigrant rather than native, regardless of the history which put them there. Russians who migrated to northern Kazakhstan, Belarus and Ukraine fit especially well this analogy, since they never crossed anything that could be considered a formal political boundary.[7] The national delimitation of 1922–36, which formally set the internal borders of Soviet Central Asia (especially beneficial to the Kazakh SSR), and the "gift" of the Crimea by the Russian SFSR to the Ukrainian SSR in 1956 are now both seen as grave errors of magnanimity by Russian rightists and much of the Russian public.

Unlike peoples of other imperial diasporas, Russians did not consider themselves to be colonizing outsiders at the time of migration, with the exception of the Cossacks, who clearly represented frontier guards. Nor did they have the "mental preparation" of a more traditional diaspora. As stated earlier, most Russians saw the Soviet Union (and Romanov Russia before it) as their homeland and therefore would not consider themselves as "immigrants" in the sense that a Scotsman in eighteenth-century Hindustan, a German in nineteenth-century Galicia or a Frenchman in twentieth-century Algeria would have viewed themselves. As Rogers Brubaker has stated, "Russianess, like 'whiteness' in the US, was in a sense invisible; it was experienced not as a particular nationality but as the general norm, the zero-value, the universal condition against which other nationalities existed as particular and particularist 'deviations'" (1996: 49). In fact, Russians in the Russian Soviet Federated Socialist Republic (RSFSR) were denied the "special rights" of nationality conferred upon other titular nations in their republics or autonomous regions. There was the perception of a type of national trade-off whereby the Russians were "at home" anywhere in the USSR, while other nationalities received extra representation within their "homeland."[8]

Russians were in effect the earliest and most enthusiastic adopters of the idea of the *sovetskii narod* (the Soviet nation) and thus saw themselves not as immigrants, colonizers or invaders, but as mobile Soviet citizens regardless of what republic they lived in.[9] With the creation of hostile successor states aggressively seeking to nationalize the state by asserting the rights of the core nation over minorities (especially the Russian minority), Russians have had keen difficulty in coming to terms with their new status (Smith 1997: 75). Severed mentally, politically and geographically from their homeland, these "new" immigrants have had to rethink what it means to be part of a diaspora community and mentally to place themselves within that conceptual space.

Despite the uniqueness of the case of Russians outside of Russia, a critical treatment of Russians in the NIS does provide some interesting theoretical parallels with ethnic and identity politics in the postmodern age. All states are multinational, with only a few exceptions (notably the Republic of Korea and Iceland). Some of the earliest nation-states (e.g., France, Spain, Great Britain, etc.) minimized the ethno-cultural fractures within their states through the long and arduous process of "nationalizing homogenization by state authorities," which allowed hierarchical empires to be "transformed into relatively egalitarian nation-states based on a horizontal notion of equal citizenship" (Suny 1997: 7). Other states (e.g., Russia, Turkey, Romania, etc.) built or maintained state structures and crafted policies that relegated peripheral ethno-cultural groups to the status of "national minorities," groups permanently enshrined in their own difference and lacking (in most cases) full participation in the activities and benefits of the state. The Soviet Union, which assumed much of the multinational Russian state in 1917, oscillated in its policy toward national groups for a brief period, but ultimately chose to institutionalize national distinction within the state. This decision has visible and resounding repercussions today, as the legacy of Soviet nationality policy bears unintended fruit in the form of "projects of redemption" for erstwhile suppressed titular majorities[10] in their newly independent states. Ethnic Russians are now on the receiving end of biased nationality policy. By looking at how Russians are responding to this challenge, it is possible to draw some tentative conclusions on how other "marooned" nationalities and archipelago nations (Magyars in Romania, Serbs in Bosnia, etc.) will respond to the new realities imposed by globalization.

Nationalizing states as a catalyst for Russian action

Before the dissolution of the Soviet empire, nationalist elements in many of the non-Russian republics were clamoring for greater recognition of the rights of the titular majorities (often at the expense of the Russian and Russian-speaking populations). Mikhail S. Gorbachev's *glasnost* (openness) created an environment where increasingly nationalistically oriented elites could and did assume power, although these politicians were still required to work within the one-party system. After independence, cultural protection and promotion of the core nationality became institutionalized through political action. The Russian diaspora became the first target for these new policies. In *Nationalism Reframed*, Rogers Brubaker describes a:

> triad linking national minorities, the newly nationalizing states in which they live, and the external national 'homelands' to which they belong, or can be constructed as belonging, by ethnocultural affinity though not by legal citizenship . . . bound together in a single relational nexus.
>
> (1996: 4–5)

This theoretical concept is perhaps nowhere better manifested than in the post-Soviet successor states of Central Asia and the Baltics, where states as disparate as pluralistic Estonia and dictatorial Turkmenistan have followed strikingly similar trajectories since sloughing off the Soviet yoke in 1991.

There has been a spectrum of responses to the presence of Russians in the newly formed states that make up the post-Soviet space of Eurasia. In the Baltics – Estonia and Latvia in particular – nationalizing states disenfranchised the Russians (and other non-indigenous nationalities) with stringent citizenship requirements, including historical residency conditions (typically stipulating that an individual or his or her forebears had to be living in the state prior to Soviet annexation in 1940), language proficiency, loyalty oaths and other benchmarks, which many Russians are unable or unwilling to meet. In the case of Estonia, the Law on Aliens (1993) went beyond simple disenfranchisement and implied (as least to the Russian government) that Russians and other non-citizens[11] may be subject to expulsion in the future. Beyond denial of citizenship, the Russian community complains of loss of jobs,[12] inability to travel abroad, attempts at forcible assimilation, and calculated policies intended to provoke people into emigrating (Laitin 1998). Thus Russians, who form majorities in many areas of these states (upwards of 95 percent in some localities), are now stateless people without the ability to vote for their leaders or run for office, and whose guarantee of basic human rights within their state of residence remains tenuous. Latvia and Estonia defend the actions taken against its minority communities as an appropriate response to illegal migration conducted under the aegis of the occupying Soviet army (Birckenbach 1995).

In many Transcaucasian and Central Asian successor states, Russians and other nationalities are barred from political organization based on ethno-national affiliation. Kazakhstan, where Russians account for nearly a third of the population, and Georgia, where Russians represent only a tiny minority, have both taken this approach. Workarounds do exist, however – in Kazakhstan there are a number of political parties that are almost exclusively Russian in composition (*Yedinstvo* [Unity], Civic Contract and Democratic Progress), but even these groups, despite the fact that they are "playing by the rules," are often denied ballot space by the Kazakh authorities. Other organizations, especially Cossack political factions, have been treated even less kindly and refused registration.

In the singular case of Moldova, popular support for unification with neighboring Romania spurred a virulent reaction among the Slavic residents located predominately in the eastern part of the country. The result was the establishment of the Transdniestrian Moldavian Soviet Socialist Republic (TMSSR) on September 2, 1990. Two years later, ethnic warfare erupted between Russians and Ukrainians, who were seeking independence under a Transdniestrian Republic or unification with Russia or Ukraine, and Moldovans attempting to hold their brittle country together.

Russia's foreign policy: protection of its countrymen and provocation of its neighbors

The Russian Federation's initial approach to marooned Russians was ambiguous. Rather than granting automatic citizenship to all 25 million ethnic Russians and possibly creating a massive immigration dilemma, or announcing that Russians would not be allowed to immigrate, the federation instead opted for a middle path:

> The Russian citizenship law allows all former Soviet citizens who feel ethnically or emotionally attached to Russia to apply for Russian citizenship. Under international law, a state has a right to protect its citizens abroad, and Russian authorities have on numerous occasions insisted that they will indeed defend the rights of Russians in the former Soviet Union.
>
> (Baev and Kolstø 2003)

Ultimately, this ambiguous approach to citizenship among the near abroad Russians opened the door for Russia to become increasingly involved in the domestic politics of its post-Soviet neighbors and has been a tool for Russia to advance its own national interest.

Tamara Resler identifies a host of mechanisms which an external state may attempt to employ to affect the treatment of national minorities, including political incentives, such as censure by the world community or admittance into international or regional organizations; economic or humanitarian aid linked to the treatment of minorities; aid given directly to national minorities by states or subnational or transnational groups; mediation of inter-ethnic conflict or other crises; bilateral and global agreements on the treatment of minorities; sponsoring educational forums and providing experts to help in developing nationality policies; and simply serving as an example of how other states ought to treat their minorities (Resler 2003). Russia has tried nearly all of these over the past decade. Within a year of the dissolution of the Soviet Union, the Russian leadership, at the behest of the radical right and the military, began making the case of Russians in the near abroad an integral part of Moscow's foreign policy. *The Guidelines of the Foreign Policy of the Russian Federation* issued in 1992 represented a "far-reaching approach according to which Russian minorities should be considered not only as a priority problem, but also as an important asset for Russia's foreign policy" (Baev and Kolstø 2003). Russia, working within the parameters of international law regarding citizens abroad, began actively to involve itself in the interests of Russians and Russian-speakers[13] in the Baltics and the Commonwealth of Independent States (CIS).

Since the early 1990s, the Russian Federation has steadily acquired additional venues to project its influence in the name of protecting ethnic (and linguistic) countrymen abroad. Within a year of joining the UN as a separate and independent state, the Russian Federation was demanding that the UN General Secretary, Boutros Boutros-Ghali, act to stop human rights violations of Russians in the Baltic states. Also in 1992, Russia raised the issue of discrimination against Russians and Russian-speakers in the Baltics with the Commission on Security and Cooperation in Europe (CSCE). Throughout the 1990s and into 2003, Russia used the CSCE, now known as the Organization for Security and Cooperation in Europe (OSCE), as a mechanism to involve itself in the affairs of its neighbors over the issue of the treatment of ethnic Russians. In 1995, Russia established the Council of Compatriots within the Duma and began setting aside funding for support of russophones and ethnic Russians in neighboring states. The same year, President Yeltsin used Russia's leadership position in the Commonwealth of Independent States to demand an end to discrimination of Russians in member states (Hagendoorn *et al.* 2001: 77).

The Baltics have been the focal point of much of Russia's multilateral posturing over the issue of its external countrymen. Perhaps this is due to the high level of integration the Baltics have pursued with Europe since independence, combined with clear signals that Estonia, Latvia and Lithuania wish to distance themselves from Russia (none joined the Russian-dominated Commonwealth of Independent States). In 1996 Russia joined the Council of Europe, which provided "an additional rostrum from which to express concern for the plight of the Russian minorities abroad" (Baev and Kolstø 2003). The following year, the VII International Session of the Social Movement "Legal Assembly," titled "The Russian Diaspora: Problems and Rights of Fellow Countrymen Abroad," noted that in a number of states of the former USSR, especially in Latvia and Estonia, "there are continuing grave violations of natural and inalienable human rights in relation to persons belonging to the Russian diaspora" (Bowring 2002).

Since assuming office, President Putin has shown he is a campaigner for the rights of offshore Russians. The president's early relations with his counterparts in the NIS were heavily informed by a desire to improve the status of Russians and Russian-speakers. In 2001, Putin called on the president of Latvia to implement "changes to the country's policy toward [Russian] 'compatriots in Latvia' – a reference to Latvian citizenship and language laws that unjustly exclude many Russians from political, civic and economic life" (*Russia Journal* 2001). In late summer of 2002, Moscow signaled that it would allocate some 470 million rubles (US$15 million) during the 2003–5 timeframe for supporting Russians abroad. Most of this will be spent on developing infrastructure for maintaining relations with the diaspora (TASS 2002). For some politicians, such as Aman Tuleev, Putin's measures do not go far enough. He and other activists continue to advocate "stiff and adequate measures" to ensure better treatment of Russians in the Baltics and Central Asia, including economic sanctions against states where the rights of Russians are being encroached upon (Vinogradov and Ilyichev 2002). The lead-up to Estonia and Latvia's popular votes to join the European Union provided a valuable opportunity for Russia to spotlight the ambiguous situation in which its countrymen would be placed after these states joined the EU.

Even in countries that have a relatively small Russian community, significant efforts are under-way to insure the continued maintenance of ties to the Russian Federation, knowledge of Russian language, history and culture, and sustained Russian identity in the face of economic and political challenges. According to Valerii Svarchuk, a member of the Council of Compatriots in the Duma, Russia provides substantial amounts of money though its embassy in Georgia to insure that ethnic Russians will have access to educational and cultural resources. Selected students from the country's 180 Russian-language schools are given the opportunity to study in Russia for free, and other forms of aid are also provided. Svarchuk believes it especially important for the Russian government to act on the behalf of its fellow countrymen in Georgia, since Russians are barred from political activity based on national affiliation (*Rosbalt* 2002).[14]

It is clear that the Russian Federation is spending a great deal of effort on foreign policy initiatives and very little on engaging in activity that could be perceived as actively encouraging a "return to the homeland." Returning Russians frequently complain that going "back" to the Russian Federation is worse than staying put (personal communication, interviews conducted with ethnic Russians in Kazakhstan). The website "Russians in Tajikistan" criticizes President Putin's policy toward returning countrymen as a form of slave labor:

The increasingly racist Moscow government has been looking for a way to prevent non-Russians from entering the country in search of jobs – especially the darker-skinned non-Russians, such as people from [the] Caucasus. As a solution, Russia now considers using ethnic Russian refugees as the buffer against other unwanted aliens. Facing the same lack of legal protection and competing for the same bottom-level jobs, due to the widespread discrimination in employment, the refugees are bound to make the settling in of other immigrant groups more difficult, or such is the Russian government's hope ... Another plan Moscow has for ethnic Russians is serving as a kind of slave force to work the lands that few Russian citizens are willing to inhabit. According to President Putin's statement, such people are most needed in Siberia and other such regions, and not in the warmer parts of the country where the refugees from the subtropical Central Asia tend to gravitate to. Putin asserted that Moscow would have to "rigidly control" where such migrants settled. One is left to guess about the form and the extent of that control. Time to dust off those old cattle cars?

(Yereshenko 2003)

According to *US News & World Report*, "only 'forced refugees' get the $411 in welcome money. The Russian government is trying to improve conditions where Russians live so that they do not return to Russia" (*Migration Point* 1994). Arguably this is due to the fact that having the Russian minority ensconced in adjacent states provides Russia with a lingering reason to involve itself in the domestic politics of its neighbors.

The diaspora's role in Russia's domestic politics

Initially, the battle cry of protecting the Russians in the "near abroad" was monopolized by the nationalist right and hard-core communist reactionaries, but the clear benefits of supporting countrymen in the near abroad quickly caused the issue to move into the Russian mainstream. In the early 1990s, the tenor of the discourse surrounding ethnic Russians in the NIS contained a strong irredentist, if not revanchist, flavor. For many policy analysts in the West, the seemingly virulent obsession with the fate of Russians in adjoining states is seen as a potentially destabilizing force, since the federation had a "permanent excuse to express concern about the status of these communities, and demand that Russian forces protect them."[15] Very public pronouncements by the Russians in their bilateral relationships with former states of the USSR demonstrated the centrality of the case of the Russian diaspora, e.g., a warning to Latvia which asserted:

the activities of the state Duma as regards the development of Russo-Latvian relations, including the creation of a legal basis for their development, will be closely connected with the normalization of a legal status of the Russian-speaking population in Latvia and full observance of its political, economic, cultural and social rights.

(TASS 1994)

Such language was not ignored by the international community concerned with Russian revanchism.

In 1990, Nobel laureate and arch-conservative Alexander Solzhenitsyn publicly called for the creation of a "Greater Slavic State" made up of Russia, Ukraine, Belarus and northern Kazakhstan to replace the USSR, setting a rather ominous precedent for the future. The leadership of the country (Putin, and Yeltsin before him) is undoubtedly influenced by the extreme right and often attempts to ride on the wave of popular sentiment created by those such as the bombast of nationalist zealots Vladimir Zhirinovskii. Zhirinovskii built his power base in the early 1990s by playing on revanchist sentiment among Russians who were marginalized by the painful shift to capitalism and the relative demise of Russian (read Soviet) influence in world politics. The mistreatment of ethnic Russians in nationalizing states, formerly under the control of Moscow, made grist for the mill. Zhirinovskii, who demanded a reconstituted Russia with all former territories, including Finland, never wielded much power, but his "call to arms" in support of offshore Russians clearly impacted policy throughout the federation at both the federal and regional level and certainly won him votes among the disaffected Russian masses.

Following Zhirinovskii's lead, a number of other "brown" politicians have trumpeted the rights of Russian countrymen in the near abroad. Most notable among these is Dmitry Rogozin. In his first interview as chairman of the International Affairs Committee of the Russian Federation in February 2000, Rogozin defined Russia's main task as insuring the safety of ethnic Russians in post-Soviet successor states:

> It is permissible to employ a full array of instruments, from the political up to and including the military, for exerting pressure upon aggressor countries. Discrimination against Russian subjects and threats to their lives, let alone taking their lives, amounts to a threat to the Russian state itself and its national security. We have 25 million compatriots in the near abroad. That problem is our number one problem, a national security problem.
>
> (Foye 2000)

Rogozin also suggested tying economic cooperation with individual states in the near abroad to the status of its countrymen in those states and converting the Russian diaspora into an "intermediary for handling major economic agreements in those countries" (ibid.).

Besides the rightists, the military also played an important part in relations with the diaspora. In fact, Russian concerns over the poor treatment of its countrymen in the Baltics proved to be a sticking point which delayed troop withdrawal for several years after independence (Simonsen 2001). General Lebed, one of the principal forces in the Russian government during the mid-1990s, took an active interest in the fortunes of Russia's countrymen in the borderlands. In 1993, *The Independent* asserted, "Much of Russian policy in this area [Russians in the near abroad], though, seems to be fixed by the military – sometimes by the Defence Ministry in Moscow, other times by local commanders such as General Alexander Lebed in Moldova" (Higgins 1993).

Lebed earned himself a worldwide reputation in the 1992–3 Moldovan conflict, as he was able to end the bloodshed while simultaneously supporting Russian and Ukrainian secessionists in Transdniestria. Lebed had traveled to Moldova incognito in early summer of 1992 and shortly thereafter took control of the Fourteenth Army in response to the advance of Moldovan troops on the city of Bendery. Lebed voiced "strong support for the regime in Tiraspol [the capital of Transdniestria] and referred to Transdniestria and even the town of Bendery [not considered part of historical Russian claims] on the west bank as constituting 'a small part of Russia'" (Kolstø *et al.* 1993). His decisive action against both the "fascists" of Moldova and the "crooks" of the Transdniester Republic earned him a solid reputation as a bastion of patriotic communism as well as the protector of the Slavs east of the Dnestr.

Lebed took a somewhat ambiguous approach to politics in the early 1990s, refusing the requests of both Boris Yelstin and, later, Alexander Rutskoi (leader of an attempted putsch in 1993) to engage in partisan politics, responding that the military should "remain neutral in such matters," although he did briefly hold a seat in the Supreme Soviet of the separatist Transdniester Moldovan Republic during the fall of 1993. In 1995, Lebed, the former chairman of the Congress of Russian Communities,[16] declared that special Russian troops should be ready to "protect the Russians in the 'near abroad'" (Hagendoorn *et al.* 2001: 77). This statement, in conjunction with his other famous quote of 1995, "First we will act, then we will explain," rather ominously underscored the nexus between Russia's concerns for its countrymen abroad, its own security, and its greater geopolitical concerns. In an interview published in *Moscow News*, Lebed addressed the issue of the near abroad head on:

> Our power must not and will not come into conflict with the Muslim world or with the Catholic world. . . . Russia, and it alone, is able to organize anew this spiritual space. . . . [T]he peoples of the former USSR already understand that until recently they lived in a great country and now survive in petty states without any help or love from a prince beyond the ocean [i.e., the United States]. Precisely together with Russia will they occupy a worthy place in the world.
>
> (Dunlop 1997)

Lebed's popularity among the working classes remained strong throughout the 1990s and for a period he seemed to be in a position to assume the presidency after Yeltsin's departure. Until his death in a helicopter accident in April 2002, he continued to be identified in and outside of Russia as an unflinching champion for the rights of the millions of ethnic Russians living beyond the borders of the Russian Federation.

Russian responses to the federation's overtures

Despite predictions to contrary, Russians are on the whole adjusting to their new found position in the non-Slavic successor states of the Soviet Union. Those

Russians who vehemently rejected the new political, cultural and economic realities of the Newly Independent States typically chose to emigrate to the federation in the early 1990s (Chinn and Kaiser 1996: 12). Those who remained have begun to assume many of the characteristics of a diaspora community. Like the Uzbeks, Ukrainians and Armenians who lived as "third-class citizens"[17] in Soviet republics where they did not form the titular majority, Russians are now coping with the demands of living and working in a society where they do not form the elite. Yet, it is clear that the Russian Federation will not abandon them to the fate faced by minorities from other states (even if that is what many ethnic Russians in the NIS would prefer). Therefore, their participation in the daily political life of the countries in which they reside is becoming increasingly important, regardless of whether or not they are allowed to participate in political organization based on ethno-national affiliation. The Newly Independent States "must find ways to manage the seemingly inherent conflicts among their multinational populations – or face an escalation of inter-national conflict that can threaten their independence and complicate an already delicate relationship between them and the Russian Federation" (ibid.: 14). Although the Russians have been sapped of much of their power in the wake of the Soviet Union's collapse, certain vestiges still remain. By playing on nationalist sentiment in the Russian Federation, ethnic Russians are able to develop a system of proxy politics that, in many cases, more than compensates for the loss of citizenship rights or the ability to form ethnically based political parties.

Such groups as the Russian Society in Latvia are stepping on to the international stage in an attempt to improve the status of disenfranchised and disaffected Russians in the NIS. On the eve of Latvia's vote to join the EU, Alexander Rzavins, minority rights adviser to the chairman of the Russian Society, criticized Latvia's ongoing reticence to address the issue of citizenship for its Russian-speaking inhabitants. Rzavins, in what has become a familiar refrain, stated, "We are not foreigners. Most of us were born here and we consider this country our country" (Harding 2003). The Russian Society of Latvia is one of several Russian activist groups in the Baltics which submits reports directly to Moscow on the conditions of Russians in the near abroad. Others include the Latvian Human Rights Committee, the Russian Community of Latvia, the Russian National and Cultural society of Daugavpils, the Russian Community of Estonia, the Estonian United Russian People's Party and the Estonian Human Rights Information Centre. These and other groups have attempted to enlist the help of the Russian Federation as well as international organizations such as the OSCE in the attempt to effect political change in their new countries of residence. Similar groups exist in Kazakhstan, including *Lad* (Harmony), the Russian Community and the Russkaya Obshchina organization, led by the outspoken Genadiy Belyakov.

In 1996, Pål Kolstø identified four possible political trajectories for Russians outside of Russia: 1) loyalty toward the historical boundaries of the Soviet/tsarist state up to and including attempts to resurrect it; 2) loyalty toward the (very large) rump state of the Russian Federation; 3) aspirations for a new (Russian) nation-state; and 4) loyalty to the (new) state of residence. However, it is increasingly apparent that most Russians outside the federation do not fit neatly into these categories. Instead, they are engaged in a complex ongoing negotiation of identity based upon a unique historical transformation (Bhabha 1994: 2). Russian elites understand that maintaining constant links with the motherland and powerful actors within the national homeland remains vital to assuring this peculiar power base. Communications technologies such as mobile phones, satellite television and the World Wide Web enable a vibrant two-way flow of information between members of the Russian nation in and outside of the federation. The Internet has proved an especially powerful tool of empowerment for the Russian diaspora in the NIS. As Frank Louis Rusciano points out, the Internet endows marginalized groups with "the ability to 'tell one's story' [and] affect one's political conditions" (2001). Russians in the near abroad, who tend to be more educated, cosmopolitan and tech-savvy than their indigene counterparts (with the possible exception of those in the Baltic states), have been well positioned to take advantage of the Internet's possibilities for national identity-building and maintaining the linkages necessary to conduct proxy politicking.[18] Russians have built (digital) bridges to compatriots in the Russian Federation, other NIS states and even farther afield (the US, Australia and Western Europe), thus resewing the seams of a nation with little regards for the boundaries of states.[19]

As Leda Cooks (2001) argues, the Internet has had a powerful effect on identities among diaspora communities, especially in relation to the concepts of state and nation; however, the peculiarities of identity formation in cyberspace do not "erase the hierarchies or annihilate the old markers of membership" among ethnic groups. Russians are scrambling to remain or regain a position of dominance in lands where Russian hegemony has been, until quite recently, an indisputable fact. Cyberspace provides the means to bypass and circumvent traditional state sovereignty and transcend geographically bound entities (Dougherty and Pfaltz-graff 2001: 156), thus allowing web-enabled communities a great deal of latitude in the way in which they confront issues of nationality, especially when large communities of co-nationals already populate the conceptual space of the Internet.

Arjun Appadurai (1996) has eloquently described the effects of the new technologies on "imagination,"[20] especially the contrived notions of state and national identity. Among the Russians beached by the ebbing of the waters that made up the Soviet Union, imagination is an extremely powerful force in identity-creating in a new world of freshly minted, yet incontestably weak states and re-emerging, reinvigorated nations. For many deterritorialized groups, the challenging confrontation with modernity and globalization, combined with the "inability" to think their way out of the imaginary nation-state, results in violence in the name of embracing the very imaginary they seek to escape (Appadurai 1996: 166). The newly realized Russian diaspora in the Russian Federation's borderlands, however, provides an interesting counter to Appadurai's theoretical "challenged" nation. As the historical shock troops of modernity, and to a lesser extent of globalization, the Russians occupy a unique niche in postmodern, postnational society that enables them to manifest a least of few of the traits that Appadurai predicts for a new paradigm based on "complex, non-territorial, postnational forms of allegiance" (ibid.). In effect, Russian national identity in the near abroad increasingly resembles *transnational*[21] rather than nationalist, anti-state or anti-national.[22] In fact, Rogozin's comments quoted earlier on the importance of off-shore Russians as economic intermediaries for the federation's interactions with the Newly Independent States reflect some foreshadowing of this new role.

Conclusion: the future of the Russian diaspora in the NIS

The Russian diaspora in the Newly Independent States is by no means uniform. A slow exodus of Russians continues from Transcaucasia and the Central Asian states (other than Kazakhstan). Poverty, lack of opportunity, and ethnic and religious strife are seen as the principal drivers of the "return" to Russia. As mentioned previously, as of 2001 there remained only 19 million Russians in the near abroad, down from 25 million in 1991 (Goble 2001). The most precipitous decline in the Russian population is in those areas where "local wars" have occurred. According to Tom Heleniak, "The rate of return among the states varies considerably, ranging from 50 percent in the three Transcaucasus states and Tajikistan to barely 1 percent from Ukraine and Belarus" (2001). The ethnic conflicts in Abkhazia, Nagorno-Karabakh and Ossetia, and the Tajik civil war, undoubtedly contribute to this vast disparity.

As Russians depart, the federation's interest in maintaining its "special relationship" with the region is unlikely to wane; however, the role of Russian countrymen in foreign policy will be significantly decreased. Yet, the states of Central Asia are not free to do as they will in regards to lingering Russians. Economically weak and politically stunted, the Newly Independent States along Russia's southern border are inextricably tied to Moscow whether they like it or not. Geopolitics dictates that, if these states engage in "nationalizing" that smacks of ethnic cleansing or apartheid vis-à-vis the Russians, the federation's reaction will surely be swift and unkind.

In the mid-1990s, Martha Brill Olcott reported that Kazakhstan's offshore Russians were finding it difficult to adapt to their nationalizing state of residence, and that the majority of the educated elite planned to leave the country when possible due to their poor chances of employment as a result of their status as a minority (2002: 177, 179). Yet, most Russians, especially those in the northern part of the country, have decided to stay, leaving a substantial population contiguous with the Russian Federation. In my own research conducted among Russian elites in the country's economic capital, Almaty, I found that a vast majority believe they will fare better by staying in Kazakhstan. Some respondents did try and "make it" in the Russian Federation but found that treatment there was worse than in their home state. The continued presence of large numbers of ethnic Russians in Kazakhstan will undoubtedly leave the door open to continued political interest from Moscow and future intrigues. Barring the unlikely event of open warfare between nationalities in Kazakhstan, the Russian Federation will probably be content to use ethno-cultural questions to advance its own national interest rather than pushing for territorial aggrandizement or autonomy for Kazakhstan's Russian populace.

Due to the undeniable benefits associated with EU accession and the economic dynamism of the region, Russians in the Baltic states are sure to stay put. Despite the inequities in Estonian, Latvian and Lithuanian society faced by Russians and Russian-speakers, the trade-off is compelling. Russia is unlikely to "abandon" its co-nationals in the Baltics, since the region represents a valuable gateway to Europe. According to Menon:

> The status of ethnic Russians in the near abroad will remain part of Russia's political discourse, given the allure of nationalism and its utility to demagogues . . . Controversies centering on the Russian diaspora have created more friction between Russia and the Baltic states (principally Latvia and Estonia) and will continue to do so. Nevertheless, the problem has been confined to the political sphere and has not involved the military for several reasons. Russia's leaders know that attempts to intimidate the Baltics would mobilize anti-Russian sentiments in the West and strengthen support for bringing them into NATO. Conversely, the leaders of Estonia and Latvia realize the need to reconcile their projects for nation building with Russia's interests. Russians in the Baltic countries have adjusted to irksome circumstances even when, as in the case of language and citizenship laws, they resent them.
>
> (Menon 2001)

The reason he gives for the last assertion is based in *realpolitik* – Russians in the Baltics are living the good life compared to their countrymen across the border. Furthermore, most Russians in the Baltics are urban-dwellers, and Russian policies for "returning" countrymen have focused mostly in relocation to the countryside (Nikolaev 1994: 120).

The Russian exodus from Kyrgyzstan dropped precipitously at the turn of the century, owing in part to President Askar Akayev's declaration of Russian as a state language and an increasing perception of ethnic equality between Kyrgyz and Russians (*Pravda* 2001). Elsewhere in Central Asia, Russia has steadily re-exerted its influence over a number of strategically important states, specifically Kazakhstan and Uzbekistan, often with concern for its countrymen informing much of the discourse surrounding its relations with these states. As mentioned earlier, there is increasing talk in Moscow and Washington of a "Russian Monroe Doctrine" that is being applied to Central Asia and the Caucasus.[23]

Rather than directly confronting the United States, which had exponentially increased its aid, presence and focus on the region in the wake of September 11th, 2001, the Russian Federation instead filled the vacuum left by the Americans as attention turned from the "War on Terror" to toppling Saddam Hussein's regime in Iraq. The following year, a Russian senator, Mikhail Margelov, asserted that "From the historical and geographical points of view, we [Russians] were and always will be there in Central Asia" (BBC 2002a). Although this type of bombast likely endangers the position of Russians in the new states of Central Asia, the benefits to domestic politics are unquestioned.[24] By stirring up nationalist sentiment among the domestic population and constantly reasserting Russia's special relationship with Central Asia, it is possible to counter the deleterious impact of the recent US military presence in the region which has been a blow to the Russian psyche (Torbakov 2003).

The case of Transdniestria remains a complicated and destabilizing influence on the Black Sea region. More than a decade after open conflict subsided, Transdniestria remains autonomous though it lacks recognition from it neighbors and the international community. According to the BBC, "a younger and apparently more energetic Russian leadership has given new confidence to Transdniestria" (BBC 2000). The Russian Federation remains ensconced in the affairs of the troubled region, yet seems to offer little in the way of solutions.

For the offshore Russians, the embrace of separatism and/or anti-titular nationalism is unlikely to produce anything except bitter fruit, since the Russian Federation has shown that its allegiance to diasporan causes is inherently self-serving. Russia has little desire to incorporate breakaway republics, as witnessed by the Abkhazian and Transdniestrian debacles. Instead, actors within the Russian Federation will exert leverage on the ethnic Russians to achieve tactical and strategic goals. Likewise, Russians have little chance of fully integrating themselves into the societies in which they live (at least in the short term). The nationalizing states of the NIS are unlikely to engage in overt apartheid, but it is clear Russians will continue to be shut out of the upper echelons of society. There is hope, however. As alluded to earlier, the Russians are beginning to assume the mantle of a transnational identity. Like the Levantines of the eastern Mediterranean, Russians of the near abroad may prove to be powerful non-state actors performing the role of go-between for the Russian Federation and its formerly co-joined neighbors.

Notes

1 Russians outside the RSFSR represented the largest group of people living outside their "homeland" or lacking a homeland. The total number of those considered national minorities in the USSR totaled 73 million (Suny 2001).

2 For an in-depth analysis of the process of identity formation among Russians outside of Russia in the immediate post-Soviet period, see Laitin 1998.

3 A national or ethnic minority is defined as any group that a) forms a numerical minority in a given state, b) does not dominate politically, c) differs from the majority population due to ethnic, linguistic or religious characteristics, and d) expresses feelings of intra-group solidarity in preserving their own culture, traditions and language (Minority Rights Group 1991: xiv).

4 I have purposefully chosen to exclude Ukraine and Belorussia from this analysis on account of the unique nature of inter-ethnic relations between Great Russians (Russians), Little Russians (Ukrainians) and White Russians (Belorussians). For a discussion of this topic, see Evgenii Golovakh, Natalia Panina and Nikolai Churilov's "Russians in Ukraine," in Shlapentokh *et al.* 1994; and Chinn and Kaiser 1996.

5 The Kazakh population was reduced by 39.8 percent between 1926 and 1937 (Masanov and Erlan 2002).

6 For an interesting analysis of the similarities of these two imperial diasporas, see Rogers Brubaker's *Nationalism Reframed* (1996). Despite Brubaker's thoughtful comparison, there

are few if any geopolitical imperatives that would cause Russia to follow the irredentist path trod by Germany in the interwar period.

7 Dmitri Trenin recounts the oft-muttered lament of Russians that the Crimea and other parts of the historical Russian state are now in foreign countries while the "alien" territory of Chechnya is still tethered to the Russian Federation (2002: 170).

8 See Suny 2001: 252.

9 Although the constituent republics were nominally separate geographic entities with the ability to secede from the union at any time, the reality was that the USSR formed a unified state in all the crucial ways.

10 Titular majority refers to the nominal majority nationality in a given republic; thus the Russians were the titular majority in the Russian FSSR, the Estonians in the Estonian SSR and so on. With the exception of the Kazakh SSR, titular majorities also formed demographic majorities.

11 Some news reports in Israel at the time theorized a connection between the measures and a resurgence of anti-Semitism in the Baltics, since Jews living in the Baltics were almost universally stripped of citizenship based on their lack of language proficiency (see, e.g., Ruby 1992). Under the USSR's nationality regime, persons of Jewish extraction were categorized as *yevrei* (Jew) on their internal passports regardless of where they were born or what language they spoke (most spoke Russian as their first language despite their republic of residence).

12 For example, the careers of pharmacist, lawyer, fireman, doctor, policeman and, of course, elected politician are no longer open to non-citizens, regardless of talent or experience.

13 From 1995 onward, there is little distinction among the two, as both are referred to as *sootechestvenniki*, or 'fellow countrymen' or 'compatriots' (Hagendoorn *et al.* 2001: 77).

14 Due to Russian migratory patters in Transcaucasia, which have historically been limited to the cities, regional organization is impossible. Other ethnic groups such as the Azeris do not face the same challenges, since their population centers are rural rather than urban.

15 See also Dunlop 2000.

16 The organization was created in 1993 by Moscow-based political entrepreneurs with the aim of reuniting a putative Russian nation within a territorially enlarged state.

17 Non-Russian immigrants to other republics benefited neither from the *korenizatsiia*, or "indigenization," that favored titular majorities, nor from imperial policy that offered better jobs, housing, etc., to Russians.

18 See Emory and Bates 2001 for more on how Internet use is especially high among the elite in formerly communist countries of Eastern Europe and the Soviet Union.

19 Christoph Engel (2000) refers to this phenomenon as the creation of "communities without propinquity."

20 Appadurai argues that technology has enabled imagination to become a collective, social fact no longer tethered to art, mythology or ritual or dependent on charismatic individuals who would manipulate imagination for their own ends (1996: 5–6).

21 As Rosenau asserts, "Transnational behavior is conceived as derived from a multiplicity of institutionalized and ad hoc arrangements though which governments and nongovernmental collectivities accommodate each other and, in so doing, come to share responsibility for the course of events" (1997: 51).

22 This type of new national identity bears some resemblance to Kolstø's theoretical "New Cossack" identity (1996). Building on Cossack identity formation in the tsarist period, Kolstø posits that some Russians in the near abroad may pick and choose aspects of their identity from the environs while maintaining a core attachment to the Russian *ethnos*.

23 In Transcaucasia, the situation is not closely tied to ethnic Russians, since very few remain in the region.

24 Even more dangerous than Margelov's antics are the isolated cases of outright political intrigue, such as the November 1999 plot by a dozen citizens of the Russian Federation and ten ethnic Russian citizens of Kazakhstan to start an uprising to seize political power

in Ust-Kamenogorsk. Their intentions were to establish a republic called "Russian Land" in north-eastern Kazakhstan.

References

Appadurai, A. (1996) *Modernity at Large: Cultural Dimensions of Globalization*. Minneapolis: University of Minnesota Press.

Baev, P., and Kolstø, P. (2003) "Russian Minorities in the Former Soviet Union," International Peace and Research Center, Oslo, Norway, online: http://www.prio.no/html/osce-russianminorities.htm (downloaded March 3, 2003).

Barrington, L. W., Herron, E. S., and Silver, B. D. (2002) "The Motherland is Calling: Views of Homeland Among Russians in the Near Abroad," online: www.msu.edu/~bsilver/Rodina2002.pdf (downloaded February 28, 2003).

BBC (2000) "Two Moldovas Celebrate Independence," *BBC Worldwide Monitoring*, August 27.

——(2002a) "Uzbek Historian Criticizes Russian Senator's Statements about Central Asia," *BBC Worldwide Monitoring*, February 17.

——(2002b) "Slav Movement Concerned over 'Pressure' on Ethnic Russians in Kazakhstan," *BBC Worldwide Monitoring*, April 21.

Bhabha, H. K. (1994) *The Location of Culture*. London: Routledge.

Birckenbach, H. (1995) "Fact-finding as Part of Preventive Diplomacy: Experience of the Citizenship Conflicts in Estonia and Latvia," *Peace Research*, November.

Bowring, B. (2002) "Austro-Marxism's Last Laugh? The Struggle for Recognition of National-Cultural Autonomy for Rossians and Russians," *Europe-Asia Studies*, vol. 54, no. 2.

Brubaker, R. (1996) *Nationalism Reframed: Nationhood and the National Question in the New Europe*. Cambridge: Cambridge University Press.

Chinn, J., and Kaiser R. (1996) *Russians as the New Minority: Ethnicity and Nationalism in Soviet Successor States*. Boulder, CO: Westview Press.

Cooks, L. (2001) "Negotiating National Identity and Social Movements in Cyberspace," in Ebo, Bosah (ed.) *Cyberimperialism?: Global Relations in the New Electronic Frontier*. Westport, CT: Praeger.

Dougherty, J. E., and Pfaltzgraff, R. L. (2001) *Contending Theories of International Relations: A Comprehensive Survey*. 5th edn, New York: Longman.

Dunlop, J. B. (1997) "Aleksandr Lebed and Russian Foreign Policy," *SAIS Review*, vol. 17, no. 1, pp. 47–72.

——(2000) "Tightening the Screws in Russia," *Weekly Standard*, January 24.

Emory, M., and Bates, B. J. (2001) "Creating New Relations: The Internet in Central and Eastern Europe," in Ebo, Bosah (ed.) *Cyberimperialism?: Global Relations in the New Electronic Frontier*. Westport, CT: Praeger.

Engel, C. (2000) "The Internet and the Nation State," in Engel, Christoph, and Heller, Kenneth H. (eds) *Understanding the Impact of Global Networks on Social, Political and Cultural Values*. Baden-Baden: Nomos Verlagsgellschaft.

Foye, S. (2000) "An Ill-Wind Blows in Moscow?" *The Fortnight in Review*, vol. 6, no. 3. Online: http://russia.jamestown.org/pubs/view/for_006_003_001.htm (downloaded February 1, 2003).

Goble, P. (2001) "Russian Presence in Former Republics Declines," *RFE/RL Newsline*, vol. 5, no. 149.

Hagendoorn, K., Linssen, H. and Tumanov, S. (2001) *Intergroup Relations in States of the Former Soviet Union: The Perception of Russians*. Hove, East Sussex: Psychology Press.

Harding, G. (2003) "Latvia's Stateless Russians," *Washington Times*, September 19.

Heleniak, T. (2001) "Ethnic Unmixing and Forced Migration in the Transition States," *Transition Newsletter* [World Bank Group], online: www.worldbank.org/html/prddr/trans/julaug99/pgspgs8–11.htm (downloaded August 23, 2003).

Higgins, A. (1993) "Russia Intent on Offering Protection to its Diaspora," *The Independent*, July 20.

Knight, A. (1993) *Beria: Stalin's First Lieutenant*. Princeton, NJ: Princeton Academic Press.

Kolstø, P. (1996) "The New Russian Diaspora – an Identity of its Own?," *Ethnic and Racial Studies*, vol. 19, no. 3.

Kolstø P., Edemsky, A., and Kalashnikova, N. (1993) "The Dniester Conflict: Between Irredentism and Separatism," *Europe–Asia Studies*, vol. 45, no. 6, p. 977.

Laitin, D. (1998) *Identity in Formation: Russian-Speaking Populations in the Near Abroad*. Ithaca, NY: Cornell University Press.

Masanov, N., and Erlan, K. (eds) (2002) "The Nationalities Question in Post-Soviet Kazakhstan," Institute of Developing Economies, November 6, online: http://www.ide.go.jp/English/Publish/Mes/51.html (downloaded March 1, 2003).

Menon, R. (2001) "Structural Constraints on Russian Diplomacy," *Orbis*, vol. 45, no. 4, pp. 579–96.

Migranian, A. (1994) "Russia and the Near Abroad," *Nezavisimaia Gazeta*, January 12; translated in *Current Digest of the Post-Soviet Press*, vol. 46, no. 6, pp. 1–4.

Migration Point (1994) "Immigration Laws," no. 12 (May).

Minority Rights Group (1991) *World Directory of Minorities*. Harlow: Longman.

Nikolaev, S. (1994) "Russians in Uzbekistan," in Shlapentokh, V., Sendich, M., and Payin, E. (eds) *The New Russian Diaspora: Russian Minorities in the Former Soviet Republics*. Armonk, NY: M. E. Sharpe.

Olcott, M. B. (2002) *Kazakhstan: Unfulfilled Promise*. Washington, DC: Carnegie Endowment for International Peace.

Payin, E. (1994) "The Empire and the Russians: Historical Aspects," in Shlapentokh, V., Sendich, M., and Payin, E. (eds) *The New Russian Diaspora: Russian Minorities in the Former Soviet Republics*. Armonk, NY: M. E. Sharpe.

Pravda (2001) "Number of Russians Willing to Move to Russia Reduces in Kirghizia," October 31.

Resler, T. J. (2003) "Foreign Influence on National Minority Rights," online: http://www.acdis.uiuc.edu/homepage_docs/pubs_docs/S&P_docs/S&P_VIII-4/foreign_influence.html (downloaded September 1, 2003).

Rosbalt (2002) "*Russkie Gruzii: potentsial migratsii ne ischerpan*" [Russians in Georgia: The migration issue is not yet settled], January 11, online: http://www.rosbalt.ru/2002/11/01/72205.html (downloaded February 14, 2003).

Rosenau, J. N. (1997) *Along the Domestic–Foreign Frontier: Exploring Governance in a Turbulent World*. Cambridge: Cambridge University Press.

Ruby, W. (1992) "The Jews of Estonia are Feeling the Heat," *Jerusalem Post*, July 21.

Rusciano, F. L. (2001) "The Three Faces of Cyberimperialism," in Ebo, Bosah (ed.) *Cyberimperialism?: Global Relations in the New Electronic Frontier*. Westport, CT: Praeger.

Russia Journal (2001) "Contested Openness," April 27.

Shlapentokh, V., Sendich, M., and Payin, E. (eds) (1994) *The New Russian Diaspora: Russian Minorities in the Former Soviet Republics*. Armonk, NY: M. E. Sharpe.

Simonsen, S. G. (2001) "Compatriot Games: Explaining the 'Diaspora Linkage' in Russia's Military Withdrawal from the Baltic States," *Europe–Asia Studies*, vol. 53, no. 5.

Smith, G. (1997) "The Russian Diaspora: Identity, Citizenship and Homeland," in Bradshaw, Michael J. (ed.) *Geography and Transition in the Post-Soviet Republics*. Chichester: John Wiley & Sons.

Suny, R. G. (1997) "The Empire Strikes Out: Imperial Russia, 'National' Identity, and Theories of Empire," paper delivered at the University of Chicago Conference "Empire and Nations: The Soviet Union and the Non-Russian Peoples," October 24–6; pubd in *A State of Nations: Empire and Nation-Making in the Age of Lenin and Stalin*, ed. R. G. Suny and T. Martin. Oxford: Oxford University Press, 2001.

——(2001) "Making Minorities: The Politics of National Boundaries in the Soviet Experience," in Burguière, A., and Grew, R. (eds) *The Construction of Minorities: Cases for Comparison across Time and around the World*. Ann Arbor: University of Michigan Press.

TASS (1994) "State Duma Denounces Discrimination of Russians in Latvia," July 15.

——(2002) "Itar-Tass News Digest of August 20."

Torbakov, I. (2003) "Russia Moves to Reassert Influence In Central Asia, Caucasus," *Eurasia Insight*, March 3.

Trenin, D. (2002) *The End of Eurasia: Russia on the Border between Geopolitics and Globalization*. Washington, DC: Carnegie Endowment for Global Peace.

Tuminez, A. S. (2000) *Russian Nationalism since 1956: Ideology and the Making of Foreign Policy*. Lanham, MD: Rowman & Littlefield.

Vinogradov, M., and Ilyichev, G. (2002) "Foreign Affairs," *Izvestia*, May 6.

Yereshenko, M. (2002) "President Putin: Refugees Should Go to Siberia," *Russians in Tajikistan*, online: members.aol.com/lotaryn/refugeesinrussia.html (downloaded August 23, 2003).

Zhanguttin, B. (2002) "Kazakhstan's Slavic Population: Demographic Characteristics and Status," *Central Asia and the Caucasus: Journal of Social and Political Studies*, no. 4 (16).

Newport Library and
Information Service

Index

Note: "n." after a page reference indicates the number of a note on that page.

Z478154